AF412205

Citizenship in a Transnational Canada

This book is part of the Peter Lang Politics and Economics list.
Every volume is peer reviewed and meets
the highest quality standards for content and production.

PETER LANG
New York • Bern • Berlin
Brussels • Vienna • Oxford • Warsaw

Augie Fleras

Citizenship in a Transnational Canada

PETER LANG
New York • Bern • Berlin
Brussels • Vienna • Oxford • Warsaw

Library of Congress Cataloging-in-Publication Data

Names: Fleras, Augie, author
Title: Citizenship in a transnational Canada / Augie Fleras.
Description: New York: Peter Lang, 2018.
Includes bibliographical references and index.
Identifiers: LCCN 2017038127 | ISBN 978-1-4331-4996-2 (hardback: alk. paper)
ISBN 978-1-4331-4997-9 (ebook pdf)
ISBN 978-1-4331-4998-6 (epub) | ISBN 978-1-4331-4999-3 (mobi)
Subjects: Citizenship—Social aspects—Canada.
Transnationalism—Canada.
State, The—Social aspects—Canada.
Multiculturalism—Canada.
Canada—Emigration and immigration—Social aspects.
Classification: LCC JL187 .F54 2018 | DDC 323.60971—dc23
LC record available at https://lccn.loc.gov/2017038127
DOI 10.3726/b11911

Bibliographic information published by **Die Deutsche Nationalbibliothek.**
Die Deutsche Nationalbibliothek lists this publication in the "Deutsche
Nationalbibliografie"; detailed bibliographic data are available
on the Internet at http://dnb.d-nb.de/.

The paper in this book meets the guidelines for permanence and durability
of the Committee on Production Guidelines for Book Longevity
of the Council of Library Resources.

For Quinn

TABLE OF CONTENTS

PREFACE

Citizenship no longer means what it once meant. The accelerated realities in a world of "posts", "trans", and "isms" are challenging those citizenship discourses and practices that no longer apply although new models are not yet ready to preempt or displace. At the crux of this discursive erasure [a reassessment without a resolution or replacement] is the pending demise of state-centric notions of citizenship that historically informed national models, yet can no longer abide by the multiple modalities of belonging and identity in a seemingly "postcitizenship" world of "here", "there", and "everywhere". Contradictions abound over the following paradoxes: the persistence of territorially bounded citizenship regimes despite a relatively unbounded world of mobility and increasingly porous borders; the paramountcy of formal citizenship rights that neither lead to substantive equality nor reflect peoples' lived-experiences; universal citizenship models that paper over the realities of a hyperdiverse world of transmigration and multi-universes ("multiversality"); a seemingly progressive commitment to inclusion that's offset by the reality of systemic exclusions in defining "who's in" and "who's out"; a one-size-fits-all citizenship narrative at odds with governance models for differently accommodating a diversity-of-diversities; and the promise of a global/cosmopolitan ideal that, ironically, remains tethered to the *realpolitik* of specific nation-states. A key theme framed as a core question captures a sense of the politics and paradox at play: *In a topsy-turvey world of transmobility, cosmopolitanism, and multicentricity, does it still makes sense to talk about a bounded national citizenship model when peoples' notions of membership, entitlements, and identity are increasingly unbounded by postnational dynamics and de-spatialized by transnational patterns?* Or differently rephrased as an answer: we no longer live in a citizenship world if defined along state-centric Westphalian lines; more accurately, ours is a postcitizenship world of diverse-diversities, transmigration and interconnectedness, identity politics and politicized identities, and the internationalization of a human rights agenda. These observations—conventional models of citizenship as increasingly obsolete; a growing realignment of citizenship as principle and practice; and a discursive shift in how we "think", "talk", and "do" citizenship—secure the basis for reframing the citizenship concept in an emerging postcitizenship era.

That the topic of citizenship is sharply contested should come as no surprise (Sejersen, 2008; Tarozzi and Torres, 2016). This domain has evolved into a field so littered with misconceptions and conceptual stretching that many despair of clarity or consensus (Bosniak, 2006; Isin and Nyers, 2014). The citizenship concept itself is riddled with an array of paradoxes and controversies that reflect divergent perspectives, competing arguments, and conflicting conclusions. Often acrimonious disputes arise over the meaning of citizenship in terms of status, rights, identity, and activity; what it means to be citizen in a world organized around a local/national/global nexus; what constitutes a meaningful citizenship in a rapidly changing and diversifying milieu; and whether citizenship still matters in postcitizenship context. Of particular note are debates over the question of, "What is citizenship for": to protect the rights of individuals; improve pathways to inclusiveness; secure socio-political stability; impose social control; enhance the accumulation of wealth; provide a platform for challenge and resistance; or advance the nation-building project? The centrality of these concerns, notwithstanding, this book concedes a dearth of consensus over the "what", "why" and "how" behind these complicated issues (also Isin and Nyers, 2014). Dissensus is the rule, not the exception, especially when polite fictions about identity, entitlement, and belonging conceal uncomfortable truths about "who belongs", "how they belong", and "what belonging entitles" (Fleras, 2017). However inconvenient or unsatisfying, a lack of agreement may not be detrimental to the overall project since answers need not overwhelm the objective of any inquiry. What counts, instead, is the asking of questions that challenge stale conventions and yield fresh perspectives.

Citizenship in a Transnational Canada offers a distinct look at reconceptualizing citizenship in a contested world of shifting narratives, evolving models, and future possibilities. The book aims to provide readers with a critically informed understanding of the politics and the paradoxes accompanying the citizenship "turn" as discourse and practice in a world of posts, trans, and isms. *Citizenship in a Transnational Canada* is predicated on the assumption that a new vocabulary is required for thinking, talking, and doing citizenship if there is any hope of formulating a narrative consistent with contested domains and emergent realities. The book is also premised on the assumption that the citizenship concept is experiencing an identity crisis ("what it is?") and a crisis of confidence ("what should it be doing?"), largely because the world we inhabit is more complexly diverse, increasingly connected yet disconnected, subject to unanticipated crises and general turmoil, and disenchanted with the certainties of the past although unsure of what lies in store (Noonan and Nadkarni 2016). The crux of the argument is fairly straightforward: New citizenship narratives and practices are emerging that challenge the conventional citizenship model of a single nation-state within a territorially-bounded framework (Mann, 2017). These discursive frames capitalize on the complexities of transmigrant identities across a networked web of transnational linkages and a postmulticultural reality of diverse-diversities. Once associated with belonging to a national community, citizenship rights are increasingly sourced and legitimated within a global framework of human rights although, paradoxically, peoples identities remain particularistic and locally defined while the nation-state continues to be the repository of formal rights and membership (Soysal, 2011). No less salient are the politics that accompany the politicization of Indigenous peoples' citizenship commensurate with their constitutional status as "the (de facto) sovereigns within" (Fleras, 2017; Maaka and Fleras, 2005). The paradoxes and possibilities that attend to the conceptual makeover of national citizenship regimes along "postcitizenship" lines are explored as well across the settler domains of Canada and (to a lesser extent) the United States, Aotearoa/New Zealand and Australia.

The content of *Citizenship in a Transnational Canada* covers a lot of ground in analyzing the politics and the politicization of citizenship. A multidimensional approach to framing, analyzing, interpreting, and redefining the meaning and practice of citizenship is advocated, including citizenship as: *a legal status* consisting of formal rights, duties, and obligations: a *state discourse* involving narratives of control and cooptation ("hegemony"); an *interpretive lens* for better understanding wider issues of belonging and identity in a diversifying world; a *heuristic device* for analyzing and assessing claims to equality, justice and inclusion that pivot around a citizenship discourse; *a normative theory* that defines a set of political expectations; a *contested site* of challenge, resistance, and transformation ("counter-hegemony"); a *set of practices* from everyday political activism to claims-making politics; and a *distributive ideal* in pursuing the principles of social justice for newcomers and Indigenous peoples (Wood, 2003). The demands of citizens from the margins (especially those involving the politics of Indigeneity) are shown to have a powerful impact in disrupting the once snug fit between territory and nationality (Rygiel, 2015). A critical citizenship perspective is applied across the board: Euro/state-centric citizenship regimes are framed as controlling and exclusionary, in contrast to those not-yet-attained citizenship models that appear more fluid and flexible, uncoupled from territory, and inclusive of diverse-diversities. The (post) settler societies of Canada, Australia, the United States, and New Zealand appears to be embracing more inclusive citizenship regime—at least in theory if not always in practice. They also appear to be moving toward the principles and practices of a postcitizenship model—a belated recognition that acquiring full citizenship status involves more than claiming inclusion on terms already established, but also entails a commitment in which the boundaries of identity and belonging are redrawn beyond the contours of a single and undifferentiated citizenship (Marback, 2016). The book ends on a high note by demonstrating the utility of reframing citizenship along postcitizenship lines, employed in the broadest sense to incorporate the dynamics and demands of new citizenship regimes in the re-making.

References

Bosniak, Linda. *The Citizen and the Alien*. Princeton, NJ: Princeton University Press, 2006.

Fleras, Augie. "Rethinking Citizenship Through Transnational Lenses." In *Citizenship in a Transnational Perspective*, edited by J. Mann, 15–48. New York: Palgrave Macmillan, 2017.

Isin, Engin F. and Peter Nyers. "Introduction: Globalizing Citizenship Studies." In *Routledge Handbook of Global Citizenship Studies*, edited by E. Isin and P. Nyers. New York: Routledge, 1–11. 2014.

Maaka, Roger and Augie Fleras. The Politics of Indigeneity: Challenging the State in Canada and Aotearoa New Zealand. Dunedin, NZ: University of Otago Press, 2005.

Mann, Jatinder. "Introduction." In *Citizenship in a Transnational Perspective*, edited by J. Mann, 1–14. New York: Palgrave Macmillan, 2017.

Marback, Richard. "Introduction." In *Representation and Citizenship*, edited by R. Marback, 1–16. Detroit: Wayne State University Press, 2016.

Noonan, Norma C. and Vidya Nadkarni. "Introduction: A Century of Challenges." In *Challenge and Change*, edited by N.C. Noonan and V. Nadkarni,. 1–11. New York: Palgrave Macmillan, 2016.

Rygiel, Kim. *Governing Through Citizenship and Citizenship from Below. An Interview with Kim Rygiel.* Movements Journal, 2015.

Sejersen, T.B. "'I Vow to Thee My Countries'—The Expansion of Dual Citizenship in the 21st Century." *International Migration Review* 42, no. 3 (2008): 523–549.

Soysal, Yasemin Nuhoglu. "Postnational Citizenship: Reconfiguring the Familiar Terrain." In The Blackwell Companion to Political Sociology, Edited by Kate Nash and Allan Scott. Oxford UK: Blackwell, 2004.

Tarozzi, M. and C.A. Torres. *Global Citizenship Education and the Crisis of Multiculturalism. Comparative Perspectives.* New York: Bloomsbury Press, 2016.

Wood, Patricia K. "Aboriginal/Indigenous Citizenship: An Introduction." *Citizenship Studies* 7, no. 4 (2003): 371–378.

PART 1
FRAMING CITIZENSHIP: PARADOXES, PROBLEMS, POLITICS

· 1 ·

CONTESTING CITIZENSHIP: AN IDENTITY CRISIS, A CRISIS OF CONFIDENCE

Introduction: Framing the Issues, Reframing the Debates

To define the domain of citizenship as topical and contested is tantamount to taking credit for reinventing the wheel. A citizenship "turn" across the disciplines of sociology, political science, global studies, and anthropology attests to its growing popularity as a field of study in its own right as well as a catalyst in challenging the inequalities of exclusion. This assessment should come as no surprise. The world may be rapidly changing and increasingly diverse in responding to the rhythms and demands of globalization, the repercussions of digital technology, and the multiplicity of social movements and identity politics. But while many governance institutions appear to be relatively unscathed by the speed and scale of these social changes (Environic Institute/Institute for Governance, 2016), the emergence of a new global disorder—sharply contested, deeply unsettled, and intensely diverse as well as digitally networked and globally interconnected—is chipping away at the edifice of a national citizenship (Ommundsen, Leach and Vandenberg, 2010). Pressure is mounting for rethinking the meanings *attached* to the citizenship concept in light of those new discourses and complex practices that speak to the different ways of becoming a citizen, being a citizen, and doing citizenship (Fleras, 2017). The problematizing of citizenship is captured by those scholarly titles that conflate citizenship with challenge and crisis, contestation and change (see Fleras, 2016). No less evident is the proliferation of terms specifying particular forms of citizenship which, at last count, totalled over seventy entries (also Fleras, 2016). Nearly as impressive as the number of titles and terms are the spate of conferences in Canada that address the politics of citizenship and the politicization of citizenship in shifting contexts.

What conclusions about citizenship are discernible from these publications, references, and conferences? First, debates over citizenship now embody a major topic of study within the social sciences, not only in addressing practical political questions, but also in reformulating theoretical debates (Marback, 2016; Turner, 1990). An outpouring of research and publications has yielded a slew of normative theories, a proliferation of typologies and terms, a deconstructing of tacitly assumed assumptions and taken-for-granted postulates, and a reframing of citizenship as an entry point for rethinking the inequalities of power and privilege (Hoffman, 2004). Citizenship as a subject of study has evolved from a relatively obscure topic of interest into a wildly popular domain for debating the politics over who belongs, how they belong, and what belonging entails. Recurrent debates and contemporary controversies reveal an uncanny knack for realigning citizenship discourses along fundamentally opposing lines, thus exposing the duality of citizenship as internally inclusive yet externally exclusive, particularly in those citizenship regimes ill-equipped for coping with the surge and demands of international migration (Bosniak, 2006; Brubaker, 1992; Joppke, 2010). Finally, much can be gleaned from the internationalization of human rights norms and cosmopolitan principles, together with the interplay of international migration, communication technologies, and globalization dynamics. Far from being a static and objective fact of law, citizenship is neither a stable phenomenon nor an anachronism from the past, but an evolving and constructed dynamic within the context of a digitally connected yet socially disconnected reality. Scholarship is disavowing the study of citizenship as a legal status with formal rights preferring, instead, to focus on the complexities and paradoxes of a lived-citizenship, both multilayered and multidimensional, and subject to political disagreements and politicized circumstances (Hoffman, 2004; Kivisto and Faist, 2008; Maas, 2013; Modood, 2007; Richez and Manfredi, 2014).

Second, the combination of titles, terms, and "talkfests" reinforces a reading of citizenship as continually contested, permanently reinvented, and conceptually stretched (Balibar, 2004; Clark et al., 2014; Isin and Nyers, 2014).

Three themes prevail that expose a burgeoning identity crisis with a corresponding crisis of confidence: (1) citizenship no longer means what it once did; (2) it's time to revisit the meaning of a meaningful citizenship beyond nation-state frames without denying the recognition of differences or the necessity of common principles (Stanford, 2011); and (3) the interplay of transnationalism, universal personhood, and identity politics is transforming how we think, talk, and do citizenship in ways that have yet-to-be-fathomed. The rights and sites as well as scales and acts of citizenship have multiplied in complexity to the point where both academics and public figures are struggling to invent a new vocabulary that aligns with emergent trends and lived-realities (Clarke et al., 2014; Isin, 2009). The politics of Indigeneity have proven particularly disruptive in unsettling the principles of a settler-centric citizenship (Green, 2017; Spoonley, 2017). References to the concept of citizenizing Indigeneity while Indigenizing citizenship invoke the possibility of Indigenous-plus citizenship models that confirm the priority rights of the "nations within" without relinquishing access to national citizenship rights (Chabot, 2007)(see Chapter 7).

Third, the homogenizing and hegemonic logic of a national citizenship is under widespread scrutiny and criticism. Pluralism theories and Indigeneity politics challenge the so-called universalism and the alleged neutrality of national citizenship models (Lightfoot, 2013); feminist theories contest the systemic androcentrism at the heart of formal citizenship rights (Lister, 2007; Munday, 2009); people with disabilities demand an inclusive citizenship that puts them in charge of their lives and in control over life-chances (Morris, 2005); and critical citizenship theories expose the racialized and Eurocentric biases embedded in a universal citizenship (Cao, 2015). Just as citizenship is gendered, i.e., systemically biased to reflect, reinforce, and advance androcentric interests as natural and normal, desirable and acceptable, so too is it racialized in ways that institutionalize the Eurocentricity of a systemic white society (Fleras, 2016). Of particular salience in decentering a state-centred citizenship are those cosmopolitan aspirations that repudiate the value and validity of a territorially-bounded Westphalian ("nation-state") model. An offer of a global citizenship that transcends national borders is proposed instead, with its connotation of universal personhood in advancing a new framework of shared global responsibilities, including planetary survival (Cao, 2015). And yet, while notions of identity and belonging are no longer the sole preserve of a national citizenship, having been eclipsed by cosmopolitan commitments and transmigrant mobilities, the locus of citizenship rights remain locked and located within the nation-state, further complicating a domain in flux and controversy.

In short, nation-state notions of citizenship are increasingly pressured *from above* by the forces of transmigration, globalization, and cosmopolitan ideologies of universal personhood. The process by which migrants sustain meaningful and transnational relations between their country of origin and the host country has disrupted conventional routines of spatiality as they relate to peoples' lived citizenship experiences beyond national borders (Stasiulis, 2017). Citizenship conventions are also unsettled *from below* by the politics of Indigeneity, initiatives to differently accommodate complex diversities, and the growing appeal of denizenship (denizens: permanent residents with rights comparable to those of citizens [Soysal, 2004]). An identity crisis of confidence is captured by Canadian academics, Yvonne Hebert and Lori Wilkinson (2002), who conclude:

> Citizenship is in transformation, its meaning is expanding, and interest in the subject is exploding. Citizenship has moved from being closed to being open, from exclusion to inclusion. Once having had a unitary stable meaning, citizenship is now diffuse, multiple and ever-shifting. Originally clearly defined by geographical borders and a common history, citizenship is increasingly in question.

References to citizenship as an unfinished project in progress accepts the inevitability of a concept in crisis (Tarozzi and Torres, 2016). Citizenship as a contested concept is now under *erasure as no-longer relevant but also in a not-yet situation of decline, one in which the old no longer applies although it's not yet entirely displaced by the new—whatever that might be* (Isin and Nyers, 2014). New modalities may be promoting new citizenship discourses, yet they are neither fully formed nor wholly functional (see Weaver, 2015). This state of liminality of neither here nor there affirms Derrida's prescient notion of erasure (1998) when it acknowledges the value of a cutting edge idea, yet remains skeptical of its application (also Isin and Nyers, 2014). Take, for example, the ongoing tension between the legal status of a national citizenship and the lived-experiences of a postcitizenship in the making. A national citizenship in a world of posts, trans, and isms may *no longer* be as relevant in defining identity, belonging, and entitlements; nevertheless, it remains the repository of citizenship rights in defining who belongs, how they belong, and what belonging entitles. By contrast, a discursive shift in how we think, talk, and do citizenship is unmistakable, although new modes of becoming, being, and doing citizenship are *not yet* ready or able to dislodge the old (Fleras, 2017). Or as Janine Brodie (2002) pointed out a few years ago (and I paraphrase), old ideas about Canada are eroding, but they have not yet been replaced with newer visions of an evolving reality that tap into the collective imagination and a shared narrative. Clearly, then, there is much to gain in framing citizenship in a permanent state of rupture and erasure as well as of redefinition and reconstruction. It confirms the necessity for a new vocabulary of citizenship (Isin, 2009) if only to underscore how the messy yet interconnected lives of people rarely dovetail with the tidy yet narrow parameters of a state-centred citizenship—especially when borders cross *peoples*, prompting people to *cross borders* in search of citizenship (Byrne, 2014).

A Contested and Contestable Concept: "What Is Citizenship for?"

Citizenship as status, discourses, and practices constitutes a lively field of study. Such a statement is hardly surprising. The concept of citizenship has long informed debates in political theory, either as a lynchpin for controversies over the ideals of freedom, autonomy, and equality or as a contested site for sorting out competing claims to rights, identity, and belonging (Kymlicka, 2016). But the 21st century is challenging conventional models that typically framed citizenship as a bundle of rights bestowed on all members of a distinct and bounded political community (Mann, 2017). The focus of a citizenship which aligns territorial boundedness with identity and belonging has shifted in recent years. An exclusive emphasis on the nation-state as the political container of like-minded citizen has given way to discourses that emphasize the centrality of human rights within the context of multilevel governance models and multilayered citizenship patterns (Strasser, 2013; Tonkiss and Bloom, 2015). The homogenizing and controlling logic of state-centric citizenship models confronts a dizzying array of challenges, including social movements (from feminist to multiculturalism to cosmopolitanism), intensified migration flows and complex diversities, competing equality and inclusiveness demands, the internationalization of a human rights agenda, and the interpenetration of the global with the national and local (Roseneil et al., 2013; Stanford, 2011; Strasser, 2013;). Disadvantaged and minoritized groups who resent their exclusion from society have forged ahead with claims for substantive equality based on lived-experiences and the principle of universal personhood (Banko, 2014). Feminists continue to critique a so-called universal citizenship as systemically androcentric in robbing recognition of female differences as grounds for belonging and identity. Denizens insist on the right to belong and claim entitlements despite lacking a passport or citizenship status, whereas transnational migrants are rewriting the boundaries of political communities by living and acting across the borders of two or more nation-states.

No one should scoff at the magnitude of the changes and controversies associated with a citizenship in motion. The concept of a national citizenship is experiencing an identity crisis in defining what citizenship means in a world of posts, trans, and isms. It's also enduring a crisis of confidence in grappling with what citizenship should mean or what it must do in a world of shifting discourses and practices. A series of questions come to the fore in framing this identity crisis of confidence: what does citizenship mean for people's notions of identity, belonging, and entitlements; what should it mean in terms of how we think, talk, and do citizenship; of what is citizenship for in a changing, contested, and diverse world; and what modalities of membership speak to the truism that every nation-state is resident to noncitizens, while every national-ity is territorially dispersed—in the process both undermining yet reaffirming notions of sovereignty, national identity, and a statist citizenship (Berg and Rodriguez, 2013). This informative passage in Ommundsen, Leach and Van-denberg (2010) pinpoints the indeterminacies unleashed by the explosive mix of global dynamics and citizenship realities:

> Destabilising boundaries between culture and state, self and others, sameness and difference, cultural citizenship in a global era brings out tensions between individual and group rights, between human and cultural rights, between principles of univer-salism and respect for cultural differences, and between the authority of the state, the rule of international law, and the seeming lawlessness of transnational capital…It has eroded some social and cultural distinctions and inequities but created others. It has undermined traditional notions of individual and group identity but given rise to an unprecedented focus on "identity politics'. It has witnessed the rise of progressive transnational social movements pursuing issues of gender and ecology and regres-sive parochial movements based on religious fundamentalism, patriarchy, and ethnic nationalism.…It has exploded the myth of the nation as an organically constituted community but produced nostalgia for and chauvinistic efforts to instill, national and ethnic traditions based on common origins and shared destinies.

On the surface, the concept of citizenship may strike many as unprob-lematic—straightforward, uncomplicated, and not particularly interesting. Traditional state-centric approaches to citizenship tended to focus on the centrality of membership in a nation-state with a corresponding set of rights and duties. The sense of belonging and bonding to others that citizens enjoyed as members of a bounded political community made it abundantly obvious: it was neither valid nor possible to detach citizenship from the authority of the sovereign nation-state (Linklater, 1998). But a closer reading and critical examination of citizenship expose new complexities. Citizenship represents a sharply disputed and keenly contested site, evolving in response to historical and political developments, and assuming a bewildering range of expressions that render it more complex and confounding than ever imagined (Bosniak, 2006; Mann, 2017). The interplay of globalization and the internationalization of human rights with that of identity politics and new social movements unsettles the viability a national citizenship in an increasingly postcitizenship world (Fleras, 2017). Further indeterminacies surface when framing citizenship outside of a legal status of formal membership. For in the final analysis, the citizenship concept is also a cultural ideal infused with moral meaning, normative principles, and value orientations against the backdrop of a specific political, social and historical context (Modood, 2007).

This book takes its cue from the necessity to deconstruct and problematize the concept of citizenship, if only to demonstrate how the concept is more political and paradoxical than previously imagined, especially in light of new patterns related to mobility, hyperdiversity, and interconnectivity (Clark and Savage, 2016; Tarozzi and Torres, 2016). Consider the following as indicative of those interactive polarities, awkward paradoxes and polite fictions that obscure inconvenient truths (see Fleras, 2016 for fuller discussion): (a) more scholarly interest in citizenship is offset by less consensus over its meaning (b) citizenship seems to matter less in a world of/in motion, yet it also matters more for precisely the same reason (c) in a complex, diverse, and changing world, a national citizenship rooted in the principles of a centuries old Westphalian model is proving both resilient yet dated, changing not fading away (d) diversity and hybridity may be the trademarks of contemporary society, yet citizenship remains rooted in unity and homogeneity while relating to citizens from an assimilationist perspective (e) is it possible to reconcile a bounded national citizenship with the realities of an increasingly unbounded postnational world? (f) citizenship as discourse goes beyond its legal status, yet its legality secures the basis of a rights-based global order (g) an emphasis on citizenship as activity and activism suggests a discursive shift in framing citizenship—from citizenship as a thing (*or noun*) to citizenship as doing (*or verb*) (h) an imagining of citizenship as transnational and cosmopolitan levels does not invalidate local and particularistic notions of belonging and identity (i) moves to liberalize and denationalize citizenship regimes are offset by countermoves to renationalize it to suit mainstream priorities (j) a commitment to the citizenship ideals of inclusiveness and equality does not discount patterns of inequality and exclusion, both deliberate and systemic (k) reference to citizenship as hegemony and controlling is balanced by its empowering potential to resist, disrupt, and transform and (l) the potential of an online citizenship as sources of political activism and social movements may conceal the disruptive side of social media.

That the domain of citizenship symbolizes a site of contestation and change is beyond dispute. The politics of citizenship not only reflect an identity crisis and crisis of confidence in defining who belongs, how they belong, and what belonging entitles. The politicization of this domain also reinforces the onset of new ways in thinking, talking, and doing citizenship. Citizenship discourses and practices are undergoing what amounts to a discursive shift in terms of what they look like, what they are doing, and what they should be doing as national citizenship space becomes increasingly contested by the transnational and the multicentric (Fox, 2005; Leggewie, 2013). Those marginalized groups formerly excluded on the basis of Indigenous, racialized, ethnic, sexual, dis/ableist, and gender identities demand recognition and accommodation in ways that expose the limits of a one-size-fits-all citizenship regime (Fleischmann et al., 2011; Isin, 2015). Women want to expand their social citizenship rights including access to safe and inexpensive childcare; racialized groups want recognition, redistribution, and representation commensurate with their formal status in society; gays and lesbians want the same rights as heterosexual partners such as spousal benefits (Field, 2007); diasporic groups want naturalization and political rights; and dis/ability groups want recognition of their abilities as fully engaged citizens (Isin, 2015). Of particular salience in debating the benefits and burdens of citizenship are the politics of Indigeneity. Indigenous peoples insist on citizenship arrangements that superimpose their group-differentiated rights as *citizens of Indigenous nations* alongside their constitutional rights as national citizens. In short, to the extent citizenship narratives are increasingly informed and reformed by those at the margins (Atac et al., 2016), the politics of citizenship are re-assessing what once was tacitly accepted, but now is problematized and politicized (Field, 2007; Hines, 2007, 2009; Wood, 2003).

The Politics of Citizenship, the Politicization of Citizenship

The politics of citizenship and the politicization of citizenship inform—and are informed by—the struggles of those at the margins (Hollander, 2014; Yashar, 2005). Challenges to the boundaries and content (meaning) of citizenship reflect—and are reflected in—minority politics and Indigenous peoples movements, some of them violent and themselves exclusionary in orientation, while others are more mindful of expanding the parameters of membership to embrace the "other" (Bond, 2016). But growing pressure on Euro/state-centric citizenship models to radically rethink the accommodation of diversity and equality (Banulescu-Bogdan, 2012) cannot dispel the now obvious. Claims to inclusion and universalism have done little to eviscerate the systemic exclusions of those national citizenship regimes mired in the biases of race, Eurocentricity, gender, sexuality, and class (Bloemraad et al., 2008; Yuval-Davis, 1999). For example, the colonialist project known as settler society-building found its strongest expression in the hierarchies of citizenship that facilitated the goal of absorption, social control, or territorial expansion (Green, 2017; Isin and Wood, 1999). Or consider how the process of naturalization is manipulated as an instrument of targeted exclusion through the introduction of formidable language requirements and complex host-country knowledge tests (Bilefsky, 2016; Skific, 2013). These systemic biases have had the effect of creating a category of second class citizens, not because as citizens they lack formal rights, but because they must exercise these citizenship rights in a lived-context that neither reflect minority daily experiences nor advance their interests or aspirations. Such systemic bias is particularly evident in debates that address the politicized relationship between citizenship and gender.

Insight Post

National Citizenships: Universal and Neutral or Gendered and Biased?

A citizenship lens provides a heuristic device for analyzing and assessing how patterns of inequality, injustice, and exclusion are created, justified, and sustained as well as how they are challenged and transformed (Fleras, 2017). Such an assessment would appear relevant when applied to the relationship between gender and citizenship if mediated through the prism of a gendered lens. The incongruity can be framed around a series of questions. Is a national citizenship as universal and value-free as some claim, or is it fundamentally gendered and biased? How has the collective action of women challenged and transformed conventional notions of citizenship at the level of policies and laws, recurrent discourses, and lived experiences? Is it possible to re-assess the current state of citizenship from the perspective of women, particularly minoritized (racialized, Indigenous, and immigrant) women? Or is the citizenship concept so suffused with systemic and androcentric biases that it's no longer salvageable in its present form (Roseneil, Halsaa, and Sumer, 2013)? Is it best to persevere with the tools at hand by looking for ways of improving the inclusiveness of a state-centric citizenship? Or perhaps a better alternative is to altogether discard a citizenship that originated in the gendered nexus of Enlightenment liberal individualism, a systematic patriarchy, and a Westphalian nation-state logic (Roseneil, 2013a)?

Discussions and debates over citizenship tended to be couched in gender neutral terms or, more precisely, a perception of citizens as explicitly genderless yet implicitly male (Lister, 2007). But citizenship as a universal concept uniformly applicable across the board is neither gender neutral nor innocent of bias when applied to principles, discourse, or practice (Butler and Benoit, 2015). Modern laws, policies, and protocols associated with citizenship may purport to be colour-blind by virtue of treating everyone equally the same. In reality, structural barriers and systemic biases preclude equitable outcomes since citizenship as a social construct is infused with androcentric norms that define some aspects of reality as normal, desirable, and necessary while dismissing other perspectives as inferior or irrelevant. For example, it's widely acknowledged that the citizenship concept was designed according to a male template (Dauvergne, 2000), with the result the exclusion of women was parlayed into a theory and practice of citizenship (Lister, 2007). The words of Ruth Lister (1997) are strikingly apropos: "The universalist cloak of the abstract, disembodied individual has been cast aside to reveal a definitely male citizen and a white heterosexual, non disabled one at that". Yasmeen Abu-Laban (2014) also draws attention to this patricentric ideal by citing a poem entitled "Citizenship" in Alfred J. Fitzpatrick's 1919 Handbook for New Canadians:

> The good citizen
> Loves God
> Loves the Empire
> Loves Canada
> Loves his own family…
> Is every inch a man

Citizenship as a concept continues to be gendered in ways that differently impact women and men. Its engenderment is often detrimental to women, resulting in their exclusion from full and equal exercise of their democratic rights (Munday, 2009). As an aspirational concept and lived reality, citizenship has long proven a mixed blessing for women and feminists since its promise of inclusion is marred by exclusionary disappointment (Predelli et al., 2013; Roseneil, 2013a,b). According to a report published by the Pew Research Center (Theodorou, 2014), twenty-seven countries continue to limit a woman's ability to transmit citizenship to her non-citizen (stateless) spouse or her children—a situation that can leave a child stateless (without nationality) in the case of a stateless father (Marlan, 2017).

A gendered citizenship entails more than the historical exclusion of women from citizenship or access to its rights. More to the point, it refers to a citizenship that is deeply and systemically androcentric in reflecting and reinforcing the logic of a citizenship regime, framed from a male perspective as the unquestioned standard or tacitly accepted norm. Feminists have long questioned the so-called universal premises that mask a systemic androcentrism (Lister, 1997, 2007; Tastsoglou and Dobrowolsky, 2006; Yuval-Davis, 1999). They point to systemic biases in a liberal citizenship that privileges the primacy of morally autonomous individuals at the expense of a citizenship more mindful of the lived-values of human interdependence and community building (Roseneil et al., 2013). Definitions of citizenship reflect and reinforce a public/private dichotomy that frames citizens as abstract and disembodied persons whose lived-experiences are silenced (Dauvergne, 2000). A focus on citizenship as status and formal rights downplays the performative dimension of participation and agency, particularly as marginalized groups mobilize to claim their rights through dialogue, association, and collective action. The intersecting and overlapping social locations of minority women (immigrant, racialized, and Indigenous) as citizens are further obscured because of exclusions based on multiple axes of discrimination and inequality. Not surprisingly, feminists tend to view citizenship less as a lived reality, but more as an aspirational ideal that must be contested and reconstructed (Predelli et al., 2013).

To sum up, citizenship is gendered inasmuch as it's anchored in the public domain, ignores or suppresses differences, elevates individual independence over community empowerment, and reflects the centrality of androcentrism in defining normalcy and acceptability (Dauvergne, 2000). Women are compelled to deny their distinctiveness by conforming to a masculine citizenship ideal rather than an inclusiveness on their own terms, while the experiences of men (white, middle class, heterosexual, and able bodied) are superimposed upon the category of women as a whole.

Yet overcoming this systemic gendered bias is trickier than it might appear. A commitment to promote women as equal citizens in a gendered system may prove insufficient because of inherent male biases that deny as they include. The formal equality of legal citizenship rights such as voting or free speech masks those inequalities of exclusion that fall outside the narrow purview of the public sphere (Dauvergne, 2000). What's required for substantive change is a commitment to balance the particular with the universalism, a universal with the particular. Or to put a slightly different spin, it's more important than ever to acknowledge the creative tension that thrives in the interplay between the formal rights of universalism with the lived experiences of diverse women (Lister, 2007; Strasser, 2013).

The Insight Post makes it abundantly clear. A focus on citizenship politics and the politicization of citizenship pushes the parameters of citizenship-making to a newer level. It demonstrates how core issues related to redistribution, representation, or recognition are increasingly constructed and framed as citizenship rights by those at the margins (Isin et al., 2008). The meaning of citizenship is often contested by those anxious to reframe patterns of identity, belonging, and entitlements around the themes of heterogeneity, inclusiveness, and people's lived-realities instead of state-centric notions of the static, singular, and abstract (Atac et al., 2016; Clarke et al., 2014; Yashar, 2005). Such a politicized domain makes it more important than ever to problematize the concept of citizenship in light of its promises and disappointments.

Problematizing Citizenship: Citizenship Promises, Citizen Disappointments

What is citizenship? What is citizenship for? What is it designed to do, for whom (Nyers, 2010)? On the surface, reference to citizenship seems simple and unproblematic; for example, in 1992, Canada's Federal Court of Appeal portrayed the term citizen as "straightforward", "unambiguous" and in need of "no interpretation at all", while the Supreme Court in 1989 disregarded any distinctions based on citizenship when it incorporated a reference to citizenship in a ruling (Richez and Manfredi, 2014). In reality, however, the citizenship concept conceals layers of complexity and contradictions that must be exposed and deconstructed if it's to move beyond a marker of membership and rights and across a spectrum of meanings related to access, identity, and entitlements in a multi-universe of mobility, connectivity and transnationality (Clark and Savage, 2016; Clarke et al., 2014; Richez and Manfredi, 2014). The chaotic nonlinearity of a hyperdiverse and politicized world undermines the legitimacy of those conventional meanings designed for a less complex and more homogeneous world. Orthodox citizenship discourses are deemed to be increasingly dated, dangerously inappropriate or even counterproductive, and in desperate need of reinvention rather than a fine-tuning of a permanent baseline (Clarke et al., 2014; Moore, 2012). Or as once put by Canada's former Minister of Citizenship, Immigration, and Multiculturalism, Jason Kenney, albeit in a more restrictive sense of making Canadian citizenship "harder to get and easier to lose" (cited in Abu-Laban, 2015), "we need a citizenship that is relevant to today's challenges, not those of 30 or 40 years ago." Michael Peter Smith (2003: 15) also writes to this effect:

> Discourses on the rights, entitlements, and obligations of citizenship have changed dramatically in the past two decades as a result of the increasingly transnational character of global migration flows, cultural networks, and sociopolitical practices. The once taken for granted correspondence between citizen and the nation and the state has been questioned as new forms of "grassroots citizenship" have taken on an increasingly trans-territorial character. What used to be defined as citizenship was rooted in a specific space, but globalization is detaching identity and belonging from any sense of residence as an actual community on the ground (Kivisto, 2008). Resident non citizens now routinely live and work in transnational cities throughout the world while maintaining social and political networks linking them to people and places in their countries of origin. At the same time, the rise of supranational institutional networks and the spread of the discourse on human rights also challenges received notions of state sovereignty.

Reference to problematizing a concept such as citizenship offers a new analytic outlook. A type of critical thinking is proposed that goes beyond the conventional in challenging how we think and talk about social reality. The process of problematizing renders problematic what is tacitly assumed and unquestioned; unfamiliarizes common sense by way of "playful inversions" that upend the self evident to yield fresh insights; unsettles convention by exposing an issue as more complicated a problem than widely assumed; and questions the familiar as a problem for criticism and analysis. A problematizing of citizenship is timely and necessary. Its disputed status as principle and practice makes it more important than ever to decentre citizenship from conventional anchors and fixed moorings, while acknowledging the dynamics of mobility and mutability as central rather than ancillary (Clarke et al., 2014). The problematizizing of citizenship by denaturalizing it uncovers its constructed status and unsettles its taken-for-grantedness while debunking those polite fictions that blanket uncomfortable truths (Bosniak, 2006). Problematizing citizenship as a socially constructed and contested governance in transition also points to a reality that no longer exists, but one in the making, albeit not yet ready to dominate (Isin and Nyers, 2014). The interplay of "the no longer but not yet" frame demonstrates how existing discourses may commit to the new realities; nevertheless, they lack the conceptual clout to superimpose or supersede. Newer concepts may better reflect new practices and developments but rarely possess the critical mass to dislodge the incumbents.

A commitment to problematizing the citizenship concept unmasks the complexities and conundrums at the heart of this books' conceptual framework. This commitment includes debates over the interactive binaries of status vs practice, membership vs claims-making, normative vs contextual, domination vs empowerment, abstracted vs lived, formal vs substantive, and national vs trans/post/national (Isin, 2009). Of particular note are the following problematics that pose key questions about the politics and politicization of citizenship when driven by the realities of globalization and universal personhood, in addition to surges in ethno-nationalism, the dynamics of cross-border flows, the complexities of a multiversal world of diverse diversities, and the proliferation of diasporic communities (Brubaker, 2005):

- *What does citizenship really mean? What is it really for?* What is the meaning of citizenship? Or perhaps more accurately, what is meant by reference to this "process" or "thing" called citizenship, especially when conventional markers no longer apply? What exactly constitutes a (good) citizen in the complex, diverse, and changing milieu of shifting loyalties and multi-layered belongings? What constitutes a meaningful citizenship in a seemingly disjointed world of shifting transnational contexts, splintered loyalties, and contested realities (Conference Notes, 2012; Friedman and Schultermandl, 2016)? For some, lived citizenship realities can no longer be squeezed into the homogenizing logic of a national citizenship. Instead, references to citizenship in a world of motion must shift conceptually toward transmigration within the context of transnational social spaces and postnational realities (Castles et al., 2013; Fong, 2011; Glick-Schiller, 2005). The transnational social field created by transmigrants requires a broader conception of citizenship so that questions of belonging, identity, and rights acknowledge the interplay of the local/national/global nexus at varying levels (Rodriguez, 2008). For others, the combination of globalized world of massive migration, transnational forms of associations, and disaporic loyalties, calls for a different line of argument. More robust conceptions of a territorially bounded and nationally anchored citizenship are necessary to offset the threat of fragmentation by securing a commitment to cohesion and control (Motomura, 2006).

- *Is a meaningful citizenship possible in a "messy" postcitizenship world?* How should the meaning and practice of citizenship address the challenges posed by the interplay and dynamics of transnationalism and postnationalism with that of postcolonialism, and postmulticulturalism? What happens when static national models can't cut it, yet the nation state remains the prime authority and primary receptacle in defining who belongs, how they belong, and what belonging entitles (Benhabib, 2007; Camilleri, 2015; Castles et al., 2013; Isin and Nyers, 2014). The heuristic value of transnational lenses used in the broadest sense as discourse and a lived-reality point to a discursive shift in how we think, talk, and do citizenship, especially when locating citizenship models within fields of flows that span national territories yet, paradoxically, remain legally locked into territorially bounded spaces (Levitt, 2004; Simmons, 2010). And since we no longer think only in hierarchies, but increasingly through networks of digital communication and online platforms, citizenship is perceived as another node in a world-wide web of a local-national-global nexus (Isin and Ruppert, 2015; Soto, 2014). Clearly, then, an inchoate world of movement, mass migration and messy boundaries exposes the folly of boxing the meaning of citizenship into a single analytical category, within a specific geographical territory and inside a singular national identity. Reference to a postcitizenship world in capturing new citizenship discourses and practices may indeed prove an idea whose time has come.

- *Is this the end of citizenship or its end as we know it?* Are we at the end of citizenship or at the end of citizenship with which we are familiar, namely, membership with rights in a territorially bounded polity whose origins and legitimacy reflect a singular commitment and uniform application (Berezin, 2003; Cairns, 1999; Isin and Nyers, 2014)? To one side, a national citizenship and corresponding rights remain a desired goal for many migrants—especially for those who are undocumented or who occupy precarious status such as temporary foreign workers. For them, nothing has displaced the centrality and desirability of state-centric citizenship with its sought-after guarantees of security and mobility (Hansen, 2009; Nunn et al., 2015; Urzi and Williams, 2016). To the other side, a Euro/state-centric citizenship as a governance model is losing its legitimacy and appeal as notions of identity and belonging become increasingly uncoupled from a specific locale in a transnational world of mobility (Antonini, 2014; Hoffman, 2004; Labelle and Rocher, 2004; Nagel and Staeheli, 2002; Stasiulis, 2017). A more robust version of postnational citizenship may prove its worth in a world where the ideal of political community and formal citizenship rarely dovetail as neatly as they once did, largely because people's identities and affiliations do not always coincide with the formal boundaries of a national citizenship model (Rodriguez, 2010). A focus on citizenship as a contested site rather than a worldwide classificatory filing system is helpful. It not only exposes its entrenchment in political projects and cultural formations (Brubaker, 1992), but also renders as problematic those assumptions that frame citizenship as universal and abstract (Clarke et al., 2014).

- *Creating commitment to an instrument of social control.* What does it mean to be a citizen of a society whose citizenship promises of equality and inclusion are betrayed by the disappointments of violence, inequality, and marginalization (Bloemraad, 2015; Gouws, 2004)? Concerns are mounting over the feasibility of instilling within racialized minorities and Indigenous peoples an emotional embrace to an institution and process that violated fundamental human rights in the drive to dominate and control (Alfred, 2009; Green, 2017; Kornelsen, 2015; Menon, 2009)? The question is whether it's feasible or desirable to reinvigorate a seemingly moribund concept often associated with the coercive—even genocidal—practices of a settler colonialism. The challenge lies in de-parochializing the citizenship concept, not only to interrogate the symbolic aggression inherent in state-centric citizenships (Roseneil, 2013a), but also to liberate citizenship from the shackles of a Western history, its origins and structure as a Eurocentric institution, and the parochialism of the Westphalian citizenship regime (Isin and Nyers, 2014; van den Boogaard, 2016). Of particular note are demands for enlarging the boundaries of citizenship to better address broader issues beyond the legal and abstracted in acknowledging the "lived-status" of doing citizenship.

- *Is it salvageable?* Is it possible to balance a one-size-fits-all citizenship with a citizenship model both inclusive and empowering as well as multicentric and multiversal (Hanvelt and Papillon, 2005; Lee, 2016; Smith and Rogers, 2016)? Or is a national citizenship so heavily-freighted a concept that it's beyond redemption as a viable alternative, despite a proclaimed universality and presumed neutrality that obscures its rootedness in Eurocentric, colonialist, racialized, and androcentric biases (Lister, 1997)? Is citizenship an ideal worth fighting for, or, is a new language required to express ideas of identity and belonging that build on yet move beyond the principles of liberal universalism (Roseneil, 2013a)? The challenge is formidable: just as the citizenship concept is systemically gendered (i.e.tailored to fit male realities by way of a public/private divide that facilitated men's involvement in the public domain (Lister, 1997)], so too is citizenship racialized insofar as it reflects largely Eurocentric experiences, principles, and priorities (Joppke, 2010; Lee, 2014; van den Boogaard, 2016). Despite these deterrents, immigrant and Indigenous peoples' struggles for equality are not only illustrative of contemporary citizenship politics, but also constitutive of them (Galvez, 2013).

- *Toward a postcitizenship citizenship.* What is the value in reframing 21st century citizenship along postcitizenship lines? Put bluntly, in a rapidly changing and increasingly diverse world, conventional models of citizenship no longer resonate with meaning or relevance as they once did. We no longer live in a Westphalian citizenship world of expectations and outcomes but in a postcitizenship citizenship world with respect to how we think, talk, and do citizenship. To be sure, reference to a postcitizenship as reality, discourse, and practice does not denote a new legal status with formal rights. Rather, it offers a new discursive framework with which to differently interpret citizenship by generating a critical awareness of the world as an infinitely more complex, contested, and diverse than convention can convey—no more so than when unsettled by an interplay of multiculturalism with postmulticulturalism, nationalism with postnationalism, colonialism with postcolonialism, and migration with transmigration across a local/national/global nexus. Finally, the "post" in postcitizenship is not employed in the sense of "after" or "rejection". It's about constructively engaging with the positives of conventional citizenship models yet moving smartly beyond them in a spirit of constructive engagement.

Content and Arguments

A paradigm shift in reframing citizenship is unmistakable. The liberalization of a citizenship agenda continues apace, despite evidence of crackdown over newcomer admission and the incorporation of civic integration tests and stricter language requirements in defining who gets to belong. Western European countries that are major immigrant destinations have generally eased access to citizenship via the introduction of a jus soli mindset, tolerance for dual nationality, more open naturalization process by simplifying residence requirements, and a more principled pathway for the acquisition of citizenship (Hampshire, 2013). Pressure is mounting for uncoupling the concept of citizenship from its traditional moorings as state-centric, bounded, singular, static, and stuck. Proposed instead is a model that acknowledges and reframes the citizenship concept as a multilayered and multiversal reality as well as a more plural, fluid, and creative dynamic. Of those factors in the forefront of change and controversy, the following developments stand out: (a) robust levels of international migration leading to dual/multiple citizenships (b) the proliferation of transmigrant links and diasporic communities in contesting a one-size-fits-all national citizenship, (c) nested and multilevel citizenships that address national minority claims for territorial autonomy (d) differentiated citizenships that embrace minority demands for protection from discrimination, exemptions from general rules and obligations, access to valued resources and respectful recognition of their distinctiveness (e) postnational dynamics of identity politics coupled with the postcolonial politics of Indigeneity and (f) the internationalization of human rights in weakening the link between citizenship and nationality in a bordered territoriality (Bernal, 2014; Bloemraad, 2004; Camilleri, 2015; Maas, 2013; Smith, 2003).

These observations—conventional notions of thinking, talking, and doing citizenship are losing relevance; the meaning of citizenship is realigning along multi-centric lines; and a citizenship from the margins is dislodging a business-as-usual mindset—secure the content and argument for *Citizenship in a Transnational Canada*. This book is predicated on the premise that an increasingly dated national ("Westphalian") citizenship model requires an ambitious rethinking, one that moves positively beyond the articulated bounds of the nation-state by incorporating: (a) the principles of inclusiveness as grounds for recognition and entitlement (Bloemraad, 2004) (b) a postmulticultural lens in acknowledging multiversality and multiplicity of a hyperdiverse reality (Fleras, 2015) and (c) a postcitizenship mindset in rethinking the basis for belonging, identity, and entitlements. The book is also premised on the assumption that the politics of citizenship and the politicization of citizenship provide a framework for analyzing patterns of social inequality, a powerful weapon in the struggle for equality and inclusiveness ("citizenship-as-strategy" [Assies, 2005]), and an entry point for demonstrating how a formal citizenship reinforces a systemic exclusion when it intersects with the diversities of gender, race, Indigeneity, and immigrant status. To ground these dynamics while putting them to the test, *Citizenship in a Transnational Canada* analyzes the contested and changing dynamics of citizenship as discourse and practice when applied to Canada and (to a lesser extent) United States, Australia, and New Zealand—each of whom is looking to modify and move the citizenship agenda but with varying degrees of success.

Mindful of these positions and oppositions, I will argue that the concept of citizenship and current citizenship models are experiencing an identity crisis and a crisis of confidence. The signs of an identity crisis of confidence are growing: (a) citizenship no longer means what it once did in a rapidly changing and increasingly diverse and interconnected world (b) it's time to rethink the meaning of a meaningful citizenship across a broader range of rights and entitlements, multiple layers of identity, and more diversely complex patterns of belonging (Simon-Kumar, 2014) (c) pressure is mounting to de-center Eurocentric citizenship models along more multicentric and inclusive lines (d) little consensus exists over the meaning of citizenship in a sharply contested domain of belonging, identity, and entitlements and (e) the emergence of a postcitizenship citizenship acknowledges a discursive shift in the way we think, talk, and do citizenship. The value of a postcitizenship lens is proposed as an invitation for reassessing new citizenship realities, discourse and practices, while drawing attention to the importance of problematizing citizenship by dismantling convenient fictions to expose layers of inconvenient truths. The increasingly outdated assumptions of a national/ Westphalian citizenship regime are offset by the principles of an emerging postcitizenship context, while acknowledging how the current realities in the CANZUS countries hover somewhere in between an increasingly unworkable present and an ambitious yet unrealized future. More specifically, Canada's citizenship model is conceptualized across a local/national/global nexus, along comparative lines that include Australia, New Zealand, and the United States, and against the backdrop of a postcitizenship world of posts, trans, and isms. Finally, this book emphasizes the need to challenge conventional ways of framing citizenship as discourse and practice, what it means to be a citizen in the 21st century, and what constitutes a meaningful citizenship beyond the parameters that once prevailed, but now are transitioning to domains beyond the parochialism of sovereign states, national agendas, and physical borders (Maas, 2013).

Citizenship in a Transnational Canada is themed around the politics of citizenship and the politicization of citizenship. Citizenship politics and the emergence of a politicized citizenship domain furnishes insights into politics of mobilization and activism, sharpen debates over national identity and the limits of diversity, and secure a measure of recognition, redistribution and/or redress for the historically excluded. The politicization of citizenship questions the legitimacy of national citizenship as discourse and practice by emphasizing the centrality of "doing" citizenship at the level of performance, activity, and activism (Fleras, 2016; Isin and Nyers, 2014). It also provides a reminder that there is nothing natural or normal about citizenship, given its status as an ideologically infused, socially constructed, and contested site that varies across time and space. Its loaded status as a discourse in defence of dominant ideology renders the meaning of citizenship subject to challenge and redefinition, especially by those at the margins. Consider, for example, how Indigenous peoples are actively remaking the concept of citizenship by reframing it along the postcolonial lines of an Indigenous citizenship (see Chapter 7) (Banko, 2014; Green, 2017; Isin, 2009). Emergent citizenship narratives are superimposing the primacy of heterogeneity, inclusiveness, and people's lived-realities over that of homogeneity, absorption, and abstract rights (Atac et al., 2016; Galvez, 2013). And yet theorizing citizenship within a multiversal and multilayered context reinforces how the politics of citizenship remain locked within the controlling logic of the nation-state and a national citizenship (also Walter, 2014). That the state remains the most important location for citizenship serves to remind us that the power of the status quo is not fading away, but changing its dynamic (Tarozzi and Torres, 2016).

This book draws inspiration from a critical citizenship perspective. References to citizenship are not limited to a focus on the formal-legal, from voting rights to passport control. More accurately, its primarily about the substantive dimensions of citizenship, including those aspects of citizenship that are concealed such as the barriers that prevent individuals and marginalized groups from equal participation and full contribution to society (Field, 2007; Young, 1990). The study of citizenship especially in the Marshallian sense may have embraced a normative ideal of equal rights, access to membership, and full participation in society ("citizenship promises"). But citizenship must also be reframed in the opposite, namely, the absence of rights, the lack of capacity to exercise agency and involvement, and subjective experiences of outsider status and non belonging ("citizen disappointments") (Roseneil et al., 2013).[1] The concept of citizenship becomes politicized when statist notions of a national citizenship no longer offer satisfying answers to perennial questions over identity, belonging, and entitlements—not because of coercive and tyrannical power but because of the unintended consequences of everyday practices of a well-intentioned liberal society (Isin, 2002; Mhurchu, 2014; Rygiel, 2014; Young, 1990). A critical citizenship approach capitalizes on this lacunae in our knowledge by demonstrating how (a) citizenship biases are largely systemic, especially when failure to incorporate differences that make a difference reinforce a one-size-fits-all format that inadvertently excludes (b) its legal status and bounded political location are proving unhelpful in realizing a truly inclusive citizenship, in part because of provisions that exclude those beyond mainstream notions of identity, belonging, and status and (c) the value of an intersectional analysis exposes settler citizenship regimes as systemically biased ("gendered", "Eurocentric", "racialized" etc.), thus amplifying the effect of multiple and overlapping inequalities of exclusion. In short, the promise of citizenship as a passport to inclusiveness and equality is compromised when the realities of peoples' lives and life-chances as citizens do not match citizenship ideals, but reflect citizenship disappointments (Roseneil et al., 2013).

Citizenship in a Transnational Canada capitalizes on the tension between a legal citizenship within a national framework and the emergence of a postcitizenship as a reality, discourse and activity in a world increasingly diverse, complex, and interconnected. We live in a postcitizenship-themed world of posts, trans, and isms which makes it doubly important to situate citizenship within a broader and changing context of the transnational and postnational as well as postcolonial and postmulticultural. Ours is a world where citizenship politics in redefining who belongs, how, and why signify a new pattern of thinking, talking, and doing citizenship (for an interesting study see Harris-Perry, 2016). To be sure, reference to a critically informed postcitizenship does not announce the death of citizenship or corresponding demise of citizenship rights. Rather, a commitment to postcitizenship as a discursive framework provides an interpretive lens for reconsidering ways of re-engaging (interacting, identifying, and belonging) with a national citizenship. This commitment also provides a critical commentary on the politics of citizenship when applied to a postcolonial world of Indigenous peoples politics, a postmulticultural embrace of differently accommodating a world of diverse-diversities, the universal personhood implicit in a postnational ethic and cosmopolitan ideals, and the multilocality of transnational links and diasporic communities. The possibility of a new interpretive lens as an entry point for analysis and assessment as well as challenge and transformation points to the value of building on yet moving beyond a national citizenship. Such a lens also acknowledges that belonging, identity, and entitlements in a post-citizenship age challenge conventional citizenship notions by stretching the concept in ways that have yet to be imagined, let alone to be lived (Levy and Massalha, 2012).

Note

1. Framing refers to a process of organizing information in a way that encourages a preferred reading, in part by drawing attention to some aspects of reality as normal, desirable, and acceptable, while others are dismissed as irrelevant or inferior. It goes without saying that what is excluded from the framed reality ("citizen disappointments") may be just as important as what is included ("citizenship promises").

References

Abu-Laban, Yasmeen. "Citizenship and Foreignness in Canada." In *Routledge Handbook of Global Citizenship Studies*, edited by E. F. Isin and P. Nyers, 274–283. New York: Routledge, 2014.

Abu-Laban, Yasmeen. "Transforming Citizenship: Power, Policy, and Identity." *Canadian Ethnic Studies* 47, no. 1 (2015): 1–10.

Alfred, Taiaiake. "First Nations Perspective on Political Identity." *First Nations Citizenship Research and Policy Series*. June 2009.

Antonini, Erica. "Rethinking Public Space and Citizenship in Post-National Times: Hannah Arendt and 'The Right to Have Rights.'" *European Journal of Research on Education* 2, no. 6 (2014): 80–87.

Arendt, Hannah. *The Origins of Totalitarianism*. New York: Houghton Mifflin Harcourt, 1951.

Atac, Ilker, Kim Rygiel, and Maurice Stierl. "Introduction: The Contentious Politics of Refugee and Migrant Protest and Solidarity Movements: Remaking Citizenship From the Margins." *Citizenship Studies* 20, no. 5 (2016): 527–544.

Balibar, Etienne. *We, the People of Europe? Reflections on Transnational Citizenship*. Princeton, NJ: Princeton University Press, 2004.

Banko, Lauren, E. "The Invention of Citizenship in Palestine." In *Routledge Handbook of Global Citizenship Studies*, edited by E. Isin and P. Nyers, 317–324. New York: Routledge, 2014.

Banulescu-Bogdan, Natalia. "Shaping Citizenship Policies to Strengthen Immigrant Integration." *MPI*, August 2, 2012.

Banulescu-Bogdan, Natalia. "Top 10 of 2015—Issue #5: Governments Increasingly Restrict Citizenship." *MPI*, December 14, 2015.

Benhabib, Seyla. "Twilight of Sovereignty or the Emergence of Cosmopolitan Norms: Rethinking Citizenship in Volatile Times." *Citizenship Studies* 11, no. 1 (2007): 19–36.

Berezin, Mabel. "Territory, Emotion, and identity." In *Europe Without Borders*, edited by M. Berezin and M. Schain, 1–22. Baltimore: Johns Hopkins University Press, 2003.

Berg, Ulla Dalum and Robyn Magalit Rodriguez. "Transnational Citizenship Across the Americas." *Identities* 20, no. 6 (2013):649–664.

Bernal, Victoria. *Nation as Networks. Diaspora, Cyberspace, and Citizenship.* Chicago: University of Chicago Press, 2014.

Bilefsky, Dan. "Becoming Danish Gets Even Harder." *New York Times*, July 16–17, 2016.

Bloemraad, Irene. "Who Claims Dual Citizenship? The Limits of Postnationalism, The Possibilities of Transnationalism, and the Persistence of Traditional Citizenship." *IMR* 38, no. 2 (2004): 389–426.

Bloemraad, Irene. "Theorizing and Analyzing Citizenship in Multicultural Societies." *The Sociological Quarterly* 56, no. 4 (2015): 591–606.

Bloemraad, Irene, Anna Korteweg, and Gokce Yurdakul. "Citizenship and Migration: Multiculturalism, Assimilation, and Challenges to the Nation-State." *Annual Review of Sociology* 34 (2008): 153–179.

Bond, Ross. "Multicultural Nationalism? National Identities Among Minority Groups in Scotland's Census." *Journal of Ethnic and Migration Studies*. Published online September 19, 2016.

Boogaard, Vanessa van den. "Modern Post-Colonial Approaches to Citizenship: Kwame Nkrumah's Political Thought on Pan-Africanism." *Citizenship Studies*. Published online, August 6, 2016.

Bosniak, Linda. *The Citizen and the Alien.* Princeton, NJ: Princeton University Press, 2006.

Brodie, Janine. "Citizenship and Solidarity: Reflections on the Canadian Way." *Citizenship Studies* 6, no. 4 (2002): 377–394.

Brubaker, Rogers. *Citizenship and Nationhood in France and Germany.* Cambridge, MA: Harvard University Press, 1992.

Brubaker, Rogers. "The 'Diaspora' Diaspora." *Ethnic and Racial Studies* 28, no. 1 (2005): 1–19.

Butler, Kate and Cecilia Benoit. "Citizenship Practices Among Youth Who Have Experienced Government Care." *Canadian Journal of Sociology* 40, no. 1 (2015): 25–41.

Byrne, Bridget. *Making Citizens.* Palgrave Politics of Identity and Citizenship Series. London: Palgrave Macmillan, 2014.

Cairns, Alan (ed.) *Citizenship, Diversity, and Pluralism: Canadian and Comparative Perspectives.* Montreal/Kingston: McGill-Queens University Press, 1999.

Camilleri Joseph. "Great Transition." *Dialogical Citizenship: Dancing Toward Solidarity. A Great Transition Initiative Essay.* Retrieved 2015. http://www.greattransition.org.

Cao, Benito. *Environment and Citizenship.* New York: Routledge, 2015.

Castles, Stephen, Hein de Haas and Marvin Miller. *The Age of Migration*. 5/e. New York: Palgrave, 2013.

Chabot, Lynn. "The Concept of Citizenship in Western Liberal Democracies and in First Nations: A Research Paper." Prepared for the Governance Policy Directorate, Lands and Trusts Services. INAC, March 2007.

Clark, Emily B. and Glenn C. Savage. "Problematizing 'Global Citizenship' In an International School." In *Educating for the 21st Century*, edited by S. Choo, D. Sawch, A. Villanueva, and R. Vinz, 405–424. Singapore: Springer Link, 2016.

Clarke, John, et al. *Disputing Citizenship*. Boston: Polity Press, 2014.

Conference Notes. "Rethinking the Transnational Perspective: Shortcomings and New Approaches." International Workshop, University of Fribourg, September 13–14, 2012.

Dauvergne, Catherine. "Citizenship, Migration Laws and Women: Gendering Permanent Residency Status." *Melbourne University Law Review* 11, 2000.

Derrida, Jacques. *Of Grammatology*. Baltimore: Johns Hopkins University Press, 1998.

Environic Institute in Partnership with Institute on Governance. *Canadian Public Opinion on Governance*. Final Report, June 2016.

Field, Ann-Marie. "Counter-Hegemonic Citizenship: LGBT Communities and the Politics of Hate Crimes in Canada." *Citizenship Studies* 11, no. 3 (2007): 247–262.

Fleischmann Aloys NM, Nancy van Styvendale, and Cody McCarroll (eds.). *Narratives of Citizenship: Indigenous and Diasporic Peoples Unsettle the Nation State*. Edmonton: University of Alberta, 2011.

Fleras, Augie. "Beyond Multiculturalism: Managing Complex Diversities in Postmulticultural Canada." In *Revisiting Multiculturalism in Canada*, edited by L. Wong and S. Guo, 297–321. Rotterdam: Sense Publishers, 2015.

Fleras, Augie. "Re-imagining Citizenship in Canada, New Zealand, and Australia: Transnational Dynamics, Postnational Complexities, Postcitizenship Possibilities." Plenary Paper, Citizenship in a Transnational Context, University of Alberta, Edmonton, July 6–7, 2016.

Fleras, Augie. "Rethinking Citizenship Through Transnational Lenses." In *Citizenship in a Transnational Perspective*, edited by J. Mann, 15–48. New York: Palgrave Macmillan, 2017.

Fong, Vanessa. *Paradise Redefined. Transnational Chinese Students and the Quest for Flexible Citizenship in the Developed World*. Palo Alto, CA: Stanford University Press, 2011.

Fox, Jonathan. "Unpacking 'Transnational Citizenship.'" *Annual Review of Political Science* 8 (2005): 171–201.

Friedman, May and Silvia Schultermandl. *Click and Kin: Transnational identity and Quick Media*. Toronto: University of Toronto Press, 2016.

Galvez, Alyshia. "Immigrant Citizenship: Neoliberalism, Immobility, and the Vernacular Meanings of Citizenship." *Identities* 20, no. 6 (2013): 720–737.

Glick-Schiller, Nina. "Transborder Citizenship: An Outcome of Legal Pluralism within Transnational Social Fields." In *Mobile People, Mobile Law. Expanding Legal Relations in a Contracting World*, edited by F. Bender, et al., 48–90. London: Ashgate, 2005.

Gouws, Amanda (ed.). *(Un)thinking Citizenship: Feminist Debates in Contemporary South Africa*. Burlington, VT: Ashgate, 2004.

Green, Joyce. "The Impossibility of Citizenship Liberation for Indigenous People." In *Citizenship in a Transnational Perspective*, edited by J. Mann, 175–188. New York: Palgrave Macmillan, 2017.

Hampshire, James. *The Politics of Immigration. Contradictions of the Liberal State*. Boston: Polity Press, 2013.

Hansen, Randall. "The Poverty of Postnationalism: Citizenship, Immigration, and the New Europe." *Theory and Society* 38 (2009): 1–24.

Hanvelt, Marc and Martin Papillon. "Parallel or Embedded? Aboriginal Self-Government and the Changing Nature of Canadian Citizenship." In *Insiders and Outsiders: Alan Cairns and the Reshaping of Canadian Citizenship*, G. Kernerman and P. Resnick, 242–257. Vancouver: UBC Press, 2005.

Harris-Perry, Melissa. "The Politicization of Beyonce." *Elle Magazine*. November 8, 2016.

Hebert, Yvonne M. (ed.). *Citizenship in Transformation in Canada*. Toronto: University of Toronto Press, 2002.

Hebert, Yvonne M. and Lori Wilkinson. *The Citizenship Debates: Conceptual, Policy, Experiential, and Educational Issues*, edited by Y. M. Hebert, 3–36. Toronto: University of Toronto Press, 2002.

Hines, Sally "(Trans)Forming Gender: Social Change and Transgender Citizenship." *Sociological Research Online* 12, no. 1 (2007).

Hines, Sally. "A Pathway to Diversity?: Human Rights, Citizenship, and the Politics of Transgender." *Contemporary Politics* 15, no. 1 (2009): 87–102.

Hoffman, John. *Citizenship Beyond the State*. Thousand Oaks, CA: Sage, 2004.

Hollander, Saskia. "Renegotiating the Social Contract." June 27, 2014. Retrieved from http://www.thebrokeronline.eu.

Isin, Engin F. *Being Political: Genealogies of Citizenship*. Minneapolis: University of Minnesota Press, 2002.

Isin, Engin F. "Citizenship in Flux: The Figure of the Activist Citizen." *Subjectivity* 29 (2009): 367–388.

Isin, Engin F. *Citizenship After Orientalism: Transforming Political Theory*. London: Palgrave Macmillan, 2015.

Isin, Engin F. and Patricia K. Wood. *Citizenship and Identity*. Thousand Oaks, CA: Sage Publications, 1999.

Isin, Engin F, Janine Brodie, Danielle Juteau, and Daiva Stasiulis. "Recasting the Social in Citizenship." In *Recasting the Social in Citizenship*. Edited by E. Isin, 3–19. Toronto" University of Toronto Press, 2008.

Isin, Engin F. and Peter Nyers. "Introduction: Globalizing Citizenship Studies." In *Routledge Handbook of Global Citizenship Studies*, edited by E. Isin and P. Nyers. New York: Routledge, 2014.

Isin, Engin and Evelyn Ruppert. *Being Digital Citizens*. London: Rowman & Littlefield, 2015.

Jenson, Jane and Martin Papillon. "Challenging the Citizenship Regime: James Bay Cree and Transnational Action." *Politics and Society* 28, no. 2 (2000): 245–264.

Joppke, Christian. *Immigration and Citizenship*. Boston: Polity Press, 2010.

Kivisto, Peter and Thomas Faist. "The Boundaries of Citizenship: Dual, Nested, and Global." In *Politics of Globalization*, edited by Samir Dasgupta and Jan Nederveen Pieterse, 356–368. Thousand Oaks, CA: Sage Publications, 2008.

Kornelsen, Derek Wayne. "Postcolonial Citizenship: Reconceiving Authority and Belonging in Settler Societies." PhD Thesis, Vancouver, University of British Columbia, 2015.

Kymlicka, Will. "Trajectories of Multicultural Citizenship." In *Representation and Citizenship*, edited by R. Marback, 52–78. Detroit: Wayne State University Press, 2016.

Labelle, Micheline and Francois Rocher. "Debating Citizenship in Canada: the Collide of Two Nation-Building Projects." In *From Subjects to Citizens: A Hundred Years of Citizenship in Australia and Canada. Proceedings of a conference in Ottawa, 2001*, edited by P. Boyer et al., 263–286. University of Ottawa Press, 2004.

Lee, Charles T. "Decolonizing Global Citizenship." In *Routledge Handbook of Global Citizenship Studies*, edited by E. Isin and P. Nyers, 75–85. New York: Routledge, 2014.

Lee, Charles. *Ingenious Citizenship: Recrafting Democracy for Social Change.* Durham, NC: Duke University Press, 2016.

Leggewie, Claus. "Eurozine." *Transnational Citizenship. Ideals and European Realities.* Retrieved from http://www.eurozine.com, February 19, 2013.

Levitt, Peggy. "Migration Policy." *Transnational Migrant: When "Home" Means More Than One Country. Migration Policy.* October 1, 2004. Retrieved from http://www.migrationpolicy. org

Levy, Gal and Mohammad Massalha. "Within and Beyond Citizenship: Alternative Educational Initiatives in the Arab Society of Israel." *Citizenship Studies* 16, no. 7 (2012): 905–917.

Lightfoot, Sheryl. "The International Indigenous Rights Discourse and its Demand for Multilevel Citizenship." In *Multilevel Citizenship.* edited by W. Maas, Philadelphia: University of Pennsylvania Press, 2013.

Linklater, Andrew. "Citizenship and Sovereignty in the Post-Westphalian State." *European Journal of International Relations* 2, no. 1 (1996): 77–103.

Linklater, Andrew. "Cosmopolitan Citizenship." *Citizenship Studies* 2, no. 1 (1998): 23–4.

Lister, Ruth. "Dialectics of Citizenship." *Hypatia* 12, no. 4 (1997): 6–26.

Lister, Ruth. "Inclusive Citizenship: Realizing the Potential." *Citizenship Studies*, 49–61. Published online, May 30, 2007.

Maas, Willem. *Multilevel Citizenship.* Philadelphia: University of Pennsylvania Press, 2013.

Mann, Jatinder. "Introduction." In *Citizenship in a Transnational Perspective*, edited by J. Mann, 1–14. New York: Palgrave Macmillan, 2017.

Marback, Richard. "Introduction." In *Representation and Citizenship*, edited by R. Marback, 1–16. Detroit: Wayne State University Press, 2016.

Marlan, Tori. No Job. No Car. No Bank Account. What It's Like to be Stateless in Canada. *The Walrus*, March 20, 2017

Menon Nivedita. "Thinking Through the Postnation." *Economic and Political Weekly* 44, no. 10 (2009): 70–77.

Mhurchu, Aoileann Ni. "Citizenship Beyond State Sovereignty." In *Routledge Handbook of Global Citizenship Studies*, edited by E. Isin and P. Nyers, 119–127. New York: Routledge, 2014.

Modood, Tariq. "Multiculturalism, Citizenship, and National Identity." *Open Democracy*, Posted, May 17, 2007.

Moore, Alan. "No Straight Lines: Making Sense of Our Non-Linear World." *Stanford Social Innovation Review*. September 2012.

Morris, Jenny. "Citizenship and Disabled People: A Scoping Paper Prepared for the Disability Rights Commission," 2005. Retrieved from http://disability-studies.leeds.ac.uk.

Motomura, Hiroshi. *Americans in Waiting. The Lost Story of Immigration and Citizenship in the United States*. New York: Oxford University Press, 2006.

Munday, Jennie. "Gendered Citizenship." *Sociology Compass* 3, no. 2 (2009): 249–266.

Nagel, Caroline and Lynn Staeheli. "Citizenship, Nation, and Transnational Migration: The Case of Arab-American Activism." Paper presented to the Globalization and Democracy Conference, Boulder, CO, April 2002.

Nunn, Caitlin, C. McMichael, S. M. Gifford, and I. Correa-Velez. "Mobility and Security: The Perceived Benefits of Citizenship for Resettled Young People from Refugee Backgrounds." *Journal of Ethnic and Migration Studies*. Published online October 6, 2015.

Nyers, Peter. "Dueling Designs: The Politics of Rescuing Dual Citizens". *Citizenship Studies* 14, no. 1 (2010): 47–60.

Ommundsen, W., M. Leach, and A. Vandenberg. "Introduction." In *Cultural Citizenship and the Challenges of Globalization*, edited by W. Ommundsen, M. Leach, and A Vandenberg, 1–24. Cresskill, NJ: Hampton Press, 2010.

Predelli, Line Nyhagen, Beatrice Halsaa, and Cecile Thun. "'Citizenship is Not a Word I Use': How Women's Movement Activists Understand Citizenship." In *Remaking Citizenship in Multicultural Europe*, edited by Beatrice Halsaa, Sasha Roseneil and Sevil Sumer, 188–201. New York: Palgrave Macmillan, 2013.

Richez, Emmanuelle and Christopher P. Manfredi. "Citizenship and the Canadian Charter." In *Migration, Regionalization, Citizenship*, edited by Katja Sarkowsky, Rainer-Olaf Schultze, Sabine Schwarze, 127–150. VS Verlag fur Sozialwissenschaften, Springer Fachmedien Weisbaden, 2014.

Rodriguez, Cristina M. "Review: the Citizenship Paradox in a Transnational Age." *Michigan Law Review* 106, no. 6 (2008): 1111–1118.

Roseneil, Sasha. "Beyond Citizenship? Feminism and the Transformation of Belonging." In *Beyond Citizenship? Feminism and the Transformation of Belonging*, edited by S. Roseneil, 1–18. New York: Palgrave, 2013a.

Roseneil, Sasha. "Beyond Citizenship?" *Huffpost Politics*. May 7, 2013b.

Roseneil, Sasha, Beatrice Halsaa, and Sevil Sumer. "Remaking Citizenship in Europe: Women's Movements, Gender, and Diversity." In *Remaking Citizenship in Multicultural Europe*, edited by Beatrice Halsaa, Sasha Roseneil and Sevil Sumer, 1–18. New York: Palgrave Macmillan, 2013.

Rygiel Kim. *Globalizing Citizenship*. Vancouver: University of British Columbia Press, 2010.

Rygiel, Kim. "Life through Death: Transgressive Citizenship at the Border." In *Routledge Handbook of Global Citizenship Studies*, edited by E. Isin and P. Nyers, 62–72. New York: Routledge, 2014.

Sejersen, T. B. "'I Vow to Thee My Countries'—The Expansion of Dual Citizenship in the 21st Century." *International Migration Review* 42, no. 3 (2008): 523–549.

Simmons, Alan. *Immigration and Canada. Global and Transnational Perspectives*. Toronto: Canadian Scholars' Press, 2010.

Simon-Kumar, Rachel. "Difference and Diversity in Aotearoa/New Zealand: Post-neoliberal Constructions of the Ideal Citizen." *Ethnicities* 14, no. 1 (2014): 136–159.

Skific, Sanja. "Citizenship as an Instrument of Inclusion and Exclusion—a Comparative Analysis of Language Requirements in Naturalization Processes in the United States, Canada, Australia, and New Zealand." *Lengua y Migracion* 5, no. 1 (2013): 5–32.

Smith, Bryan and Pamela Rogers. "Towards a Theory of Decolonizing Citizenship." *Citizenship Education Research Journal* 5, no. 10 (2016): 59–72.

Smith, Michael Peter. "Transnationalism and Citizenship." In *Approaching Nationalisms*, edited by Brenda Yeoh, 15–38. Boston: Kluwer, 2003.

Soto, Jorge. "What Does Citizenship Mean in the 21st Century?" *Huffpost Impact*. January 21, 2014.

Soysal, Yasemin Nuhoglu. "Postnational Citizenship: Reconfiguring the Familiar Terrain." In *The Blackwell Companion to Political Sociology*, edited by Kate Nash and Alan Scott. Oxford UK: Blackwell, 2004.

Spoonley, Paul. "Renegotiating Citizenship: Indigeneity and Superdiversity in Contemporary Aotearoa/New Zealand." In *Citizenship in a Transnational Perspective*, edited by J. Mann, 209–224. New York: Palgrave Macmillan, 2017.

Stasiulis, Daiva. "Respatializing Social Citizenship and Security Among Dual Citizens in the Lebanese Diaspora." In *Citizenship in a Transnational Perspective, Canada, Australia, and New Zealand*, edited by J. Mann., 49–78. New York: Palgrave Macmillan, 2017.

Stanford. "Citizenship." *Encyclopedia of Philosophy*. Retrieved from https://plato.stanford.edu, 2011.

Strasser, Sabine. "Rethinking Citizenship in a Multicultural Europe. Critical Encounters with Feminist, Multicultural, and Transnational Citizenship." In *Remaking Citizenship in Multicultural Europe*, edited by Halsa, Beatrice, Sasha Roseneil and Sevil Sumer, 21–43. New York: Palgrave Macmillan, 2013.

Stromquist, Nelly P. "Theorizing Global Citizenship: Discourses, Challenges, and Implications for Education." *Inter-American Journal of Education for Democracy* 2, no. 1 (2009).

Tarozzi, M. and C.A. Torres. *Global Citizenship Education and the Crisis of Multiculturalism. Comparative Perspectives*. New York: Bloomsbury Press, 2016.

Tastsoglou, E. and A. Dobrowolsky (ed.). *Women, Migration, and Citizenship: Making Local, National, and Transnational Connections*. Burlington, VT: Ashgate Publishing, 2006.

Theodorou Angelina E. "27 Countries Limit a Woman's Ability to Pass Citizenship to Her Child or Spouse." *Pew Research Center*, August 5, 2014.

Tonkiss, K. and T. Bloom. "Theorising Noncitizenship: Concepts, Debates, and Challenges." *Citizenship Studies* 19, no. 8 (2015): 837–852.

Triadafilopoulos, Triadafilos. *Review of Citizenship in Transformation in Canada.* Institute of
   Public Administration in Canada 46, no. 4 (2003): 533–534.

Turner, Bryan S. "Outline of a Theory of Citizenship." *Sociology* 24, no. 2 (1990): 189–217.

Urzi, Domenica and Colin Williams. "Beyond Post-national Citizenship: An Evaluation of the
   Experiences of Tunisian and Romanian Migrants Working in the Agricultural Sector of
   Sicily." *Citizenship Studies.* Published online, November 10, 2016.

Walter, Maggie. "The Race Bind: Denying Australian Indigenous Rights." In *Indivisible: Indigenous Human Rights,* edited by J. Green, 43–64. Halifax: Fernwood, 2014.

Weaver, Hilary. "Reframing New Frontiers for Indigenous Peoples." *Journal of Sociology and
   Social Welfare* XL111, no. 3 (2015): 25–39.

Wood, Patricia K. "Aboriginal/Indigenous Citizenship: An Introduction." *Citizenship Studies* 7,
   no. 4 (2003): 371–378.

Yashar Deborah J. "Citizen Regimes and Indigenous Politics in Latin America." Proto-Paper
   prepared for "Claiming Citizenship in America," a Conference Organized by the Canadian Research Chair in Governance and Citizenship. May 27, 2005.

Young, Iris Marion. *Inclusion and Democracy.* New York: Oxford University Press, 1990.

Yuval-Davis, Nira. "The 'Multi-layered' Citizen. Citizenship in the Age of 'Glocalization.'"
   International Feminist Journal of Politics 1, no. 1 (1999): 119–136.

· 2 ·

CONCEPTUALIZING CITIZENSHIP

Introduction: Citizenship Matters

Those fortunate enough to be born in Canada or the United States rarely need to dwell on the benefits that citizenship confers (also Shachar, 2009). Members of the the so called "lucky ovarian club" automatically receive the full rights and entitlements associated with a birthright citizenship regardless of their parent's citizenship or parental residence status. A similar scenario prevails in New Zealand and Australia, although there are strings attached to a birthright citizenship if neither parent is a citizen nor permanent resident. Such a breezy attitude is not necessarily shared by those who must acquire citizenship through naturalization and whose acquisition is a desired prize that can mean the difference between life and death (Nunn et al., 2015). Citizenship is often a salient issue in many civil wars and situations of sectarian violence, especially in those societies that divide population into the "haves" (citizens) and the "have nots" (subjects or aliens). Worse still is the prospect of statelessness: International law regards statelessness as a condition in which a person is not considered a national (or generally speaking, not a citizen, although there are cases of individuals with citizenship but effectively stateless without state protection of rights [Bloom, 2017]). The UN

High Commissioner for Refugees estimates that statelessness afflicts upwards to 10 million persons worldwide, including 1,690 individuals who self-defined as stateless according to Canada's 2011 National Household Survey (Marlan, 2017). Or consider how the Myanmar (Burmese) government passed a law in 1982 that stripped the Rohingya minority of their citizenship and voting rights, thus rendering them stateless and without fundamental protections from violence and the ethnic cleansing they now endure (Goodspeed, 2017). The status of statelessness can arise in four ways: absence of citizenship such as stateless refugees; voluntary renunciation of citizenship; removal of citizenship (a woman in Morocco or Vietnam (until recently) lost her citizenship and became stateless if her marriage to a foreigner ended in divorce or her husband acquired a new citizenship); and cases of failed or collapsed states. To be stateless (without citizenship) runs the risk of serious humanitarian implications, from a loss of legal protection or a right to participate in the political process, to the increased likelihood of sexual and physical violence, poor employment prospects, and inadequate access to health care or education. Stateless individuals may also lack basic documentation related to the certification of births, marriages, and deaths (Blitz, 2011). In other words, citizenship makes us human, or as Arendt pointed out in the *Origins of Totalitarianism* (1951), to be deprived of citizenship (a state of statelessness without a right to have rights) was tantamount to invisibility and beyond the pale of humanity.

Put bluntly, citizenship matters. Possessing citizenship or having a nationality provides individuals with access to membership and identity, rights to claims-making, grounds for participation, security and protection from arbitrary government actions, and benefits from a body of common political knowledge (Abowitz and Harnish, 2006; Joppke, 2010). As Ayelet Shachar (2014) reminds us, our basic right to have rights is fragile and insecure if we can be deprived of membership in an organized political community. Attainment of citizenship offers the full panoply of civil, social, economic, and political rights accorded by the nation state, including security from arbitrary arrest, immunity from deportation for minor offences, the right to vote and stand for political office, a passport for travel across international borders, diplomatic protection in foreign countries, access to jobs and occupations denied to non citizens, eligibility for various public benefits and social services, and the option to sponsor overseas parents, children and relatives (Bloemraad, 2015; Hampshire, 2013). Possession of citizenship bolsters economic prospects. Studies indicate that citizenship by birth or choice reduces the risk of employment precarity, notably for racialized persons, thus underscoring the importance of incorporating legal status into the mix (Goldring and Joly, 2014; Urzi and Williams, 2016).

That citizenship matters is hardly surprising. Talk of a "post"-citizenship world of discursive shifts, notwithstanding, people still inhabit real if multiple physical sites that often arouse strong emotional bonds of loyalty and commitment (Berezin, 2003). A sense of identity and belonging to politically bounded community continues to be valued, despite the realities of rapid communications, more permeable borders, global mobility patterns, the rise of multiple citizenships, and a growing cosmopolitanism based on universal personhood (Mann, 2017). Last but not least, the health, governability, and stability of modern democratic systems are partly dependent on the qualities of citizenship and the attitudes of citizens across a variety of fronts. Citizenship secures a framework that bundles together a related set of political, social, and civil principles for promoting the virtues of public spiritedness, a sense of civility and tolerance, a shared notion of solidarity, and the bonds of trust in establishing a community of "us". Additional attributes of a functioning citizenship include a public acceptance of diverse ethnocultural or religious identities; a willingness to tolerate and cooperate with others who differ from them; and an openness to participate in the political process for enhancing the public good, preserving the environment or promoting social justice (Kymlicka, 2001). Not surprisingly, debates over inequality are often coded in the language of citizenship rather than the analytical categories of redistribution or recognition (Holston, 2009; Isin et al., 2008: 4).1

Of particular importance is the role of citizenship as a gateway (portal) in accessing and securing the full range of human rights. The citizenship concept may be a fashionable political topic or a scholarly buzzword. But it also represents a very real pathway to rights and recognition, inclusion and belonging (Roseneil et al., 2013). Or as famously articulated by Hanna Arendt (1951), "citizenship is about the right to have rights", that is, the guarantee, expression, and enforcement of universal human rights depend on access to a national citizenship (also Gormley, 2014; Shachar, 2014). And in a globalizing world of international migration and transnational forms of association, territorially-anchored national citizenships may be more relevant than ever in mooring a person to a nationality (Motomura, 2006) In truth, possessing citizenship does not always offer full panoply of these rights if minorities are denied a sense of belonging to the imagined community of a nation-state (Bonjour and Block, 2016). The mere possession of citizenship is neither a magical wand that whisks away inequality nor a quick-fix formula to ensure inclusion (Bloemraad, 2015). For instance, the 14th Amendment in 1868 may have guaranteed the federal citizenship for Black Americans, but not the right to vote, no access to educational opportunities or decent jobs, and no protection from lynchings in the past or police brutality at present. Despite this gap between ideals and reality, citizenship matters because it's a difference that makes a difference. It enhances the probability of making generally good things happen, not only in accessing core rights without undue government interference, but also in not having to prove one's bona fides for exercising these rights (Sobel, 2016).

This chapter capitalizes on the assumption that citizenship is one of those concepts that everyone thinks they intuitively understand, yet rarely do, resulting in the equivalent of a "paralysis by analysis". Debates over the nature, characteristics and benefits of citizenship as a contested terrain pose a series of tricky and under-theorized questions: "what is the meaning of citizenship in a changing and diverse world"; "what does it mean to be a citizen" at the intersection of a local, national, and global nexus; "what constitutes a meaningful citizenship" in a world of posts, trans, and isms? "How does citizenship provide an interpretative lens with which to better understand behaviour, predict success or failure, mobilize people into action groups and legalize claims-making activities"? "Is it possible to reconcile the tension between citizenship as a formal/legal status and the realities of a lived-citizenship as an activity, practice, or a performance ("doing" citizenship)"? "Does citizenship as concept still retain utility in a world where citizenship and nationhood are increasingly contested as organizational principles of society and the basis of international law" (Bloemraad et al., 2008; Kivisto, 2008)? "Does it still make sense to talk about a bounded citizenship as a governance model when migrant notions of identity and belonging are increasingly untethered from singular space" (Stasiulis, 2017b)? Responses to these loaded questions usually elude consensus or rarely yield a definitive answer.

The citizenship domain represents a contested site subject to struggles of interpretation and situated within the context of shifting regimes, contested discourses and prevailing practices. Such complexity makes it crucial that we problematize the concept of citizenship in the hope of exposing patterns, politics, and paradoxes that are not readily discernible, yet may conceal more than they reveal (Isin and Nyers, 2014). This chapter addresses each of the following issues, namely, defining and conceptualizing citizenship; situating a national (or Westphalian) citizenship model within a historical context; rethinking the meaning of citizenship under challenging circumstances and acknowledging the centrality of "doing" (or "lived"-) citizenship as a vital feature. The chapter also demonstrates how the parameters of citizenship within specific regimes continue to expand in ways that embody emergent realities, evolving discourses, and contested domains. The content of this chapter will set the stage for later discussions on how a discursive shift in postcitizenship precepts and practices is challenging the exclusive authority of the nation-state in defining how we think, talk, and do citizenship.

Citizenship in Historical Perspective: Toward a National (Westphalian) Citizenship Model

Citizenship represents one of the world's oldest systems of governance for organizing human relations [Cao, 2015; Hanvelt and Papillon, 2005). From Aristotle and Arendt to contemporary scholars such as Will Kymlicka, Jane Jenson, and Engin Isin, the concept of citizenship provides a forum for contemporary debates over the nature of freedom, autonomy, and equality, while securing a site for contesting competing debates over nationalism and identity, the right-to-have-rights claims, and conditions for recognition and acceptance (DiGregorio and Merolli, 2016). The earliest manifestations of citizenship focused on identifying and rewarding those individuals who provided a core service such as protection to the community (Chabot, 2007). Citizenship was deemed a privilege for a minority of the population, that is, citizens possessed rights that were withheld from non citizens such as women, the unpropertied, and slaves. Its genesis in the Western world was rooted in the ancient Greek notion of polis (specific territory) in which the highest calling reflected political engagement in a male-only public domain. Both the ancient Greeks and Romans depicted citizenship as a status superior to the private sphere, occupied by male patricians enjoying public political life in the polis, and informed by the concept of a political community and civic involvement (from jury duty to military service) in which the ideal citizen put aside the private interests for the sake of the public good (Dominelli, 2014a; Marback, 2016). The Roman Republic developed an alternative rights-oriented model—in part justified on the need to incorporate conquered populations across the Empire through legal protection instead of civic participation—that established a precursor to Western traditions of citizenship around a juridical concept of legal status and formal rights (Bloemraad et al., 2008; Stanford, 2011).

Over time, the medieval polity in feudal Europe displaced Greco-Roman notions of citizenship as political activity. Pre-modern ideas of citizenship as membership in city-states were forged in the crucible of religious wars in Europe, the industrial and scientific revolutions, the transition to capitalism, European competition for colonial empires, and the formation of constitutionally limited monarchies and nation states (Assies, 2005; Jenson and Papillon, 2001; Strasser, 2013).The modern states that emerged out of disintegrating empires sought to establish sovereignty over internally diverse communities by promoting an ideology of national homogeneity while imposing a tight fit between nationality and territorial boundaries. This new national status gradually replaced kinship, town, guild, and gender as the determinant of access to rights, resources, identity and belonging for those defined as part of the nation (Tambini, 2001). Of particular salience in the evolutionary trajectory of citizenship was the consolidation of the modern nation-state in the aftermath of the French Revolution. The state was no longer synonymous with the monarch as a dominant political authority and primary source of peoples' rights (Maas, 2013; Noonan and Nadkarni, 2016). Rather, as Brubaker (1992) points out, the French Revolution modernized the meaning of citizenship as an attachment to a specific territorial regime whose rulers monopolized the right to proclaim rights and impose obligations. The concept of nationalism not only undermined the principles underlying empire in favour of ideas of related to democracy, rule of law, and popular sovereignty; it also embraced the moral and emotional sentiments that differentiated citizens from non-citizens (Noonan and Nadkarni, 2016). The industrial revolution, followed by 19th century state-building regimes, proved equally adept in shifting the locus of citizenship from a city/state/principality regime to one rooted in a sovereign and territorially bounded political community ("nation-state") of rights bearing individuals (Bloemraad, 2015; Labelle and Rocher, 2004; Paehlke, 2014; Stanford, 2011). Or as pithily put by Richard Marback (2016: 2) in capturing the interplay between private and public, whereas the interests of the state become the interests of the citizens in ancient Greece, the interests of the citizen gradually become the interests of the state from the French revolution onwards.

The Treaty of Westphalia in 1648 marked the origins of the modern nation state and national citizenship as the dominant form of political authority, citizen affiliation, and social organization (Maas, 2013). The foundational framework proposed by the Treaty eventually incorporated the following governance principles: (1) each nation state exercises de jure sovereignty over territory, borders, and domestic affairs without external interference (2) each state respects the territorial integrity of other states and refrains from interfering with their domestic affairs (3) each state is equal in international standing regardless of how small (Linklater, 1996; Sarkar, 2015). The outlines of national citizenship model that emerged conformed with the Westphalian principle of territorial sovereignty, an attendant claim to external closure and internal control, the legal autonomy and equality of nation-states, and a promise of non-interference in the affairs of other states (Mulcaire, 2014; Robertson, 2007). Citizenship was increasingly aligned with nationality as the legal expression of an exclusive national membership with a corresponding package of rights, duties, and identities (Brown, 2014; Cao, 2015; Dominelli, 2014b; Hettne, 2000; Tully, 2014). Westphalian concepts of citizenship increasingly dwelt on the rights of citizens/individuals rather than on duties to the state, so that obligatory and active civic duty was not always a requirement of citizenship (Chabot, 2007). They also reflected a state-centric belief that identities were zero sum, that is, someone could be one or the other, but not both—at least not without inducing disorder or fomenting division (Robertson, 2007). Membership in a political community superseded all other affiliations, while a one-size-fits-all citizenship ensured that everyone belonged and identified in the same way regardless of whether they liked it or not.

How does the status of Westphalian citizenship regime (the concept of regime will be discussed in the last section of this chapter) align with the principles and practices of contemporary citizenship (Peled, 2007)? Can a Westphalian model continue to exert an homogenizing and controlling role it fulfilled in the previous centuries, namely, a bounded state's sovereign power over a particular territory including the authority to issue or withdraw citizenship (Schuck, 2009; Stanford, 2011)? Is the Westphalian notion of citizenship (and concept of nation-state) slipping into irrelevance in light of a changing and diverse world, little more than an anachronism or obsolescence in an era of transmigration, hyperdiversities, globalization, and cosmopolitanism (Hettne, 2000; Linklater, 1996; Sarkar, 2015)? Or is it more accurate to say that what we are witnessing is not the end of citizenship but rather the end of a Westphalian citizenship model as we know it, with its privileging of the nation-state as the unfettered final authority in defining membership, identity, and entitlements. A combination of factors are challenging state-centric models of national citizenship, including the internationalization of human rights, economic globalization and globalized mobility, extension of rights to non citizens ("denizens"), a dispersal of political authority across sub- and supra-national institutions, and mobilization around collective and group-specific rights (Soysal, 2004).

No less important in unbundling the once cozy fit between territory and nationality is the declining boundedness of citizenship because of more fluid yet brittle citizen attachments to the nation state and national identity. A post-Westphalian reality points to the inescapable: territorial-bounded nation states are relinquishing their exclusive grip as the sole authority in defining belonging, identity, and entitlements. For example, globalization as a complex and nuanced process constitutes a fundamental challenge to Westphalian ideals of sovereign statehood and exclusive citizenship (Sassen, 1996; Guha, 2017). The myriad patterns of interconnectedness and corresponding reduction of barriers under globalization continue to weaken a nation-state's entitlement to unqualified and supreme rule and the ability to regulate and control the citizenship agenda within a delimited territory without undue external influence. As a result, the politics of citizenship are increasingly played out at a variety of different levels and across a local/national/global nexus (Hettne, 2000), while both the protective and enabling aspects of citizenship are extended to transmigrants, members of diasporic communities, and non-citizen residents ("denizens") (Peled, 2007).

The future appears to be no less unsettling. Disruptions to citizenship as principle, discourse, and practice reflect advances in communication and transportation, global trade and economic integration, and the internationalization of a human rights agenda (Paehlke, 2014). Such re-conceptualization is driven by the belief that we are all global citizens whether we choose to acknowledge this or not; accordingly, the meaning of citizenship encompasses globally oriented obligations and duties, including rights as both planetary and national citizens. By contrast, narrow and nationalistic loyalties are thought to be outmoded by virtue of posing a threat to global security and prosperity. Challenges and controversies over the parameters (boundaries) and content (meaning) of citizenship embody a multitude of politics, movements, and confrontations, some of them violent and themselves exclusionary in orientation. Others are inclined toward a more inclusive citizenship that provides the historically disadvantaged with the opportunities to participate and contribute as equals (also Morris, 2005). Not unexpectedly, the salience of a Westphalian citizenship model is under attack in a world where mobility rather than permanent migration is a norm, resulting in overlapping linkages in two or more countries, a majority of whom now recognize some form of dual citizenship in principle or practice. Nonetheless, predictions about the demise of the nation state as the bedrock of citizenship rights and responsibilities are premature at best; after all, the nation state remains the primary receptacle for enforcing universally defined rights even in matters involving international conventions (Kalu, 2013). In other words, there is much to commend in the claim that defining citizenship as membership in the nation-state conceals so much that it's analytically pointless (Isin and Nyers, 2014: 1). Still, there remains considerable utility in prioritizing a Westphalian model as a starting point for analyzing and debating citizenship as a contested site of claims and counterclaims (Joppke, 2010).

Conceptualizing Citizenship, Contesting Definitions

Everyone agrees that citizenship matters in specifying who belongs, how they belong, and what belonging entitles. But agreement stiffens when defining what citizenship means (or more accurately, what is the meaning attached to this "thing" or "process" called citizenship), who's included and excluded, and how citizenship is differently experienced from the vantage point of the disadvantaged (Fleras, 2016; Isin and Nyers, 2014; Kabeer, 2005; Urzi and Williams, 2016). Citizenship possesses meanings that are deeper and more subtle than owning a passport or doing jury duty. It defines a person's relationship to a nation-state which makes it difficult to separate what citizenship means without reference to related concepts such as nationalism and democracy (The Times Editorial Board, 2014). Many reject essentialist notions of citizenship that assume a fixed, true, and unchanging meaning to the concept. They prefer a citizenship couched in the language of a fluid and politically contested domain, subject to change and operating at multiple levels and across overlapping jurisdictions. Citizenship is thought to have no fixed or proper meaning but a diversity of complex meanings that are applied as the situation arises (Clarke et al., 2014). Others are critical of stretching the meaning of citizenship to the point of distortion; as a result, it no longer means what it says or says what it means but means whatever people want it to mean depending on the context or criterion. Not surprisingly, experts in the field such as Linda Bosniak (2006) propose eliminating the term altogether because of its lack of specificity.

The scope of citizenship is substantial and expanding. Citizenship may be framed in the following ways: political engagement; collective identity; social contract; membership and belonging; formal legal status; a capacity to exercise and enjoy these rights; performance and activism; and a claims-making activity that challenges as it transforms (Baubock, 2008; Berg and Rodriguez, 2013; Bloemraad, 2015; Bosniak, 2000; Hampshire, 2013; Leggewie, 2013;

Pitty, 2009). A legal definition of citizenship emphasizes a set of rules about access, membership, and rights. But a focus on the social (performative), political (claims making), and ideological dimensions of citizenship offers a discursive frame beyond the formal and the abstract. Distinctions involving formal citizenship (membership in a nation-state) differ from substantive citizenship (meaningful possession of social, civil, and political rights), which, in turn, differ from differentiated citizenship (customizing patterns of belonging and entitlements) (Shipper, 2010).

Legal definitions would appear to be relatively straightforward, based as they are on membership, rights, and mutual obligations (Enjolras, 2007). At its most elemental level, citizenship is about membership in territorially-bounded political community involving a reciprocal set of rights and duties, coupled with a commitment to a shared identity and the centrality of civic virtues and practices (Baubock, 2008; Joppke, 2007). For T.H. Marshall, citizenship consisted of a unified package of multiple rights, including the civil rights of organization and expression, political rights to vote, and social rights to a minimum living standards and entitlement to social program in the hope of offsetting the inequalities of exclusion (Balta and Altan-Olcay, 2016; Cattapan, 2009; Yashar, 2005). Citizenship can also be defined as a relationship between a person and a political community and state institutions, ideally enshrined in law, and focused on individual rights over property, security, and entitlements (Berenschot et al., 2017). Isin and Nyers (2014: 1) offer a definition along these lines: Citizenship as an institution (used in a very broad sense) that mediates the rights and relationships between the subject of politics and the polity to which the subjects belong.

By contrast, non-legal approaches are proving trickier to define, given how the term is employed across a range of ideas and practices pertaining to national identity, attachment to country, political participation and voting, and civic enactments (Jedwab, 2008; Richez and Manfredi, 2014). Citizenship represents a complex concept of diverse dimensions and multiple modalities. It may be disaggregated into four analytical dimensions (belonging and collective identity, rights, status, and participation or claims making activity [Bloemraad et al., 2008; Bosniak, 2000]), at multiple and overlapping levels (urban, tribal, national, international, transnational), across shifting domains (civil, social, political, sexual, cultural) along a multiplicity of actors and sites (courts, streets, media), and among a host of competing claims to justice and inclusiveness (Brown, 2012; Isin, 2009). That alone makes it impossible to bundle all meanings and uses into a single definition, especially those aspects of citizenship at the extreme fringes of the concept's boundaries (Baubock, 2008).

Complicating the definition domain are different models of citizenship based on membership in a polity with a corresponding set of expectations (Berenschot et al., 2017; Fonseca, 2014; Schuck, 2009). They include *liberal* models with their focus on rights, legal guarantees, individualism, market fundamentalism, and passive subject status such as compliance to laws; *republican* models are duties based, privilege the collective, prioritize public good, and promote civic engagement and active involvement in the political process; and *communitarian* models that emphasize community belonging, social embeddedness, and cultural embrace (Cao, 2015; Maas, 2013; Stanford, 2011). While the liberal model isolates the citizen as an autonomous individual whose rights and freedoms depend on collective guarantees, a republican model defines the citizen as an involved and contributing member of a political community. Whereas liberal models see citizenship as a legal status for maximizing civil rights, a republican model frames citizenship as a desirable practice involving virtuous citizens and civic virtues (from political engagement to volunteering involvement). By contrast, communitarian models envisage citizenship as a shared identity within a community of like-minded individuals (Low, 2016). The point of departure for communitarians is not the liberal individual but the political community since rights and freedoms depend on the integrity of the social order and a robust public domain. In addition to these widely cited models, Castles and Miller (2009) recognize four ideal citizenship types also based on membership patterns: an imperial model (belonging based on subject status to some ruling power); ethnic model (belonging to nation because of ethnicity (common descent, language, culture)); republican model (or civic) (belonging based on acquiring membership in a political community along with adherence to political rules and national culture); and multicultural model (belonging based on newcomer retention of identities and communities provided they conform to national laws).

Clearly, the concept of citizenship eludes an easy definition (Isin and Nyers, 2014). A slippery concept at the best of times whose contested meanings and complex practices have fluctuated over time and across space in response to internal and external factors (Dominelli, 2014c; Dominelli and Moosa-Mitha, 2014; Mhurchu, 2014), the term itself is subject to such an array of applications that the absence of any fixed reference point may derail the prospect of communication or consensus (Clarke et al., 2014). References to citizenship once revolved around a constellation of identity, belonging, and entitlements situated within the bounded confines of the nation-state and national citizenship (Mann, 2017). Now, however, the concept is splintered into multiple affiliations and shifting identities that transcend borders at once more porous yet also more militarized. The potential for a flow and movement of people across borders has unshackled cultural identities and liberated membership from physical space, while reinforcing a growing identification with a universal personhood and a cosmopolitan web of interconnectedness (Soysal, 2011; Singh, 2017). The fractious relationship between the citizens and the state is further fractured by clashes among those whose identities—from Indigenous nations to supra-national (global or cosmopolitan) perspectives—fall outside a conventional wisdom (Kabeer, 2005). Such a challenge raises the question of whether a more expansive framework can advance a inclusive citizenship, one that differently accommodates a diversity of meanings without foreclosing a meaningful link to a national citizenship. In short, this array of sweeping circumstances, interests, and dynamics in constructing and contesting citizenship as status, discourse, and practices serves as an important reminder. It reinforces the value of Engin Isin (2009: 370) prescient notion that the real issue is not about "what is citizenship" but, more accurately, about deconstructing the idea of "what is *called* citizenship".

The Multidimensionality of Citizenship

It should be obvious that social phenomenon such as citizenship can be differently defined and analysed based on (1) what something looks like (2) what it says its doing (3) what it is really doing or (4) what it should be doing. Citizenship as a concept also possesses multiple dimensions that roughly correspond with these definition typologies. They include a legal dimension (what it looks like), a normative dimension (what it should be doing) and an interactive dimension (what it is doing) (also Kivisto and Faist, 2008). A fourth dimension—a critical dimension or what citizenship is *really* doing—is also discussed by way of Insight Posts in this chapter on birthright citizenship and the politics of gendered citizenship in the first chapter.

Legal Dimensions

In legal parlance, citizenship entails formal membership in a politically constituted community (Delanty, 2007). A legal–political contract is established involving a transaction of mutual benefit to all parties, including a reciprocal exchange of rights and duties that connects individuals to membership in the state (Hebert and Wilkinson, 2002; Squires, 2007). According to this line of thought, citizenship embraces three bundles of rights: civil rights (from the right to free speech to equality before the law; political rights (the right to vote or stand for office); and social rights (from basic economic welfare to a right to education and security according to prevailing societal standards). Individual citizens rely on the state to protect their rights and freedoms; in turn, the state expects citizens to fulfill certain duties, obligations, and responsibilities. For citizens of Canada, these rights and freedoms encompass the following entitlements: equality rights, democratic rights, legal rights, mobility rights, language rights, the right of re-entry, freedom of religion, freedom of expression, and freedom of assembly and association. In return, Canadian citizens are obliged to obey Canadian laws, participate in the democratic process, respect the rights and freedoms of others, serve on jury duty when required, and recognize Canada's linguistic duality and multicultural heritage.

People can legally acquire citizenship along two pathways: at *birth (birthright)* or by *choice (naturalization)*. Citizenship by *birthright* transmits citizenship status through birth on a territory (jus soli) or from parentage (jus sanguinis). Birth under jus sanguinis assigns primacy to the citizenship of parents regardless of where the child is born; as a result, citizenship is restricted to those who share a common bloodline or who can trace their genealogy (descent) to a citizen (Young, 1998). A commitment to blood citizenship can make it extremely difficult for the foreign-born to become citizens (Howard, 2008; Nathans, 2004; Winter, 2016; Winter et al., 2016). For example, the recent movement of asylum seekers into Germany raises a thorny question: How does a country that historically defined itself as an ethnic nation broaden its self-concept to incorporate newcomers who pose a threat to its national identity (Mounk, 2017)? (Keep in mind that Germany since 2000 has shifted from a focus on jus sanguinis as the sole basis for granting German citizenship to the introduction of jus soli as principle and practice and, more recently, acceptance of an unqualified dual citizenship [Willhelm, 2016; Winter, 2016]). All states allow their citizen parents to automatically transmit citizenship on to their children. Nevertheless, there are country-by-country variations in the number of generations that a citizen living abroad can transmit their citizenship to their offspring (Macklin and Crepeau, 2010).

With jus soli, citizenship is obtained by virtue of birth place regardless (in theory) of the citizenship of parents (Young, 1998). In reality, however, the acquisition of citizenship by birth in a territory often depends on parental legal status (Baubock, 2008). Relatively few countries (Canada and the

United States are exceptions) confer automatic and unconditional citizenship to anyone born on their territory regardless of parental "legal" status, citizenship, or nationality. Countries such as New Zealand and Australia allow citizenship by birth, but only if one of the parents holds lawful resident status. As Bauder (2012) notes, most nation-states prefer one principle over another; for example, countries formed through immigration such as Canada and Australia tend to emphasize the principle of jus soli as a pathway to integration; by contrast, the out-migration countries of Europe promote the jus sanguinis principle in the hope of securing the nationality of children of expatriates [Stoker, 2011]). In reality, most states employ a combination of principles in assigning citizenship to their subjects (Baubock, 2008; Willhelm, 2016: 4).

The concept of birthright citizenship has come under criticism. A national citizenship based on the principles of jus soli and jus sanguinis is thought to be inherently and unjustly exclusive. A birthright citizenship resembles the feudal membership in medieval societies insofar as an accident of birth shapes the lives and life chances of its resident citizens (Baubock, 2008; Carens, 1987). The exclusiveness of the nation-state as the ultimate authority and repository of citizenship rights puts the onus on advancing a higher ethical plane of entitlements to offset this injustice (Nekvapil, 2011). The Insight Post below provides one example of addressing this dilemma.

Insight Post

Birthright Citizenship: Choose Your Parents Carefully

Everyone once in a while a book comes along that really ruffles conventional thinking by problematizing what is widely taken for granted. Ayelet Shachar's The Birthright Lottery (2009) is no exception to this rule, thanks to her provocative take on the concept and privileges of birthright citizenship (Bagley, 2009; Coyne, 2009). According to Shachar, possessing citizenship may well constitute the single most important institution of the modern era for allocating goods, rights, and opportunities. Yet the global citizenship regime system awards its benefits and blessings to individuals primarily on the accident of birth, so that the benefits of affluent countries (from security to prosperity) accrue to those lucky enough to be born in a specific territory (jus soli) or to a particular parent (jus sanguinis). Under a birthright citizenship, the relatively wealthy can transfer rights, opportunities, and property to children. For example, consider those well-to-do families from non-North

American countries who pursue arrangements to ensure the birth (and automatic citizenship) of their children on American soil (Balta and Altan-Olcay, 2016). By contrast, poor people who by another accident of birth and through no fault of their own are locked into political and economic systems that limit their fortunes (Bennion, 2012). For example, if one is lucky to be born a Canadian, they have won first prize in the lottery of life: a life expectancy of 82 years in 2014 and cradle-to-grave care in a prosperous and stable country. Those with the misfortune to be born in Liberia will be lucky to live to 48 years of age, eking out a precarious existence in a violent and unstable society (Gibney, n.d). No wonder Joseph Carens (1987) compares modern citizenship to feudal status in the medieval world, assigned at birth and impacting a person's life and life chances.

The repercussions of a citizenship based on fortuitous circumstances deserve attention. The legal principles of jus soli and jus sanguinis not only legitimize a morally questionable citizenship regime; they also perpetuate patterns of global inequality for, in the final analysis, the intergenerational transfer of birthright citizenship resembles a special kind of untaxed property inheritance, an entitlement not unlike that of the aristocratic transfer system of feudal Europe. But an intergenerational transfer system based on unearned privilege contravenes the very notion of what Western societies stand for. First, the accident of birth in a particular state or to specific parents should not determine a person's access to rights and benefits that, as a matter of redistributive justice, should be enjoyed universally rather than nationally (Schuck, 2009). Second, such arbitrariness is also incommensurate with the democratic principles of a liberal society, violates the principles of meritocracy, and contradicts the rule of contract and choice that underpin the foundational logic of civic (rather than ethnic) society (Isin, 2012; Shachar, 2009).

Shachar proposed two remedies to alleviate the most glaring inequalities of a system based on a chance encounter. First, she articulates a new legal principle for defining membership—jus nexi—to complement extant principles of belonging by blood or soil. According to the doctrine of jus nexi, a commitment to meaningful involvement and continuous residency in a community should also provide a platform for bestowing citizenship and its benefits to resident stakeholders, especially for those who migrated in contravention of international or national law or who find themselves stateless. After all, who is more deserving of citizenship? Those who commit to a country by choice yet are denied access versus those who happen to be born in a country yet underappreciate their good fortune (Higgins, 2009). Second, Shachar advances the idea of a global wealth transfer mechanisms as a way of compensating those on the wrong side of the birthright divide. Wealthy countries would pay to poor countries a birthright privilege levy by way of an inheritance tax, thus creating a global system of distributive justice not unlike the concept of a social safety net or that of foreign aid. Clearly, then, Shachar's proposals are a call to action for addressing the problem of global inequality. To date, however, there appears little appetite for putting these principles into practice.

Most people acquire citizenship by birth rather than by naturalization, defined as a formal and professed attachment to a polity other than a person's birthplace). Such an assertion is hardly surprising since less than 4 percent of the world's population are classified as immigrants or foreign born with residence in another country. In theory, citizenship by *naturalization* (jus domicile) suggests something that is made natural or conforms with the so-called laws of nature such as aligning a person's residence with nationality (Fortier, 2013). In reality, a naturalized citizenship is not acquired automatically (or naturally) either through marriage or simple residence. Rather, citizenship must be applied for, approved, and its acquisition may entail addressing a set of stringent requirements (also Young, 1998). A naturalized citizenship is offered to those foreign-born who are legal residents, fulfill certain residency requirements, make an effort to acquire language competency and knowledge of host country, and comply to the rule of law and shared values of that country (Griffith, 2016). The politics of naturalization should not be underestimated, especially in ethnic nation-states, since belonging is generally contingent on blood or descent (jus sanguinis). Compare this to the relative ease of acquisition in territorial-based nation-states (jus soli) with its commitment to core values and the rule of law (Vink, 2013).

Governments are known to vacillate between more facilitative or more restrictive approaches to the naturalization of would-be citizens. To one side, lowered hurdles to naturalization increasingly prevail, including, reduced residency requirements, less focus on cultural assimilation, more principled decision making on the part of the state, more emphasis on jus soli principle vis-à-vis that of jus sanguinis, and growing acceptance of dual citizenship (Joppke, 2010; Willhelm, 2016). Not surprisingly there is talk of expanding citizenship to those who can demonstrate de facto permanent residence based on an individual's right to choose a political home regardless of ancestry, immigrant status, or birthplace (Bauder, 2016; Shachar, 2009). To the other side, the liberalization of citizenship in some parts of the world are offset by mounting restrictions over the naturalization of newcomers, particularly in Europe. Barriers include tougher language and civic integration tests, lengthened residency requires, and increased government powers to revoke the citizenship from dual citizens for serious infractions against the state. In short, what prevails at present is a citizenship that's is harder to get, but easier to lose (Griffith, 2016), in effect transforming naturalization into a privilege rather than a right or, alternatively, a reward for integration rather than a pathway to integration (Puzzo, 2016).

Finally there is the contentious issue of citizenship by residence: Citizenship by *jus nexi* reflects the principle of de facto residence, a lived-belonging, and meaningful participation in a community (Bauder, 2012). Access to citizenship is determined not by an accident of birth in a political territory (jus soli) or inherited like blood from parents (jus sanguinis). Rather citizenship is determined by place of residence regardless of legal status, actual and ongoing participation in the community, a genuine connection to society, and a commitment to its values and rules (Bauder, 2016; Shachar, 2009). For example, an endorsement of the jus nexi principle would extend citizenship status to low-skilled temporary foreign workers in Canada. As it stands now, they contribute to growing the economy yet their "citizenshipless" status renders them vulnerable to exploitation. They are slotted into a predetermined occupation, cannot freely switch employers, and are barred from residency in Canada upon expiry of their employment and residence visas (Austin & Bauder, 2012; Fleras, 2015). In other words, citizenship under a jus nexi principle reflects the reality of actual residence and lived-links to a political territory regardless of documented status (Shachar, 2009).

Normative Dimensions: Ideals as Aspirations

Citizenship is more than a legal status involving instrumental benefits, although the primacy of a formal status prevails since citizenship per se has no legal authority, logic or moral force outside the political framework of a nation state (Hansen, 2009). The real meaning of citizenship goes beyond owning a passport or casting a ballot (The Times Editorial Board, 2014). It entails a psychological commitment and an "emotional investment" (Fortier, 2013) for living ethically by focusing on what we expect and what is expected of us, our rights and responsibilities to others, and our relationship to the state. In other words, while the legal matters, the normative matters too; after all, nation-states do not see themselves as an arbitrary collection of individuals with formal rights and legal status, but as communities of values embracing people of good character who share common ideals (Anderson, 2014). The normative dimensions of what citizenship should be are critical as well in posing the question of "what for is the political community" (Richez and Manfredi, 2014). In going beyond citizenship as a legal-political status, a normative dimension frames it as an aspirational ideal that invokes varying visions of the good and just society, together with the nature of the state in promoting social justice (Schuck, 2009). And while perceptions and theories of normativity have changed over time, citizenship's normative core remains constant. Citizens should enjoy equal rights as a matter of course, but also receive equal consideration and differential treatment when the situation arises (Stanford, 2011).

Therein lies a dilemma at the heart of normative citizenship. The appeal of a national citizenship based on the universality of individual freedoms and equal rights regardless of race, gender, or Indigeneity may conflict with the particularistic demands of cultural identity or aggrieved status which entail differential treatment on grounds of vulnerability or historical injustice (Chatterjee, 2006). Balancing the polarities reinforces the importance of framing citizenship politics from the perspective and struggles of non-citizens "from below" (Swerts, 2014). For example, the human rights logic implicit in a normative dimension is pivotal in securing the individual rights and group protection for those who reside in cruel and despotic states, live outside the boundary of their nationality, and risk inhumane treatment in immigrant-unfriendly regimes (Schuck, 2009). In brief, citizenship embraces a sense of the normative through participation with others in the struggle for recognition and redistribution, including the right to political engagement or claims-making in challenging the inequities of injustice and exclusion (Bloemraad, 2015).

An Interactive Dimension: "Doing" Citizenship

Formal definitions and official policies that flow from legal provisions are important and influential. Yet any understanding of citizenship is not solely determined by statutory distinctions. Framing citizenship in a universal, abstract, and objective manner (i.e., a legal status or formal membership) tends to downplay how its practiced, articulated, and experienced within a specific political, legal, social and historical context (Butler and Benoit, 2015). Just as important in conceptualizing citizenship as the legal bond between the state and the individual (although this legal status is fundamental to the enjoyment of basic human rights [Stasiulis, 2017a]) are the routine ways in which citizenship is accomplished through localized forms of social activities and how it's lived in often contradictory ways. Whereas a legal citizenship consists of full membership of a political community with equal rights that are universally shared, a lived-citizenship insists these rights are meaningful only when applied to the everyday since notions of identity and community are negotiated and enacted rather than given or assumed (Stasiulis, 2017b). Reframing citizenship from a normative dimension to everyday experiences in particular contexts is significant (Robins et al., 2008). Citizenship recast as performity (from activism to the everyday acts) calls into question the traditional assumptions about citizenship as a package of rights and responsibilities (Isin et al., 2008). Framing citizenship as everyday practice (Isin, 2009; Lister, 2007; Robins et al., 2008; Tan, 2015; Tully, 2014) emphasizes lived-citizenship as a human accomplishment, actively engaged and constructed, and involving different ways in which social actors impart meaning to "doing" citizenship, from volunteering to the micro-politics of a "citizen-centred democracy" (Cherubini, 2011; Clarkson, 2014; Kallio et al., 2015; Kivisto and Faist, 2008). The "rootedness" of lived-citizenship also provides a reminder that, in doing citizenship, we are no longer passive ciphers but active and activist agents (Isin, 2009; Kallio et al., 2016).

An activist commitment has a long pedigree: The ancient Greek polis and (to a lesser extent) the Roman republic associated citizenship with democratic participation of individuals in political affairs. Contemporary citizenship may also be framed as a set of practices and lived-rights that embody spatial experiences rather than a fixed legal entity (Kallio et al., 2015; Robins et al., 2008; Tan, 2015). At one level, reference to an engaged citizenship focuses on agency and activism through individual acts and collective resistances that rupture the normality of everyday life, promote public dialogue and democratic governance over a range of issues, and challenge existing social and political order (Bali, 2014; Bloemraad, 2015; Isin and Nielson, 2008; Isin and Nyers, 2014). As Isin et al. (2008: 7; also Kingwell, 2001) point out in demonstrating the importance of a lived-citizenship in making us human:

> Citizenship involves the art of being with others, negotiating different situations and identities, and articulating ourselves as distinct yet similar to others in our everyday lives, and asking questions of justice. Through these social struggles, we develop a sense of our rights as others' obligations and others' rights as our obligations. It is in this deep and broader sense of enactment that citizenship is social.

In a similar vein, Mark Kingwell (2001; also Hove, 2003) argue that traditional models of citizenship based on blood, belief, rights or law are increasingly irrelevant in today's churning political, social, and cultural milieu. A new citizenship model is required based on the act of participation itself—not simply expecting action from existing citizens because it's their duty—but as constitutive of the very notion of citizenship itself.

The benefits of framing citizenship as "lived" or "doing" cannot be underestimated (Stasiulis, 2017a). Framing citizenship as a lived accomplishment (Lister, 2007; Tully, 2014) acknowledges that citizenship is not just passively accepted. More to the point, it must be actively engaged, experienced, and constructed in light of the different ways that social actors give meaning and practice to citizenship as rights, belonging, and participation at local, national, and global levels (Cherubini, 2011; Grundy and Smith, 2006; Kivisto and Faist, 2008). Think of how a lived-citizenship space represents the site where migrants and transmigrants forge and sustain multi-stranded social relations that link their society of origins with the society of settlement. Emphasis must also focus on concept of citizenship as performity when applied to how people understand their rights and responsibilities as well as negotiate claims to belonging and identity (Isin and Nyers, 2014; Lister, 2007). As Harrington (2014: 18; also Kingwell, 2001) reminds in linking citizenship and the struggles that actually comprise it: "citizenship rights are not simply gained through struggle but constituted by it as an act in itself." For in the final analysis, citizenship is not just about the right to participate but also constructed in the process of doing so.

A Critical Dimension, A Contested Site

The political struggles of migrants and minorities are central in opening up new ways of thinking about citizenship as principle or practice (Atac et al., 2016). Attention is directed at those political dynamics involving migrants and supportive groups who articulate notions of being a citizen through acts of citizenship or, alternatively, through the creation of new citizenship forms around claims-making challenges to existing regimes (Bloemraad, 2015; Chopra et al., 2011). Take, for example, the concept of an insurgent citizenship: As James

Holston (2009) points out, while the 20th century urbanization has intensified poverty throughout the world, the struggle of city citizens for basic resources (from housing and sanitation to adequate shelter) and daily survival has generated what he calls insurgent citizenship. A counterhegemonic citizenship discourse is proposed by marginalized groups who unthink the content and boundaries of a Eurocentric citizenship regime along lines consistent with their lived-reality and socioeconomic circumstances (Field, 2007). Citizenship transforms itself into a contested site of struggles for progressive possibilities rather than a state-centric space of sovereignty in regulating membership and doling out entitlements. Even non citizens can engage in acts of activist citizenship in the process reinforcing how citizenship is constituted by, and constitutive of, the perspectives and practices of those at the margins.

Citizenship Regimes: The Bigger Picture

Citizenship as formal status or lived-reality is situated within a citizenship regime. The concept of citizenship as a regime may be interpreted at different levels. It can be defined as a sociopolitical field of ideas and ideals, as well as a set of rules and regulations at a particular historical moment, that inform the principles and practices of citizenship as both a normative framework and lived-experience. A citizenship regime may also be defined as a system of governance practices including those democratic rules and institutional mechanisms that enable participation in civic life, provide fora for public debate, secure pathways to representation, and acknowledge the legitimacy of specific claims-making activities. Included here are those policy initiatives, prescriptive rules, institutional arrangements, and statutory laws pertaining to rights and membership that govern the relationship between citizens and the state. This complexity of institutional rules and arrangements not only guides policy decisions and citizen claims-making activities, but also shapes patterns of inclusion/exclusion with respect to entitlements, belonging and identity (Dobrowolski and Jenson, 2004; Dupre, 2012; Field, 2007; Guillaume, 2014; Jenson, 2001, 2011; Jenson and Papillon, 2001). The most obvious example of a citizenship regime is the Westphalian citizenship model discussed earlier in this chapter.

A citizenship regime is thought to be successful when it secures a degree of socio-political stability. Nevertheless, citizenship regimes are known to experience redefinition and overhaul in response to ideological shifts at particular points in history (Jenson, 2001). For example, Jenson (2001) writes of Canada's postwar citizenship regime that sought to create a pan-Canadian identity based on the seemingly opposed values of individualism and social solidarity. Regimes that once defined citizenship in terms of property or belonging to a political community (liberal regimes) now embraced the principle of social citizenship, with its connotation of universal entitlements and social rights through the redistributive intervention of the state (Duchastel, 2009). Reference to social citizenship within the context of an expanding welfare state was framed as a status that ensured a freedom from material restraints or societal restrictions (Ben-Ishai, n.d.). Social entitlements from health to pensions were tied to citizenship insofar as Canadians by virtue of their status as citizens possessed the right of access to programs and basic levels of social welfare. A social citizenship also promoted the idea of full citizenship rights for marginalized groups since socioeconomic inequalities imposed limits on exercising citizenship rights (Humpage, 2015; Warr and Williams, 2015).

In recent years, a regime shift has followed in the wake of another ideological transformation. A commitment to neoliberalism displaced a postwar Keynesian system of economic and social rights citizenship which provided discursive space for minorities and women to make equality claims (Jenson and Phillips, 1996; but see Siltanen, 2002). Neoliberalism as ideology and a policy perspective endorses an economic system suffused with the principles of more market (market competition, free trade and investment, and deregulation), less government intervention (paring back welfare programs), and more individual autonomy and responsibility in looking after themselves and their families (Fleras, 2017; Haque, 2008; Houdt et al., 2011; Humpage, 2015). But neoliberalism is more than a shift in wealth production and distribution from state to market. It also entails applying market values and rules to society, resulting in more than a market economy but also a market society that regulates and commodifies all aspects of social life, including notions of citizenship (Cao, 2015). The prioritization of market fundamentalism as the organizing principle of society elevates private interest over public good, while government interventions into private spheres are dismissed as an unwelcome and counterproductive intrusion (Deckhard, 2016). Entitlements to social programs remain tied to citizenship, albeit through their status as freewheeling individuals rather than in their collective status as responsible citizens. The introduction of market mechanisms into public administration and social services also reinforces the idea of citizens as consumers (and vice versa) who freely select the optimal output based on rational cost—benefit calculations (Assies, 2005).

To be sure, an unfettered market approach to neoliberalism is "under repair". A social investment approach is designed to increase market capacity by embedding both social and economic activities within the context of sustainability, partnership, and collaboration. Conventional neoliberal notions of disdain for interventionist activities are offset by a commitment to social investment model that assigns the state a new role in fostering socio-economic outcomes. The objectives are geared toward better preparing individuals for entry and success in the marketplace, particularly for those under-performing in the new economy. The goal is to minimize intergenerational transmission of poverty, to impart skills for an economic future with less job security and more precarious work contracts, and to ensure a citizenship fully conversant with the principles and practices of self-reliance (Jenson, 2011).

A neoliberal imprint on the meaning of citizenship and citizenship regime has proven transformative. Neoliberalism in Canada is transforming citizenship from an emphasis on rights to that of duties, from equal conditions to equality of opportunity, and from state provision of services to the promotion of partnership with private sectors (Dobrowolsky and Jenson, 2004). Citizenship is less tied to social rights but increasingly linked to participation in the market economy through employment and consumption; the good citizen, in turn, acknowledges the limits of state provisions by embracing the holy grail of self-reliance (Brodie, 2002). Citizens are no longer holders of rights but consumers in a market, with a corresponding reduction in the collective provision of social needs and welfare services (Humpage, 2015; Larner, 2006; Morel et al., 2012). A contractual view of the relationship state and society reframes citizenship less as a right but more of a privilege or prized possession that must be earned or lost if not properly cultivated (Houdt et al., 2011). A naturalized citizenship is increasingly viewed as a reward for a successful integration into society instead of stepping-stone to facilitate settlement and integration. The hollowing out of the welfare state and accompanying erosion of social rights as wasteful, counterproductive, and contrary to individual choice and freedom further amplifies a shift from a rights discourse to a duties discourse (Cao, 2015).

Note

1. The value and status of citizenship may vary over time and place. Holston (2009) points out that, in Brazil, peoples' rights are conferred by alternative forms of status—say workers—other than citizenship. Reference to citizen reflects a category of individuals without meaningful relations—an anonymous 'other' often because of unfortunate circumstances. Elsewhere the concept of citizenship evokes negative connotations and republican overtones, for example, citizens as people who participate in violent overthrow overthrow of monarchic regimes (US and French revolution) (Chesterman and Galligan, 1997). In 60s and 70s, leftist dismissed citizenship as a bourgeois convention since it announced who had propertied stake in the community, thereby exercising informal power over the unpropertied (Hoffman, 2004).

References

Abowitz, K. K. and J. Harnish. "Contemporary Discourses of Citizenship." *Review of Educational Research* 76, no. 4 (2006): 653–690.

Assies, Willem. "Some Notes on Citizenship, Civil Society, and Social Movements." *Rozenberg Quarterly*, 2005.

Anderson, Bridget. "Exclusion, Failure, and the Politics of Citizenship." *Ryerson Centre for Immigration and Settlement*, Working Paper No 2014/1. January 2014.

Arendt, Hannah. *The Origins of Totalitarianism*. New York: Harcourt, 1951.

Atac, Ilker, Kim Rygiel, and Maurice Stierl. "Introduction: The Contentious Politics of Refugee and Migrant Protest and Solidarity Movements: Remaking Citizenship From the Margins." *Citizenship Studies* 20, no. 5 (2016): 527–544.

Austin, Carly and Harald Bauder. "Jus Domicile: A Pathway to Citizenship for Temporary Workers." In *Immigration and Settlement*, edited by H. Bauder, 21–36. Toronto: Canadian Scholars Press, 2012.

Bagley, Sasha. Book Review. "The Birthright Lottery: Citizenship and Global Inequality, Ayelet Shachar." *Osgoode Hall Law Journal* 47, no. 1 (2009): 151–158.

Bali, Maha. "Critical Citizenship for Critical Times." *Open Democracy*, April 14, 2014.

Balta, E. and O. Alton-Olcay. "Class and Passports: Transnational Strategies of Distinction in Turkey." *Sociology*. 50, 6. (2016): 1106–1122_.

Baubock, Rainer. "Citizens on the Move: Democratic Standards for Migrant's Membership." *Canadian Diversity* 6, no. 4 (2008): 7–11.

Bauder, Harald. "Jus Domicile: In Pursuit of a Citizenship of Equality and Social Justice." *Journal of International Political Theory* 8, no. 1–2 (2012): 184–196.

Bauder, Harald. "Domicile Citizenship, Migration, and the City." In *Migration Policy and Practice, Interventions and Solutions*, edited by Christian Mathies, 79–99. New York: Palgrave, 2016.

Ben-Ishai, Elizabeth n.d. "Toward a Revised Conception of Social Citizenship: An Autonomy Focused Model." 1–17. Retrieved from https//www.cpsa-acsp.ca.

Bennion, David. "The Birthright Lottery and Global Political Equality Movement." Review of Shachar's book. Retrieved 2012 from http://www.citizenorange.com.

Berenschot, W., H. S. Nordholt, and L. Bakker. "Introduction: Citizenship and Democratization in Postcolonial Southeast Asia." In *Citizenship and Democratization in Southeast Asia*, edited by W. Berenschot, H. S. Nordholt, and L. Bakker, 1–30. London: Brill, 2017.

Berg, Ulla Dalum and Robyn Magalit Rodriguez. "Transnational Citizenship Across the Americas." *Identities* 20, no. 6 (2013): 649–664.

Berezin, Mabel. "Territory, Emotion, and Identity." In *Europe Without Borders*, edited by M. Berezin and M. Schain, 1–22. Baltimore: Johns Hopkins University Press, 2003.

Blitz, Brad. "News, Kingston University London." *The Cost of Statelessness*. Retrieved 2011 from http://www.kingston.ac.uk.

Bloemraad, Irene. "Theorizing and Analyzing Citizenship in Multicultural Societies." *The Sociological Quarterly* 56, no. 4 (2015): 591–606.

Bloemraad, Irene, Anna Korteweg, and Gokce Yurdakul. "Citizenship and Migration: Multiculturalism, Assimilation, and Challenges to the Nation-State." *Annual Review of Sociology* 34 (2008): 153–179.

Bloom, Tendayi. "Problematizing the Conventions on Statelessness." *UNU-GCM Policy Report* 02/01/2017. Institute on Globalization, Culture, and Mobility.

Bonjour, Saskia and Laura Block. "Ethnicizing Citizenship, Questioning Membership. Explaining the Decreasing Family Migration Rights in Europe." *Citizenship Studies*. Published online, June 1, 2016.

Bosniak, Linda. "Citizenship Denationalized" (the State of Citizenship Symposium). *Indiana Journal of Global Legal Studies* 7, no. 2 (2000): 447–512.

Bosniak, Linda. *The Alien and the Citizen*. Princeton, NJ: Princeton University Press, 2006.

Brodie, Janine. "Citizenship and Solidarity: Reflections on the Canadian Way." *Citizenship Studies* 6, no. 4 (2002): 377–394.

Brown, Cameron J. H. "Global Hegemony and Place-Based Resistance: Citizenship, Representation, and Place in Canadian Multiculturalism and the Zapatista Movement." *The Arbutus Review* 3, no. 2 (2012): 37–56.

Brown, Marion. "Gender Inclusion and Citizenship." In *Reconfiguring Citizenship: Social Exclusion and Diversity within Inclusive Citizenship Practices*, edited by L. Dominelli and M. Moosa-Mitha, 157–166. Burlington, VT: Ashgate, 2014.

Brubaker, Rogers. *Citizenship and Nationhood in France and Germany*. Cambridge, MA: Harvard University Press, 1992.

Butler, Kate and Cecilia Benoit. "Citizenship Practices Among Youth Who Have Experienced Government Care." *Canadian Journal of Sociology* 40, no. 1 (2015): 25–41.

Cao, Benito. *Environment and Citizenship*. New York: Routledge, 2015.

Carens, Joseph. "Aliens and Citizens: the Case for Open Borders." *Review of Politics* 49, no. 2 (1987): 251–273.

Castles, Stephen and Mark J. Miller. *The Age of Migration. International Population Movements in the Modern World*. 4/e New York: The Guilford Press, 2009.

Castles, Stephen, Hein de Haas, and Marvin Miller. *The Age of Migration*. 5/e. New York: Palgrave, 2013.

Cattapan, Alana. "Theorizing Transgender Citizenship in Canada." Paper Presented to the Annual Meeting of the Canadian Political Science Association, Carleton University, Ottawa, May 27, 2009.

Chabot, Lynn. "The Concept of Citizenship in Western Liberal Democracies and in First Nations: A Research Paper." Prepared for the Governance Policy Directorate, Lands and Trusts Services. INAC, March 2007.

Chatterjee, P. *The Politics of the Governed*. New York: Columbia University Press, 2006.

Cherubini, Daniela. "Intersectionality and the Study of Lived Citizenship: A Case Study on Migrant Women's Experiences in Andalusia." *Graduate Journal of Social Science* 8, no. 20 (2011): 114–126.

Chesterman John and Brian Galligan. *Citizens without Rights: Aborigines and Australian Citizenship*. Melbourne: Cambridge University Press, 1997.

Chopra, Deepta, Philippa Williams, and Bhaskar Vira. "Politics of Citizenship, Experiencing State-Society Relations From the Margins." *Contemporary South Asia* 19, no. 3 (2011): 243–247.

Clarke, John et al. *Disputing Citizenship*. Boston: Polity Press, 2014.

Clarkson, Adrienne. *Belonging: The Paradox of Citizenship*. Toronto: Penguin, 2014.

Coyne, Andrew. "Our Feudal Immigration Policy." *Literary Review of Canada*. July 2009.

Deckhard, Natalie Delia. "After Postnational Citizenship: Constructing the Boundaries of Inclusion in Neoliberal Societies." *Sociology Compass* 10, no. 4 (2016): 294–305.

Delanty, Gerard. "Theorising Citizenship in a Global Age." In *Globalisation and Citizenship: The Transnational Challenge*, edited by W. Hudson and S. Slaughter, 15–29. New York: Routledge, 2007.

DiGregario, Michael and Jessica L. Merolli. "Introduction: Affective Citizenship and Politics of Identity, Control, and Resistance." *Citizenship Studies* 20 (2016): 933–942.

Dobrowolsky, Alexandra and Jane Jenson. "Shifting Representations of Citizenship: Canadian Politics of 'Women' and 'Children.'" *Social Politics* 11, no. 2 (2004): 154–180.

Dominelli, Lena. "Problematising Concepts of Citizenship and Citizenship Practices." In *Reconfiguring Citizenship: Social Exclusion and Diversity within Inclusive Citizenship Practices*, edited by L. Dominelli and M. Moosa-Mitha, 13–22. Burlington, VT: Ashgate, 2014a.

Dominelli, Lena. "Critical Theories: Reflecting on Citizenship Status and Practices." In *Reconfiguring Citizenship: Social Exclusion and Diversity within Inclusive Citizenship Practices*, edited by L. Dominelli and M. Moosa-Mitha, 253–262. Burlington, VT: Ashgate, 2014b.

Dominelli, Lena. "Conclusions." In *Reconfiguring Citizenship: Social Exclusion and Diversity within Inclusive Citizenship Practices*, edited by L. Dominelli and M. Moosa-Mitha, 263–266. Burlington, VT: Ashgate, 2014c.

Dominelli, Lena and Mehmoona Moosa-Mitha. "Introduction." In *Reconfiguring Citizenship: Social Exclusion and Diversity within Inclusive Citizenship Practices*, edited by L. Dominelli and M. Moosa-Mitha, 1–12. Burlington, VT: Ashgate, 2014.

Duchastel, Jules. "Multiculturalism: What are Our Discontents About?" *Canada Watch*, Fall 2009, 31–33.

Dupre, Jean-Francois. "Intercultural Citizenship, Civic Nationalism, and Nation-Building in Quebec: From Common Public Language to Laicite." *Studies in Ethnicity and Nationalism* 12 (2012): 227–248.

Enjolras, Bernard. "Toward a Post-national European Model of Citizenship." Paper presented to CINEFOGO Midterm Conference "European Citizenship: Challenges and Possibilities." Roskilde University, Denmark, 2007. 1–3.

Field, Ann-Marie. "Counter-Hegemonic Citizenship: LGBT Communities and the Politics of Hate Crimes in Canada." *Citizenship Studies* 11, no. 3 (2007): 247–262.

Fleras, Augie. "Provisional Status and Precarious Work. Customizing Immigration, Commodifying Migrant Labour." In *Migration, Regionalization, Citizenship*, edited by Katja Sarkowsky, Rainer-Olaf Schultze, and Sabine Schwarze, 27–66. New York: Springer, 2015.

Fleras, Augie. "Re-imagining Citizenship in Canada, New Zealand, and Australia: Transnational Dynamics, Postnational Complexities, Postcitizenship Possibilities." Plenary Paper, Citizenship in a Transnational Context, University of Alberta, Edmonton, 6–7 July 2016.

Fleras, Augie. *Inequality Matters*. Toronto: Oxford University Press, 2017.

Fonseca, E. N. "In the Interstices of Citizenship: the Inevitable Urgent Character of the Dimensions of Civic Virtue in Education." *Educacao e Pesquisa* 40, no. 1 (2014): 1–12.

Fortier, Anne-Marie. "What's the Big Deal? Naturalisation and the Politics of Desire." *Citizenship Studies* 17 (July 6, 2013).

Gibney, Matthew, n.d. "Statelessness and the Right to Citizenship." Retrieved from matthew.gibney@qeh.ox.ac.uk.

Goldring, Luin and Marie-Pier Joly. "Immigration, Citizenship and Racialization at Work: Unpacking Employment Precarity in Southwestern Ontario." *Just Labour: A Canadian Journal of Work and Society* 22 (2014): 94–107.

Goodspeed, Peter. "It is Time for Canada to Stand up for Rohingya." *Toronto Star* August 30, 2017.

Gormley, Shannon. "The Right to Have Rights." *Ottawa Citizen*. November 9, 2014.

Griffith, Andrew. "Canadian Citizenship: From Harder to Get and Easier to Lose to a New Balance." *Policy Options*, March 7, 2016.

Grundy, John and Miriam Smith. "The Politics of Multiscalar Citizenship: the Case of Lesbian and Gay Organizing in Canada." *Citizenship Studies*. Published online August 19, 2006, 389–404.

Guha, Sagnik. "Globalization and the State: Assessing the Decline of the Westphalian State in a Globalizing World.". *Inquiries Journal* 9, no 3 (2017):1–14.

Guillaume, Xavier. "Regimes of Citizenship" In *Routledge Handbook of Global Citizenship Studies*, edited by E. Isin and P. Nyers. New York: Routledge, 2014.

Hansen, Randall. "The Poverty of Postnationalism: Citizenship, Immigration, and the New Europe." *Theory and Society* 38 (2009): 1–24.

Hanvelt, Marc and Martin Papillon. "Parallel or Embedded? Aboriginal Self-Government and the Changing Nature of Canadian Citizenship." In *Insiders and Outsiders: Alan Cairns and the Reshaping of Canadian Citizenship*, edited by G. Kernerman and P. Resnick, 242–257. Vancouver: UBC Press, 2005.

Hampshire, James. *The Politics of Immigration. Contradictions of the Liberal State*. Boston: Polity Press, 2013.

Harrington, Jack. "Navigating Global Citizenship Studies." In *Routledge Handbook of Global Citizenship Studies*, edited by E. Isin and P. Nyers. New York: Routledge, 2014.

Haque, M. Shamsul. "Global Rise of Neoliberal State and Its Impact on Citizenship: Experiences in Developing Nations." *Asian Journal of Social Sciences* 36 (2008): 11–34.

Hebert, Yvonne M. and Lori Wilkinson. *The Citizenship Debates: Conceptual, Policy, Experiential, and Educational Issues*, edited by Y. M. Hebert, 3–36. Toronto: University of Toronto Press, 2002.

Hettne, Bjorn. "The Fate of Citizenship in Post-Westphalia." *Citizenship Studies* 4, no. 1 (2000): 35–46.

Higgins, Peter. "Book Review; Ayelet Shachar, The Birthright Lottery." *Ethics* 120, no. 1 (2009).

Hoffman, John. *Citizenship Beyond the State*. Thousand Oaks, CA: Sage Publications, 2004.

Holston, James. "Insurgent Citizenship in an Era of Global Urban Peripheries." *City & Society* 21, no. 2 (2009): 245–267.

Houdt, Friso van, Semin Suvarierol and Willem Schinkel. "Neoliberal Communitarian Citizenship: Current Trends Toward "Earned Citizenship" in the United Kingdom, France and the Netherlands." *International Sociology* 26, no. 3 (2011): 408–432.

Hove, Thomas. "Review of The World We Want, Mark Kingwell, 2001." *Workplace* 11 (2003): 218–221.

Howard, Marc Morje. "The Causes and Consequences of Germany's New Citizenship Law." *German Politics* 17, no. 1 (2008): 41–62.

Humpage, Louise. *Policy Change, Public Attitudes and Social Citizenship*. Boston: Polity Press, 2015.

Isin, Engin F., Janine Brodie, Danielle Juteau, and Daiva Stasiulis. "Recasting the Social in Citizenship." In *Recasting the Social in Citizenship*, edited by E. Isin, 3–19. Toronto: University of Toronto Press, 2008.

Isin, Engin F. "Citizenship in Flux: The Figure of the Activist Citizen." *Subjectivity* 29 (2009): 367–388.

Isin, Engin F. "Citizens without Nations." *Environment and Planning D: Society and Space* 30, no. 3 (2012): 450–467.

Isin, Engin F. and Greg Nielson (eds.). *Acts of Citizenship*. New York: Zed Books, 2008.

Isin, Engin F. and Peter Nyers. "Introduction: Globalizing Citizenship Studies." In *Routledge Handbook of Global Citizenship Studies*, edited by E. Isin and P. Nyers. New York: Routledge, 2014.

Jedwab, Jack. "Ask What You Can do for your Country and Not What it Can do for You. Is Canadian Citizenship Really Being Taken for Granted?" *Canadian Diversity* 6, no. 4 (2008): 155–159.

Jenson, Jane. *Governance and Citizenship in the European Union: What is the White Paper on Governance Suggesting About Citizenship*. Paper presented to the fifth biennial conference of the European Community Study Association—Canada, 2001.

Jenson, Jane. "Redesigning Citizenship Regime after Neoliberalism. Moving Toward Social Investment." In *Towards a Social Investment Welfare State?: Ideas, Policies, and Challenges*, edited by N. Morel, B. Pallier, and J. Palme. Boston: Policy Press, 2011.

Jenson, Jane. "Women's Citizenship in the Democracies of the Americas: Canada." *Inter-American Commission of Women*, August 2013.

Jenson, Jane and Martin Papillon. "The Changing Boundaries of Citizenship: A Review and a Research Agenda." CPRN, April 6, 2001.

Jenson, Jane and Susan Phillips. "Regime Shift: New Citizenship Practices in Canada." *International Journal of Canadian Studies* 14 (1996): 111–135.

Joppke, Christian. *Immigration and Citizenship*. Boston: Polity Press, 2010.

Kabeer, Naila. *Inclusive Citizenship: Meanings and Expressions*. London: Zed Press, 2005.

Kallio, K. P., J Hakli, and P. Backlund. "Lived Citizenship as the Locus of Political Agency in Participatory Policy." *Citizenship Studies* 19, no. 1 (2015): 101–119.

Kallio, Kirsi Pauliina and Katharyne Mitchell. "Re-Spatializing Transnational Citizenship." *Global Networks* 16, no. 3 (2016): 259–267.

Kalu, Kalu N. "Postmodern Citizenship." In *Remaking Citizenship in Multicultural Europe*, edited by Beatrice Halsaa, Sasha Roseneil and Sevil Sumer. New York: Palgrave Macmillan, 2013.

Kingwell, Mark. *The World We Want: Restoring Citizenship in a Fractured Age*. Rowman and Littlefield, 2001.

Kivisto, Peter. "Conclusion: The Boundaries of Citizenship in a Transnational Age." In *Dual Citizenship in Global Perspective: From Unitary to Multiple Citizenship*, edited by T. Faist and P. Kivisto, 272–284. New York: Palgrave Macmillan, 2008.

Kivisto, Peter and Thomas Faist. *Citizenship:Discourse, Theory, and Transnational Prospects*. Oxford: Blackwell, 2008

Kymlicka, Will. *Politics in the Vernacular: Nationalism, Multiculturalism, and Citizenship*. Toronto: Oxford University Press, 2001.

Labelle, Micheline and Francois Rocher. "Debating Citizenship in Canada: the Collide of Two Nation-Building Projects." In *From Subjects to Citizens: A Hundred Years of Citizenship in Australian and Canada*, edited by P. Boyer et al., 263–286. Ottawa: University of Ottawa Press, 2004.

Larner, Wendy. "Brokering Citizenship Claims: Neo-Liberalism, Biculturalism, and Multiculturalism in Aotearoa New Zealand." In *Women, Migration, and Citizenship*, edited by E. Tastsoglou and A. Dobrowolsky, 131–146. Burlington, VT: Ashgate, 2006.

Leggewie, Claus. "Eurozine." *Transnational Citizenship: Ideals and European Realities*. Retrieved from http://www.eurozine.com, February 19, 2013.

Linklater, Andrew. "Citizenship and Sovereignty in the Post-Westphalian State." *European Journal of International Relations* 2, no. 1 (1996): 77–103.

Lister, Ruth. "Dialectics of Citizenship." *Hypatia* 12, no. 4 (1997): 6–26.

Low, C. C. "The Politics of Citizenship in Divided Nations. Policies and Trends in Germany and China." *Communist and Post-Communist Studies* 49, no. 2 (2016): 123–135.

Maas, Willem. *Multilevel Citizenship*. Philadelphia: University of Pennsylvania Press, 2013.

Macklin, Audrey and Francois Crepeau, "Multiple Citizenship, Identity, and Entitlement in Canada." *IRPP*, June 22, 2010.

Mann, Jatinder. "Introduction." In *Citizenship in a Transnational Perspective*, edited by J. Mann, 1–14. New York: Palgrave Macmillan, 2017.

Marback, Richard. "Introduction." In *Representation and Citizenship*, edited by R. Marback, 1–16. Detroit: Wayne State University Press, 2016.

Marlan, Tori. "Universally Undocumented." *The Walrus*. April 2017, 20–22.

Mhurchu, Aoileann Ni. "Citizenship Beyond State Sovereignty." In *Routledge Handbook of Global Citizenship Studies*, edited by E. Isin and P. Nyers. New York: Routledge, 2014.

Morel, N., B. Palier, and J. Palme. "Toward a Social Investment Welfare State?: Ideas, Policies, and Challenges." *Policy Press Scholarship Online*, May 2012.

Morris, Jenny. "Disability Studies." *Citizenship and Disabled People: A Scoping Paper Prepared for the Disability Rights Commission*. Retrieved 2005 from http://disability-studies.leeds.ac.uk

Motomura, Hiroshi. *Americans in Waiting. The Lost Story of Immigration and Citizenship in the United States*. New York: Oxford University Press, 2006.

Mounk, Yascha. "Echt Deutsch." *Harpers*. April 2017, 66–72.

Mulcaire, Camille. "E-International Relations." *How Westphalian is the Westphalian Model?* February 3, 2014, Retrieved from http://www.e-ir.info.

Nathans, Eli. *The Politics of Citizenship in Germany*. Oxford, UK: Berg Publishers, 2004.

Nekvapil, Emrys. "Beyond Foreignness." *Why Global Citizenship?* April 3, 2011. Retrieved from http://beyondforeigness.org.

Ng-A-Fook, Nicholas, Linda Radford, and Tasha Ausman. "Living a Curriculum of Hyph-E-Nations: Diversity, Equality, and Social Media." *Multicultural Education Review* 4, no. 2 (2013): 91–128.

Noonan, Norma C. and Vidya Nadkarni. "Introduction: A Century of Challenges." In *Challenge and Change*, edited by N. C. Noonan and V. Nadkarni, 1–11. New York: Palgrave Macmillan, 2016.

Nunn, Caitlin, C. McMichael, S. M. Gifford, and I. Correa-Velez. "Mobility and Security: The Perceived Benefits of Citizenship for Resettled Young People from Refugee Backgrounds." *Journal of Ethnic and Migration Studies.* Published online October 6, 2015.

Paehlke, R. *Hegemony and Global Citizenship.* New York: Palgrave Macmillan, 2014.

Peled, Yoav. "Towards a Post-Citizenship Society? A Report from the Front." *Citizenship Studies* 11, no. 1 (2007): 95–104.

Pitty, Roderick. "Indigenous Citizenship as Unfinished Business." In *Does History Matter? Making and Debating Citizenship, Immigration, and Refugee Policy in Australia and New Zealand*, edited by K. Newman and G. Tavan, chapter 2. Canberra: ANU Press, 2009.

Puzzo, Catherine. "UK Citizenship in the Early 21st Century: Earning and Losing the Right to Stay." *French Journal of British Studies* xxi, no. 1 (2016).

Richez, Emmanuelle and Christopher P. Manfredi. "Citizenship and the Canadian Charter." In *Migration, Regionalization, Citizenship.* Part of the series, *Politikwissenschaftliche Paperbacks.* Springer Link, 2014.

Robertson, Susan L. "Globalisation, Rescaling National Education System, and Citizenship Regimes." In *Changing Notions of Citizenship Education in Contemporary Nation-states*, edited by K. Roth and N. Barbules. Rotterdam: Sense Publishers, 2007.

Robins, Steven, Andrea Cornwall, Bettina von Lieres. "Rethinking Citizenship in the Postcolony." *Third World Quarterly* 29, no. 6 (2008): 1069–1086.

Rodriguez, Cristina M. "Review: the Citizenship Paradox in a Transnational Age." *Michigan Law Review* 106, no. 6 (2008): 1111–1118.

Roseneil, Sasha, Beatrice Halsaa, and Sevil Sumer. "Remaking Citizenship in Europe: Women's Movements, Gender, and Diversity." In *Remaking Citizenship in Multicultural Europe*, edited by Beatrice Halsaa, Sasha Roseneil and Sevil Sumer, 1–18. New York: Palgrave Macmillan, 2013.

Sarkar, J. "Debating a Post-Wesphalian International Order." *Mainstream Weekly.* L111, no 15 (April 4, 2015).

Sassen, Saskia. "Losing Control? Sovereignty in an Age of Globalization". The 1995 Columbia University Leonard Hastings Schoff Memorial Lecture. New York: Columbia University, 1996.

Schuck, Peter H. "Three Models of Citizenship." Yale Law School, Public Law Working Paper No 168, July 15, 2009.

Shachar, Ayelet. *The Birthright Lottery: Citizenship and Global Inequality.* Boston: Harvard University Press, 2009.

Shachar, Ayelet. "Introduction: Citizenship and the 'Right to Have Rights'." *Citizenship Studies* 18, no. 2 (2014): 114–124.

Shipper, A. W. "Politics of Citizenship and Transnational Gendered Migration in East and Southeast Asia." *Pacific Affairs* 83, no. 1 (2010): 11–26.

Siltanen, Janet. "Paradise Paved? Reflections on the Fate of Social Citizenship in Canada." *Citizenship Studies* 6, no. 4 (2002): 395–420.

Singh, Jyotsna G. "Introduction." In *The Postcolonial World*, edited by J. G. Singh and David D. Kim, 1–30. New York: Routledge, 2017.

Sobel, Richard. "FifteenEightyFour, Academic Perspectives from Cambridge University Press." *The Citizenship Controversies*. Retrieved November 2, 2016. http://www.cambridgeblog. org/2016/11/the-citizenship-controversies/

Soysal, Yasemin Nuhoglu. "Postnational Citizenship: Reconfiguring the Familiar Terrain." In *The Blackwell Companion to Political Sociology*, edited by Kate Nash and Alan Scott. Hoboken, NJ: Blackwell, 2004.

Soysal, Yasemin Nuhoglu."Postnational Citizenship: Rights and Obligations of Individuality." Heinrich Boll Stiftung. Migrations Politisches Portal. May 18, 2011. Retrieved from https://heimatkunde.boell.de.

Squires, Judith. *Negotiating Equality and Diversity in Britain: Towards a Differentiated Citizenship*. Philadelphia: Taylor and Francis, 2007.

Stanford. "Stanford Encyclopedia of Philosophy." *Citizenship*. August 1, 2011. Retrieved from http://plato.stanford.edu.

Stasiulis, Daiva. "The Extraordinary Statelessness of Deepan Budlakoti: The Erosion of Canadian Citizenship Through Citizenship Deprivation." *Studies in Social Justice* 11, no. 1 (2017a): 1–26.

Stasiulis, Daiva. "Respatializing Social Citizenship and Security Among Dual Citizens in the Lebanese Diaspora." In *Citizenship in a Transnational Perspective. Canada, Australia, and New Zealand*, edited by J. Mann. 49–64, New York: Palgrave, 2017b.

Stoker, Gerry. *Prospects for Citizenship*. London: Bloomsbury Academic, 2011.

Stokes, Bruce. "What it Takes to Truly Be 'One of Us.'" Pew Research Center, February 1, 2017.

Strasser, Sabine. "Rethinking Citizenship in a Multicultural Europe. Critical Encounters with Feminist, Multicultural, and Transnational Citizenship." In *Remaking Citizenship in Multicultural Europe*, edited by Beatrice Halsaa, Sasha Roseneil and Sevil Sumer, 21–43. New York: Palgrave Macmillan, 2013.

Swerts, Thomas. "Non-Citizen Citizenship in Canada and the United States." In *Routledge Handbook of Global Citizenship Studies*, edited by E. Isin and P. Nyers. New York: Routledge, 2014.

Tambini, Damian. "Post-National Citizenship." *Ethnic and Racial Studies* 24, no. 2 (2001): 195–217.

Tan, Kathy-Ann. *Reconfiguring Citizenship and National Identity in the North American Literary Imagination*. Detroit: Wayne State University Press, 2015.

The Times Editorial Board. "The Meaning of U.S. Citizenship." *Los Angeles Times*, October 4, 2014.

Tully, James. *On Global Citizenship: James Tully in Dialogue*. New York: Bloomsbury Publishing, 2014.

Urzi, Domenica and Colin Williams. "Beyond Post-national Citizenship: An Evaluation of the Experiences of Tunisian and Romanian Migrants Working in the Agricultural Sector of Sicily." *Citizenship Studies*, 136–150. Published online November 10, 2016.

Vink, Maarten Peter. *Migration and Citizenship Attribution: Politics and Policies in Western Europe*. New York: Routledge, 2013.

Warr, Deb and Richard Williams. *The Shifting Terrain of Citizenship: A Wayfarers Guide. Scoping Report for the Melbourne Social Equity Institute*. Melbourne: University of Melbourne, 2015.

Willhelm, Cornelia. "Introduction." In *Migration, Memory, and Diversity: Germany from 1945 to the Present*, edited by C. Willhelm, 1–18. New York: Berghahn, 2016.

Winter, Elke. "Balancing Citizenship Rights in an Era of Globalization. Lightening Policy Brief Series—March." Carleton University Centre for European Studies/Canada-Europe Transatlantic Dialogue, 2016.

Winter, E., A. Diehl, and A. Patzelt. "Ethnic Nation No More? Making Sense of Germany's New Stance on Dual Citizenship By Birth." *Review of Russian and European Affairs* 9, no. 1 (2016): 1–12.

Yashar Deborah J. "Citizen Regimes and Indigenous Politics in Latin America." Proto-Paper prepared for "Claiming Citizenship in America," A Conference Organized by the Canadian Research Chair in Governance and Citizenship. May 27, 2005.

Young, Margaret. "Canadian Citizenship Act and Current Issues." Law and Government Division, BP–445E, 1998.

PART 2
UNSETTLING CITIZENSHIP REGIMES IN THE SETTLER SOCIETIES

· 3 ·

CITIZENSHIP IN SETTLER SOCIETIES: CITIZENSHIP PROMISES, CITIZEN DISAPPOINTMENTS

Introduction: Surveying the Settler Terrain

It should come as no surprise that the settler societies of Canada, Australia, New Zealand and the United States (CANZUS) are at the forefront of initiatives for facilitating the naturalization ("citizenization") of newcomers (Fleras, 2016b, 2017; Mann, 2017). That much can be expected, given their historical status as societies of immigrants to populate the land and "grow the economy" as well as normative status as principled immigration societies (or regimes). Yet their lofty status conceals a key challenge: Each of these settler societies is under pressure to create a social and political climate for expediting the incorporation of immigrants into the national fold, thereby ensuring their loyalty and commitment to the host country (Janoski, 2010). They are also being pressured to dismantle those polite fictions that extol citizenship promises yet paper over the inconvenient truths of citizen disappointments. Not surprisingly, the citizenship regimes in the CANZUS countries encompass a number of commonalities, thanks to their positioning as immigration societies, a commitment to the principle of diversity and inclusion ("multicultural societies"), and claims they are becoming increasingly postcolonial with respect to the treatment of Indigenous peoples.

This chapter takes advantage of this "confluence of commitments" to describe the citizenship regimes in each of the CANZUS countries both in the past and at present (Fleras, 2017). A brief comparison provides an overview of core similarities in defining who belongs, how they belong, and what belonging entitles in terms of rights and responsibilities (also Spoonley, 2015). Differences are no less discernible, despite numerous overlaps, especially in their approach to the citizenship of Indigenous peoples (This topic will be further addressed in Chapter 7). But while the citizenship regimes in Australia, New Zealand, and the United States may be evolving along an exclusion-inclusive trajectory, including acceptance of dual citizenship and denizen rights, gaps persist between what citizenship offers ("promises") and what it delivers ("disappointments"). The chapter also takes a brief look at the citizenship program in the U.S. This excursion not only fosters insight into the world's foremost society of immigrants (in terms of numbers and desired destination); it also casts into sharper relief America's citizenship domains vis-à-vis that of the CANZ countries. Chapters 4 and 5 will discuss the concept of citizenship in a changing and diverse Canada.

Citizenship Commonalities Across the CANZ Countries

Canada, Australia, and Aotearoa/New Zealand have much in common, including the same head of state (a constitutional monarchy), similar Parliamentary and common law tradition, highly developed economies, and generally positive human rights records (Fleras, 2017). They share a history of immigration including the settlement of diasporic communities (Akbari and MacDonald, 2014; Forrest and Dunn, 2006); extensive experiences with integrating newcomers into the body politic; and a relatively tolerant attitude toward cultural diversity. These once staunchly white societies eventually discarded their open supremacy—Canada in 1962 when nationality was dropped as a criteria for newcomer admission; Australian in 1973 when the Whitlam government officially terminated a white Australia policy; and New Zealand in the 1974 when the Kirk government renounced the racialization at the heart of the country's immigration program (Atkinson, 2016). They also possess an open path to naturalization, fostered in part by easy tolerance of dual citizenship, modest residence and accessibility requirements (in contrast to some European countries where mandatory integration tests prevail [Marwah and Triadafilopoulos, 2009]) and a near automatic route to citizenship based on the principles of jus soli (membership by birth on territory) and jus domicile (membership on the basis of ideals) —unlike European notions of citizenship membership derived from parental descent or blood ties (jus sanguinis) (Joppke, 2013).

Evolving notions of citizenship regimes are in evidence as well. Of particular note is the decline of Britishness in defining the national identities of CANZ countries, including a corresponding shift from an ethnic-centred (British) citizenship (Mann, 2012, 2016; McMillan, 2014; Sassen, 2002), to a more civic-oriented citizenship rooted in the principle of universalism (Soysal, 1994). To be sure, initiatives in recent years to tighten up the rules of citizenship, from revoking citizenship to rethinking birthright citizenship in advancing a more muscular ("integrative") citizenship, have proven consequential in creating a cohort of second class citizens and a two-tier citizenship (Dauvergne, 2016; Winter, 2014; but see Joppke, 2013). For example, during the Harper regime in Canada (2006–2015), the concept of a full and permanent citizenship in Canada was transformed from a near automatic right acquired at birth or through naturalization into a conditional privilege that was harder to get but easier to lose (Abu-Laban, 2014; Stasiulis, 2017). Nevertheless, the politicization of both Indigenous peoples and ethno-racialized minorities promises to unsettle conventional notions of citizenship along more innovative lines despite the obvious challenges of working in and around the homogenizing logic of the settler state.

Cross-national differences in the citizenship domain can also be discerned (Spoonley, 2015). Unlike Australia and Canada, permanent residents in New Zealand do not require citizenship status to vote in national and local elections (some European countries allow non residents to vote in local elections). One year of permanent residency in New Zealand entitles a person to cast a ballot (but not run for political office) (McMillan, 2014, 2016). Political rights vary as well: Canadians who reside abroad for more than 5 years cannot vote or stand in national elections unless they resume residency, whereas the US allows an American national to vote in federal elections for a lifetime (as long as they pay American taxes on overseas income) (Macklin and Crepeau, 2010). Citizenship obligations vary as well. Australian citizens are obligated to vote in national elections; Canadian citizens are under obligation to do jury duty when requested [Macklin and Crepeau, 2010]). In terms of birthright citizenship, Canada (and the U.S.) continues to confer citizenship to anyone born on Canadian soil regardless of their parental immigrant status. But Australia and New Zealand restrict this right to someone born of a permanent resident or citizen. This restrictive turn in Antipodean citizenship is perceived by some as a polite way of excluding racialized migrants (Menzel, 2013). No less varied are citizenship expectations The moral contract between newcomers and Australian citizenship is more explicit than in Canada or New Zealand in terms of what is expected of citizens and what they can expect (Paquet, 2004). Whereas Canadian mindsets toward citizenship appear largely indifferent or passive, and focused on legal status and formal entitlements instead of active participation, Australians consolidate a bottom up commitment to citizenship at local, state, and commonwealth levels, thereby solidifying the identities, commonalities, and the social glue that binds Australians (Paquet, 2004). The fact that Australia celebrates an annual Citizenship Day speaks volumes of its symbolic importance.

Still, what is most striking among the CANZ countries are the commonalities that formally define who can become a citizen and how. The citizenship program for naturalizing newcomers in these countries exhibit many common features in terms of residence requirements prior to application for citizenship (a minimum of between three to five years), a declaration of intent to reside (except the U.S.), host country language requirements, knowledge of a host country's history and culture usually assessed via a citizenship test, an evaluation of an applicant's character through an interview or written test, a host of citizenship benefits, including passport issuance, security from deportation, and access to government jobs and political office, and a fee schedule that runs into several hundreds of dollars (Elgersma, 2014; Markus, 2017; US Department of Citizenship and Immigration, 2017). Shared similarities in the naturalization protocols in each of these settler regimes are matched by three foundational principles that inform the politics of citizenship governance:

1. CANZ = *Immigration Regimes*. The CANZ countries are usually defined as societies of immigrants ("what is") as well as immigration regimes ("what should be"). An immigration regime is based on five normative principles: rule based admissions to ensure newcomers are legal, "liberal", and "labour"-ready; perceptions of newcomers as valued assets for nation-building; centrality of migration and migrants to national identity; programs such as multiculturalism to facilitate their settlement and integration; and expectation of citizenship pathways for migrants and refugees (Fleras, 2016a). A normative immigration society thus reinforces a mutually reciprocating relationship between immigrants and citizenship (Korteweg and Elrick,

2014; Macklin, 2017; Spoonley and Bedford, 2012). Immigrants are expected to become citizens, while the promise of easy-to-access citizenship may sway the decision of potential migrants.

2. *CANZ = Multicultural Societies.* The CANZ countries are normally defined as multicultural societies that purport to abide by the principles of multiculturalism (New Zealand is multicultural in practice rather than in policy [Spoonley, 2017]). Reference to an official multiculturalism as diversity governance is not about celebrating differences or promoting cultural communities. To the contrary, a multicultural governance promulgates the idea that a society of many cultures is possible provided (a) certain rules are in place to ensure cohesion and cooperation, (b) everyone is equal before the law regardless of race or ethnicity (exemptions that facilitate integration are permitted when necessary), (c) individual and group differences do not preclude access to equal participation and full inclusion, and (d) ethnicity is depoliticized to ensure a public domain both safe *from* ethnicity yet safe *for* diversity (Fleras, 2009). More specifically, multiculturalism as official policy in Canada and Australia commits to creating an inclusive society by integrating migrants and minorities into the existing framework through removal of discriminatory barriers and fostering respect for cultural differences. This commitment to multiculturalism as diversity governance articulates a new way of being a citizen, namely, the right to be same yet different without paying a penalty in the process. Or to put it differently, individuals can identify and belong as national citizens through their ethnicity if they so choose, and on their own terms and pace.

3. *CANZ = Postcolonial Societies* The settler societies of CANZ share a history of colonization, dispossession, and exclusion of Indigenous peoples (Spoonley, 2015). The exclusionary agenda ranged from open neglect and coercive assimilation to compulsory integration and a strings-attached conditional autonomy framework (Fleras and Elliott, 1991; Papillon and Consentino, 2004). Founded as "white nations" (Baldwin et al., 2011; Hage, 1998), the CANZ countries could be described as racialized liberal democracies with a dominant race inscribed into the founding assumptions and foundational principles of an unwritten constitutional order (Sandercock, 2003). But the CANZ countries believe they have evolved beyond their status as white societies preferring, instead, to see themselves as postcolonial

(and cosmopolitan) societies that have dismantled the most egregious expressions of colonialism as part of the decolonizing process. To be sure, not everyone agrees with this assessment, with critics pointing to the patterns of systemic colonialism that punctuate the logic and dynamics of a neocolonial regime (Alfred, 2009,; Green, 2017; Monchalin, 2015). Even a belief in the rhetoric rather than reality of a postcolonial (and a postracial) society conceals those liberal-universal principles that underpin a national citizenship. That is, our commonalities as freewheeling citizens outweigh our differences as members of racially distinct groups, at least for purposes of recognition and reward. However commendable this sentiment, problems arise when national minorities and Indigenous peoples want their differences to be taken seriously by virtue of taking into account their group specific citizenship rights. How then have the CANZ countries responded to citizen demands and citizenship politics?

Aotearoa/New Zealand: Doing Citizenship Differently

The Oath:
I {name} swear [solemnly and sincerely affirm for the Affirmation] that I will be faithful and bear true allegiance to her Majesty Queen Elizabeth the Second, Queen of England, Her heirs and successors according to the law, and that I will faithfully observe the laws of New Zealand and fulful my duties as a New Zealand citizen. So help me God.
In Maori, Te Oati [Whakautanga] Haumi

Aoteoroa New Zealand constitutes a fusion of diverse population groups—Indigenous, settler, and immigrant (Ghosh and Leckie, 2015). They include Pakeha (white European), Indigenous Maori tribes, Pacific Islanders, and ethnic others (Simon-Kumar, 2014). In 2011, 69 percent of the population identified as of European (Pakeha) descent, 14.6 percent Maori, 9.2 percent Asian (12.8 in 2013), and 6.9 Pacific Islanders. The resulting tripartite relations of power—Indigenous peoples, settlers, and others—establishes both a framework and a governance challenge for accommodating diversity (Pearson, 2004; Spoonley et al., 2003). As well, the existence of an overseas diaspora consisting of some 500,000 adults and 300,000 of their children represents an embedded reality for New Zealand citizenship, immigration, and political system (Every Kiwi Counts, 2015; Gamlen, 2007; Waldron, 2011). To be sure, New Zealand does not subscribe to an official multiculturalism, nevertheless, it endorses the principles of multiculturalism, in part through a government body that oversees ethnic issues (Multiculturalism Policy Index, 2016), against the backdrop of a binational form of biculturalism (Fleras and Spoonley, 1999; Maaka and Fleras, 2005).

Timeline

Prior to passage of the British Nationality and New Zealand Citizenship Act in 1948, membership in the New Zealand political community was legally defined as that of a British subject—a status held in common by all those with formal membership in the British Empire (McMillan, 2014). According to Kate McMillan (2004), New Zealand citizenship originated from of a 19th century idea of imperial belonging which in turn reflected an essentially feudal concept of subjecthood (also Carens, 1987). For example, women were treated as property under citizenship protocols. "Alien" women who married British subjects including naturalized British subjects (the concept of naturalization was introduced in 1844) became British subjects, while wives and children of men whose citizenship was rescinded automatically lost their citizenship (this double standard was revoked in 1923) (Green, 2005). With the 1948 Act which came into effect in January 1949, New Zealanders transitioned from British subjects to New Zealand citizens (Spoonley, 1997) whose rights and duties reflected membership in the New Zealand community instead of their British subjecthood, although,legally, they remained British subjects with New Zealand citizenship until 1983. An amendment in 1975 permitted individuals normally resident in New Zealand to vote in general elections, although only citizens could stand as candidates. The Citizenship Act 1977 marked the end of the British/alien divide as well as the distinction between Commonwealth and foreign citizens; accordingly, the only legal distinction that mattered distinguished New Zealand citizens from others (McMillan, 2004; Spoonley, 1997). The Act also allowed citizenship by descent to be passed on through mothers as well as fathers (Green, 2005).

The 2005 Citizenship (Amendment) Act amended aspects of the 1977 Act. Citizenship could be acquired in three ways: by birth in New Zealand to a parent who was a citizen or permanent resident at time of birth; by descent to someone born outside of New Zealand to a New Zealand parent; and by grant ("naturalization") upon fulfilling certain requirements (Green, 2005). To receive a grant of New Zealand citizenship (ie naturalization), a person must fulfil certain criteria such as residency requirements and demonstrable English language competence unless they qualify for a special exemption (for example, a child born overseas of a New Zealand citizen). An amendment to New Zealand Citizenship Act imposed a set of restrictions on the concept of dual citizenship: A person born in New Zealand, Niue, Tokelau, and Cook Islands automatically became a New Zealand citizen if born before January 1, 2006. To quality for citizenship, at present, an Islander born in New Zealand must have at least one parent who is a New Zealand (or Australian) citizen or who posseses a permanent residence status in one of the above four jurisdictions (Waldron, 2011).

Insight Post

Voting and Denizenship

Should non citizens (denizens) be allowed to vote in local or national elections? Should they be able to run for political office at local or national levels? Should a certain period of permanent residency be enforced as a precondition for voting at any level? What are the benefits or risks in allowing voting rights to non citizens?

New Zealand represents one of few countries in the world that permit non citizens after one year of permanent residency to vote in local and national elections (McMillan, 2014, 2017). According to Fox (2005), some European countries and U S localities permit non citizen voting in local elections, while other countries such as Mexico allow migrants to run for office—from mayoralty level to state and federal party lists. Reaction to these arrangements vary: Some say yes. Siemiatycki (2006) argues such a concession symbolizes the warmth of a welcoming community, enhances accountability of political leaders, ensure migrant issues are on the political agenda, and hasten integration into community and society. Others argue that non citizens should be able to vote in those local elections where they live, work, pay taxes and educate children and participate in municipal decisions that affect their lives. Others disagree: they contend that allowing non citizens to vote cheapens the attainment citizenship. It also undermines the political process since non citizens are perceived to be lacking the knowledge to make informed decisions.

It remains to be seen if voting rights for permanent residents will be extended to other countries. The growing appeal of denizenship (rights of permanent residents as similar to that of citizens [Soysal, 1994]) would suggest, yes.

New Zealand's Multilayered Citizenship Regime

Like Canada and Australia, New Zealand initially subscribed to the principles of a universal citizenship regime. A one-size-fits-all concept of citizenship was applied evenly and equally to all who qualified. This universality did not historically apply to non white immigrants, including Chinese residents who, between 1908 and 1951, were denied the right to apply for permanent residency (McMillan, 2014). Even then, Chinese New Zealanders as "Aliens" (non British subjects) continued to bear the brunt of discrimination; for example, of the first 400 applicants following the lifting of restrictions, only 20 of the most highly assimilated were approved (Green, 2005). Over time, however, New Zealand citizenship models have incorporated more inclusive patterns of belonging and identity consistent with the "constitutional" status and the lived-realities of those domiciled in its domain.

Dual Citizenship and Pacific Transnationalism

Dual or multiple citizenships in some form or another have existed in New Zealand since passage of the Citizenship Act in 1948. The impetus for this duality reflects historical antecedents. Both the Cook Islands and Niue became New Zealand territories in 1901, while Tokelau achieved this status in 1916. As British subjects, citizens of these islands automatically acquired New Zealand citizenship. Membership in New Zealand political community is highly prized, particularly in countries that have experienced the legacy of New Zealand colonial relationships in the South Pacific. They include Pacific Island residents that form part of New Zealand territory (Tokelau) and the inhabitants of self-governing states in free association with New Zealand (Cook Islands and Niue). Nationals of Niue and the Cook Islands retain full New Zealand citizenship rights, thus confirming their status as dual citizens with corresponding rights in each jurisdictions (McMillan 2004). The conferral of dual citizenship addressed the issue of Pacific Island migration which encompassed an inherently transnational web among Pacific Islanders without compromising a commitment and connections to kin at home (Lee, 2009). Western Samoans are Samoan citizens rather than New Zealand citizens; nevertheless, they retain unencumbered entry into New Zealand based on an annual quota.

Indigenous Maori Citizenship

Binational states such as New Zealand confront formidable challenges in the governance of deep diversities. The challenge lies in asserting the primacy of a singular (or "universal") citizenship that reinforces the idea of similar rights applied to everyone in the same way, regardless of their differences, disadvantages, or legal status. But a universal citizenship model runs the the risk of denying minority group members the right to live and choose freely and to participate fully and equally on their own terms. For, as many have noted, a citizenship that frames people as individuals with formal rights under the law (Kymlicka and Norman, 2000) sounds good in theory. In reality, not everyone is positioned to fully practice the same rights or entitlements. For example, migrants and minorities may possess the same legal rights, yet they must express these rights in host country contexts neither designed to reflect their realities nor designed to advance their interests. The establishment of group differentiated rights that supersedes universal citizenship rights is no less critical. Such collective rights not only serve to offset the past disadvantages or overcome present-day barrier but also better account for the politics of both substate national minorities and Indigenous nations (Maaka and Fleras, 2005). The citizenship regime in New Zealand conveys a distinctive bicultural (or more accurately, a binational [Fleras and Spoonley, 1999]) reading of citizenship. The Indigenous Maori as the *tangata whenua* ("peoples of the land") possess a de facto dual citizenship based on the constitutionally protected reference to the principle of *tino rangatiratanga* ("self-determining autonomy") as stipulated by the 1840 Treaty of Waitangi/ Te Tiriti o Waitangi (Jones and Linkhorn, 2017; Larner, 2006; Stephens 2017). Chapter 7 will explore this claim in detail.

Australia: A Fair Go Citizenship?

The Oath for Citizens by Choice Not Birth: From this time forward, under God, [affirmation deletes reference to God] I pledge my loyalty to Australia and its people, whose democratic beliefs I share, whose rights and liberties I respect, and whose laws I will uphold and obey

Australia is a bit of paradox when applied to citizenship and diversity despite the adopton of more liberal and accommodative citizenship laws over a 70 year period (Jupp, 2008; also Smyth, 2016). First, nearly 30 percent of Australian identify as foreign born—in effect making Australia the world leader in the proportion of newcomers to the total population. Nevertheless, the overwhelming majority of Australian identify as European or claim European ancestry, while a small percentage are of Asian origins and identity. Fewer, still, are defined as Indigenous Australians. Moreover, while a large percentage of new Australians become citizens, including about 80 percent of those eligible for naturalization (Markus, 2017; Smith et al., 2010), Australia remains the only Western democracy without a national bill of rights specifying key citizenship rights—an omission that compromises the potential of citizenship as an instrument of empowerment (Crock, 2007; Galligan, 2017). Second, Australia may be defined as an immigration society because of a principled commitment to the admission and settlement of newcomers. Yet the international community has condemned it for its program of detaining, processing, and the offshore resettling of massed asylum seekers. Particularly controversial under its Pacific Solution intervention is the concept of outsourcing Australia's international human rights obligations by offloading boat-borne asylum seekers to Papua Guinea (Manus Island for detention) and to Nauru for processing and settlement, while declaring certain Australian controlled islands as non Australian territory for the purpose of denying refugee claims (James, 2014). Paradoxically, while Australians may be supportive of Australia's humanitarian program in resettling overseas refugees (i.e., those selected by Australia), they also support the government's Pacific Solution in warehousing those who dare to self-select for admission (Markus, 2016). Fears over the integrity of its immigration program and loss of public confidence in the country's ability to control its borders further reinforce public antipathy toward the *en masse* arrivals of asylum seekers.

Third, Australia has expressed a strong commitment to an official multiculturalism since 1973 (Bouma, 2016; Multiculturalism Policy Index, 2016). Yet the fortunes of multiculturalism at state and commonwealth levels are known to fluctuate, with most governments displaying a mixed enthusiasm (Galligan, 2017), particularly during the John Howard era (1996–2007) when the Office of Multiculturalism Affairs was rebranded as Office of Citizenship and Immigration, while the meaning of citizenship was realigned with a sense of national belonging based on a nostalgic, and insular past (Warr and Williams, 2015). Consider the contrasts: To one side, seven basic principles underpin Australian citizenship: respect and care for the land; adhere to the rule of law and ideal of equality; commit to Australia as a representative liberal democracy; uphold the principles of Australia as tolerant and fair; endorse Australia as inclusive multicultural society; foster the well being of all Australians; and recognize the unique status of First Australian peoples. To the other side, a national identity under Australian citizenship reinforces the principle of liberal nationalism by privileging British cultural traditions while repositioning ("reimagining") the civic nation along Anglo-Eurocentric lines (Levey, 2013; Voloder, 2013; also Hage, 1998). To the extent that multiculturalism exists, the provisions of the 1989 National Agenda for a Multicultural Australia remain in place in specifying that all Australians must have an overriding and unifying commitment to Australia and its core structures, values and principles (Galligan, 2017).

Fourth, Australia may celebrate an Australian Citizenship Day on the 17th of September; however, the Howard government manipulated citizenship as a tool to explicitly exclude those who did not commit to Eurocentric (liberal) values, Judeo Christianity tradition, and an Anglo-Saxon heritage (Fozdar, 2013). For Howard, in other words, citizenship was perceived as a community of values and a union of people modelled along familiar and familial lines (Joppke, 2013). Contrast this nativist position with that of former prime minister Bob Hawke, who defined a citizen as someone who lives here, obeys the laws, and pays taxes. The conclusion seems inescapable: The possibility that nearly one half of all Australians in an online survey endorse a move to curb the admission of Muslims suggests a continued affinity with Howards' restrictive turn (Essential Report, 2016).

Finally, Australia takes pride as a decent, humanitarian, multicultural and egalitarian society (Ricatti, 2016). Yet the collective status of Indigenous Australians (namely, Aborigines and Torres Strait Islanders) remains appalling regardless of the metrics employed (Galligan, 2017). As Mercer (2003) scathingly observes, Australia has the dubious distinction of being the only modern nation-state where Indigenous males on average are unlikely to live long enough to claim a retirement pension. Worse still, indicators suggest a growing deterioration of their collective status. When the Royal Commission report on Aboriginal deaths was published in 1991, Indigenous Australians comprised 14 percent of all prisoners but less than 3 percent of the population; 25 years later, they now comprise 27 percent of the prison population but still less than 3 percent of Australia's populace (Daley, 2016). (It should be noted that Indigenous peoples also account for about 25 percent of inmates in Canada's federal prison system, but only 4 percent of the country's population). Clearly, then, if there is any truth to Dostoyevski's claim that the quality and character of a society can be judged by its prisons and the treatment of prisoners, Australia's reputation takes a hit. To compound the injury and insult, Indigenous land rights are heavily qualified in favour of the commonwealth and mining companies who perpetuate a regime of dispossession, marginalization, destruction, and disconnection (Daley, 2016). Chapter 7 will explore the second class status of Indigenous Australians as citizens-minus (Chesterman and Galligan, 1997) or citizens without rights (Peterson and Sanders, 1998).

Citizenship Timeline: From Subjects to Citizens

The concept of Australian citizenship was linked to patterns of immigration and immigrant accommodation, developed through government administrative structures, and reflective of changes to its national identity as a white society (Klapdor et al., 2009; Rubenstein, 2008). Prior to federation in 1901, expressions of citizenship to the extent they existed were folded into the governance structures in each of the Australian states/colonies. Passage of the 1901 Australian Constitution Act established a starting point for formulating a national Australian citizenship. To be sure, the rights of Australian citizens were not articulated in the 1901 Act which remained silent on this issue, although as many as 30 subsequent amendments to the Act expanded on the specifics of what Australian citizenship meant and what constituted a good Australian citizen. A white supremacist logic prevailed (Galligan, 2017). The Act excluded the entry of non British people such as mainland Chinese, and non-white members of the Commonwealth (Indians and Hong Kong Chinese). The new federal government was charged with controlling immigration and naturalization to deter the admission of inadmissables—prompting Mary Crock (2007: 1058) to comment that "…the first Australian citizens were like the hole in the doughnut: they were the residue when all of the excluded or excludable people were defined." Clearly, the earliest forms of citizenship were exclusionary and manipulated as an instrument of immigration control for excluding undesirables or by whitewashing the diversity within. And while references to whiteness are rarely articulated in political or public discourse at present, the moral superiority of a white Australia has arguably remained central to Australia's national identity and the collective image of the Australian nation (Ricatti, 2016).

Passage of the Australian Nationality and Citizenship Act of 1948 came into effect in late January 1949. The Act legally defined the concept of

Australian citizenship (included Indigenous Australians): Australians were recognized as citizens of their own country although they remained British subjects until a 1984 amendment to the Citizenship Act (Galligan, 2017). The Act provided for citizenship by birth, by descent, and by grant; it also established a protocol for regulating the acquisition of Australian citizenship through naturalization ("by grant"). But because the Act didn't spell out the rights of citizenship, numerous amendments have transpired in response to changes to immigration policies, immigrant source countries, settlement philosophies, and notions of national identity (Klapdor et al., 2009). A series of amendments to the Nationality and Citizenship Act between 1955 and 1993 further stripped away the assumption of Britishness at the heart of Australian citizenship and identity. Admittedly, while citizenship possesses significant symbolic value for Australians in formally establishing membership in the national community, it has little practical effect on the material and social situation of permanent residents who retain access to welfare, medicare, public education, and special settlement services. Nevertheless citizenship provides advantages, including, immunity from deportation, access to an Australian passport, and eligibility for permanent government employment and the armed services (Klapdor et al., 2009).

The meaning of citizenship took a turn toward inclusiveness in 1973. The repeal of a white Australia policy coincided with the introduction of an official multiculturalism policy as a diversity governance model (Mann, 2012). With multiculturalism, an Anglo-national identity as a white ethnic nation-state was no longer synonymous with Australia's national identity. An official multiculturalism was aimed at the integration of newcomers though removal of discriminatory and prejudicial barriers. A liberal nationalism continued to prevail, despite references to Australia as an open and evolving society, since a federal (or commonwealth) multiculturalism continued to emphasize the priority of Australian values and institutions. A commitment to the principle of a multicultural inclusiveness was captured by Ien Ang in an address to NSW History Council in 2001 when proposing a new citizenship narrative that enabled all citizens to claim a sense of ownership and belonging to Australia (cited in Edmundson et al., 2009):

> "How can we recognize diversity as integral and intrinsic to the nation's history, and not just as a decorative afterthought? How can we develop a more diverse, shared, as well as open and living sense of heritage, something that all groups and communities contribute to, including those whose stories and voices are generally marginalized from the canonical national history."

Citizenship legislation continued to modify the notion of Australia citizenship. Modification to its birthright protocols in 1986 meant that children born in Australia no longer would acquire automatic citizenship without one parent as a citizen or permanent resident. To assist and advise the Government on citizenship-related issues, the Australian Citizenship Council was established in 1998 (Klapdor et al., 2009). A 2000 Report on Australian Citizenship for a New Century (Millbank, 2000) resulted in amendments to the Citizenship Act allowing both the introduction of dual citizenship and the extension up to the age of 25 of citizenship for children born overseas to an Australian citizens. The Australian Citizenship Act 2007 restructured the 1948 Act by introducing several measures pertaining to national security. It also extended the period of residency prior to application (from two to four years), ostensibly to improve newcomer integration by consolidating their grasp of Australian laws and values (Smith et al., 2010). More importantly, the Act summarized key substantive aspects of citizenship, including the meaning of citizenship, the right to full and formal membership, a common bond based on reciprocal rights and duties, respect for diversity, pledges of loyalty to Australia and its people, and the centrality of democratic beliefs, individual rights and liberties, and Australian laws (Galligan, 2017). Australian Citizenship Amendment (Citizenship Testing) Act of 2007 introduced new test requirements for citizenship applicants related to knowledge of the English language, Australian history and values, and the rights and duties of citizenship. Citizenship became less inclusive while the multiculturalism agenda redirected its focus to harmony and social cohesion rather than a corpus of citizenship rights and obligations (Castles, 2016). Another Bill in 2009 sought to further clarify changes to the 2007 Amendment Act. These changes in restricting access to citizenship stand in contrast to previous amendments which sought to make citizenship easier to acquire (Klapdor et al., 2009).In 2015 the Australian government proposed amendments to the Citizenship Act for revoking the citizenship and deporting those dual citizens accused of treason or terrorism-related acts.

Australia's citizenship regime resembles that of Canada. Both are civic and liberal-universal in orientation, with an attendant loyalty to polity, territory, and values rather than a particular national culture as basis for membership and entitlements (cultural nationalism) (Joppke 2013). It is estimated that 80 percent of migrants with more than ten years of residence have acquired Australian citizenship—a figure that nearly replicates Canada's 85 percent attainment rate (Smith et al., 2010). As is the case in Canada, possessing an Australian citizenship has little practical effect in everyday life since permanent residents possess similar access to services and benefits, although only citizens possess a passport, eligibility to permanent government employment, the right to vote in government elections, and immunity from deportation (Smith et al., 2010). Differences between Canada and Australia can also be discerned, albeit difficult to measure or verifty (Paquet, 2004). Evidence suggests greater citizen commitment to a social/moral contract in Australia, one that is more proactive and explicit in articulating the terms of citizenship, leading to debates about the limits to tolerance. Whereas Canadian citizenship is focused on legal status and abstract rights, with little attention to civic participation with the exception of an obligation to serve on duty when requested, Australia's more republican-oriented approach emphasizes involvement and the forging of multiple relationships. This distinction would appear consistent with the difference between liberal citizenship model (rights based, individual focus, market oriented and passive (just obey the laws) vs republican models of citizenship (duties based, centrality of the collective, public good oriented, and active citizenship participation) (Cao, 2015; Chabot, 2007; Maas, 2013). It should be noted that not everyone concurs with this assessment; for example, Jack Jedwab (2008) challenges the allegation that Canadians take their citizenship for granted. Besides, it might be argued, Canada's more casual approach and less dogmatic reference point might prove a better strategy in a globalized world of diversity and change. The resiliency implicit in such "ad-hocery" (Paquet, 2004: 257) may dampen those acrimonious debate and partisan divisions that incite inter-ethnic strife or sectarian violence.

Citizenship in America: Ideals vs. Realities

All persons born or naturalized in the United States, and subject to the jurisdiction thereof, are citizens of the United States and of the State wherein they reside. Citizenship clause of the 14th Amendment to the Constitution, 1868

The United States is often portrayed as a welcoming and inclusive democracy. It possesses a history of extending citizenship rights to an unusually diverse population as part of its founding myth as a home for the world's huddled masses (Orleck, 2003). At various points in its history, the United States has proven a world leader in expanding citizenship numbers and the diversity of people with access to citizen rights. To be sure, only property owning white males were considered full citizens at the time of the Constitution. Nevertheless, the granting of citizenship rights for voting reflected a progressive arc across an ever-broadening cross section of Americans, eventually extending to all white men in the 1830s, black males (1868), women (1920), Native (Indigenous) Americans (1924), eighteen year olds (1972), and at present to those who lawfully reside in the U.S.

This bucolic image of America as a citizenship utopia is more fiction than fact (Orleck, 2003). Not only were large number of individuals excluded from full rights and protections of citizenship for prolonged periods of time, but the expansion of citizenship rights did not materialize without a fierce and protracted struggle because of restrictive laws and fierce opposition from entrenched white interests (Orleck, n.d.). The first set of restrictions focused on race in curbing access to citizenship rights. The 1790 Alien Naturalization Act made it abundantly clear that non whites could never become American or citizens. It took the Civil War—including 600,000 dead and a million wounded—to constitutionally enshrine the 14th Amendment principle that entitled all individuals born in the United States to equal treatment under the law, with the exception of those beyond the jurisdiction of the United States such as members of the diplomatic corps, children of enemy aliens during wartime, and Native Americans whose tribal allegiance rendered them to be "alien nations" (Finkelman, 2015). In theory, the 15th Amendment in 1868 guaranteed universal suffrage (the right to vote) irrespective of race, colour, or previous condition of servitude (but not gender). In reality, it took until 1920 and years of political protest for women to win the citizenship right to vote, while African Americans engaged in a century long civil rights activism after the abolition of slavery to overturn Jim Crow segregation laws in the American south (Oleck, n.d.). African American women in the Jim Crow south were denied access to the ballot box until passage of the Voting Rights Act in 1965. People of Asian origins (South or East Asian) remained outside the orbit of citizenship rights well into the middle of the 20th century. Native Americans were also denied citizenship rights and the right to vote on grounds they did not fall under American jurisdiction. Rather they were defined and dismissed as uncivilized members of foreign nations ("tribes") or as hapless wards of the state that disqualified them as either subjects or citizens.

The overall immigrant population in the US totalled 43.3 million in 2015 or 13.5 percent of the total American population (Zong and Batalova, 2017). In 2015, 1.38 million foreign born individuals moved to the US, a 2 percent increase from 2014. India was the leading country of origin for recent immigrants (180,000), followed by China, Mexico, Philippines, and Canada. Mexicans continue to account for 27 percent of all migrants living in the US, followed by India (6%) and China and the Philippines (5%). The top five states by the number of immigrants were California (10.7 million), Texas, New York, Florida, and New Jersey; however, between 2000 and 2015, the five states with the largest percentage growth were North Dakota (137%), Tennessee, South Dakota, South Carolina and Wyoming. Around 48 percent of immigrants in the US were naturalized US citizens, while the remaining 52 percent consisted of lawful permanent residents, unauthorized immigrants, and legal residents on temporary visas (such as students). A total of 29 percent of immigrants aged 25 and older possessed a university degree (compared to 31 percent of the general population); nevertheless, educational attainment is rising for recent arrivals, with 48 percent of those arriving between 2011 and 2015 in possession of a postsecondary education.

At present, US citizenship is generally acquired by birth on American soil and those territories subject to American jurisdiction which extends to Guam, Puerto Rico, Northern Mariana Islands, US Virgin Islands and the District of Columbia. Children of American citizens are US citizens regardless of where they were born, that is, children born abroad to an American parent possesses birthright citizenship by parentage. Naturalized citizenship by persons born overseas is covered by Acts of Congress regulations and subject to fulfillment of certain requirements related to residency, English language skills, and tests that examine for American values. Citizenship entails (a) a set of rights, including the right to reside and work, enter and leave the United States, to vote in federal elections, and to stand for public office; (b) a package of benefits including consular protection outside the US, sponsorship of relatives living abroad, ability to invest in US property, transmission of citizenship to children born overseas, and protection from deportation; and (c) duties such as jury duty and payment of taxes (Spiro, 2008).

The US may be one of the more citizenship-friendly countries in the world; nevertheless, this lofty status does not preclude the inevitability of controversy and debates. Disputes over the value of dual citizenship continue to pit those who favour its potential benefits versus those who reject it on the basis of perceived costs (Renshon, 2005) (U.S. law permits dual and multiple citizenships although a naturalized American citizen must in theory renounce allegiance to the other country). The presence of a large number of undocumented migrants (between 11 and 12 million) transforms the politics of citizenization into a contentious issue. Moreover, naturalization law seemingly imposes few demands on potential citizens such as residency requirement, minimal English skills, and symbolic commitment to the Constitution while offering only few specific rights or obligations exclusive to citizenship, including the right to vote, the right to remain in the United States, and the obligation to jury duty, while military service is no longer obligatory. Put bluntly, the real prize is legal residency, not citizenship (Spiro, 2008: 159). And in a country where nearly 6 million peoples are ineligible to vote based on felony convictions (25% of those ineligible are Black), pressure is mounting to restore voting rights as part of any meaningful rehabilitation (Blessett, 2016).

Debates over who qualifies as an American citizen and who is entitled to the benefits of American citizenship have evolved into a hot button issue. Critics including President Trump dispute the validity of a law that grants citizenship to nearly every person born on American soil (Finkelman, 2015). For some, birthright citizenship is defined as a right guaranteed by 14th amendment. U.S.-born children of undocumented immigrants are automatically endowed with US citizenship. Other dispute the fact that children of parents in transit or with illegal status can acquire automatic citizenship and receive benefits, including the probability of making it harder to deport undocumented parents (Smith, 2015). How, critics ask, can such a blanket rule allow for the admission of individuals into the political fold with no meaningful connection to society simply by accident of birth on American or Canadian soil (Kivisto, 2008). Why should citizenship be offered to children of tourists ("birth tourism") who have no intention of living or committing to the US when, by contrast, hardworking undocumented labourers who pay taxes are often barred (Kivisto, 2008)? Those in favour of retaining existing birthright privileges argue that its removal would create a humanitarian catastrophe. Stripping citizenship from the country they were born in would render children both stateless and without a legal status, with little access to political processes, health care and education, few job prospects, and vulnerability to crime (Schatz, 2015). Supporters also argue that birth on territory represents an investment in long term loyalty and commitment to an American polity. But what was true in the past when migration patterns were linear, one-way, and final may be is less relevant at present. As Cristina Rodriguez (2010) points out, in a world of enhanced mobility, transmigration, and circular migration, the presumption of birthright citizenship is a questionable proxy for belonging since the parameters of citizenship (i.e. territorial presence or communal attachment or national identity) do not always coincide with notions of identity and belonging. In any case, the fact that such a jus soli rule remains in effect serve to remind that 19th century citizenship rules may prove an ill fit with 21st century realities.

References

Abu-Laban, Yasmeen. "Citizenship and Foreignness in Canada." In *Routledge Handbook of Global Citizenship Studies*, edited by E. F. Isin and P. Nyers, 274–283. New York: Routledge, 2014.

Abu-Laban, Yasmeen. "Transforming Citizenship: Power, Policy, and Identity." *Canadian Ethnic Studies* 47, no. 1 (2015): 1–10.

Akbari, Ather H. and Martha MacDonald. "Immigration Policy in Australia, Canada, New Zealand, and the United States: An Overview of Recent Trends." International Migration Review 48, 3 (2014): 801–822.

Alfred, Taiaiake. "First Nations Perspective on Political Identity." *First Nations Citizenship Research and Policy Series*. June 2009.

Atkinson, David. *The Burden of White Supremacy: Containing Asian Migration in the British Empire and the United States*. Chapel Hill: University of North Carolina Press, 2016.

Baldwin, Andrew, Laura Cameron and Audrey Kobayashi (eds.). *Rethinking the Great White North*. Vancouver, UBC Press, 2011.

Blessett, Brandi. "PA Times Online." *Rethinking the Dimensions of Citizenship*. 2016, http://patimes.org.

Bouma, Gary D. "The Role of Demographic and Socio-cultural Factors in Australia's Successful Multicultural Society: How Australia is Not Europe." *Journal of Sociology* 52, no. 4 (2016): 759–771.

Cao, Benito. *Environment and Citizenship*. New York: Routledge, 2015.

Carens, Joseph. "Aliens and Citizens: the Case for Open Borders." *Review of Politics* 49, no. 2 (1987): 251–273

Castles, Stephen. "Rethinking Australian Migration." *Australian Geographer* 47, no. 4 (2016): 391–398.

Chabot, Lynn. "The Concept of Citizenship in Western Liberal Democracies and in First Nations: A Research Paper." Prepared for the Governance Policy Directorate, Lands and Trusts Services. INAC, March 2007

Chesterman John and Brian Galligan. *Citizens without Rights: Aborigines and Australian Citizenship*. Melbourne: Cambridge University Press, 1997.

Crock, Mary. "Defining Strangers: Human Rights, Immigrants, and the Foundations for a Just Society." Lecture delivered to the Key Directions Public Lecture Series, University of Sydney, May 2, 2007.

Daley, Paul. "25 Years of Reconciliation and What Do We Have to Show For It?" *The Guardian* June 3, 2016.

Dauvergne, Catherine. *The New Politics of Immigration and the End of Settler Societies*. New York: Cambridge University Press, 2016.

Dodson, Mick. "Aboriginal and Torres Strait Islander People and Citizenship." Speech at the Complex Notions of Civic Identity Conference University of New South Wales, August 20, 1993.

Edmundson, Anna, Kylie Message, and Ursula Frederick. "Introduction: Compelling Cultures: Representing Cultural Diversity and Cohesion in Multicultural Australia." *Humanities Research* XV, no. 1 (2009): 1–6.

Elgersma, Sandra. "Canada's Changed Citizenship Law—An International Comparison." Library of Parliament, Ottawa, October 15, 2014.

Essential Report. "Ban On Muslim Immigration," September 21, 2016. Retrieved from http://www.essentialvision.com

Every Kiwi Counts Survey. Report by Colmar Brunton for KEA—New Zealand's Global Network, 2015.

Finkelman, Paul. "Citizenship and Constitution: A Legal History Lesson for Our Times." *Huffington Post* September 15, 2015.

Fleras, Augie. *The Politics of Multiculturalism: Multicultural Governances in Comparative Perspectives.* New York: Palgrave Macmillan, 2009.

Fleras, Augie. *Unequal Relations.* 8/e. Toronto: Pearson, 2016a.

Fleras, Augie. "Re-imagining Citizenship in Canada, New Zealand, and Australia: Transnational Dynamics, Postnational Complexities, Postcitizenship Possibilities." Plenary Paper, Citizenship in a Transnational Context, University of Alberta, Edmonton, July 6–7, 2016b.

Fleras, Augie. "Rethinking Citizenship Through Transnational Lenses: Canada, Australia, and New Zealand." In *Citizenship in a Transnational Perspective: Canada, Australia, and New Zealand,* edited by J. Mann., 15–48. New York: Palgrave, 2017.

Fleras, Augie and Jean Leonard Elliott. *The Nations Within.* Toronto: Oxford University Press, 1991.

Fleras, Augie and Paul Spoonley. *Recalling Aotearoa.* Auckland: Oxford University Press, 1999.

Forrest, James and Kevin Dunn. "Core Culture Hegemony and Multiculturalism." *Ethnicities* 6, no. 2 (2006): 203–230.

Fox, Jonathan. "Unpacking 'Transnational Citizenship.'" *Annual Review of Political Science* 8 (2005): 171–201.

Fozdar, Farida. "Constructing Australian Citizenship as Christian: Or How to Exclude Muslims from the National Imagining." In *Migration, Citizenship, and Intercultural Relations: Looking Through the Lens of Social Citizenship,* edited by F. Mansouri and M. Lobo, 33–49. Burlington, VT: Ashgate Publishing, 2013.

Galligan, Brian. "Australian Citizenship in a Changing Nation and World." In *Citizenship in a Transnational Perspective,* edited by J. Mann, 79–96. New York: Palgrave Macmillan, 2017.

Gamlen, Alan. "Making Hay While the Sun Shines: Envisioning New Zealand's State-Diaspora Relations." *Policy Quarterly* 3, 4 (2007): 12–23.

Ghosh, Gautam and Jacqueline Leckie (eds.). *Asians and the New Multiculturalism in Aotearoa New Zealand.* Dunedin: Otago University Press, 2015.

Green, David. "Te Ara—the Encyclopedia of New Zealand." *Citizenship—1840–1948: British Subjects.* February 8, 2005. https://teara.govt.nz/en/citizenship/page-1.

Green, Joyce. "The Impossibility of Citizenship Liberation for Indigenous People." In *Citizenship in a Transnational Perspective,* edited by J. Mann, 175–188. New York: Palgrave Macmillan, 2017.

Hage, Ghassan. *White Nation: Fantasies of White Supremacy in a Multicultural Society*. New York: Routledge, 1998.

James, Paul. "Fears of Globalization and the Borders of States: From Asylum Seekers to Citizens." *Citizenship Studies* 18, no. 2 (2014): 208–223.

Janoski, Thomas. *The Ironies of Citizenship: Naturalization and Integration in Industrialized Countries*. New York: Cambridge University Press, 2010.

Jedwab, Jack. "Ask What You Can do for your Country And Not What it Can do for You. Is Canadian Citizenship Really Being Taken for Granted?" *Canadian Diversity* 6, no. 4 (2008): 155–159.

Jones, Carwyn and Craig Linkhorn. "'All the Rights and Privileges of British Subjects': Maori and Citizenship in Aotearoa New Zealand." In *Citizenship in a Transnational Perspective*, edited by J. Mann, 139–158. New York: Palgrave Macmillan, 2017.

Joppke, Christian. "Through the European Looking Glass: Citizenship Tests in the USA, Australia, and Canada." *Citizenship Studies* 17, no. 1 (2013): 1–15.

Jupp, James. "Citizenship in Australia." *Canadian Diversity* 6, no. 4 (2008): 21–26.

Kivisto, Peter and Thomas Faist. *Citizenship: Discourse, Theory, and Transnational Prospects*. Oxford: Blackwell, 2008.

Klapdor, Michael, Moira Coombs and Catherine Bohm. *Australian Citizenship: A Chronology of Major Developments in Policy and Law. About Parliament, Parliamentary Departments, Parliamentary Library Research Publications*. Background Notes, Index Page 2009–2010. September 11, 2009.

Korteweg, Anna and Jennifer Elrick. "Citizenship Research Synthesis 2009–2013." A CERIS Report Submitted to Citizenship and Immigration Canada, Ottawa, 2014.

Kymlicka, Will and Wayne Norman (eds.). *Citizenship in Diverse Societies*. New York: Oxford University Press, 2000.

Larner, Wendy. "Brokering Citizenship Claims: Neo-Liberalism, Biculturalism, and Multiculturalism in Aotearoa New Zealand. " In *Women, Migration, and Citizenship*. edited by E. Tastsoglou and A. Dobrowolsky, 131–146. Burlington VT: Ashgate, 2006

Lee, Helen. "Introduction." In *Migration and Transnationalism: Pacific Perspectives*, edited by Helen Lee and Steve Tupai Francis. 1–6. Canberra: ANU Press, 2009.

Levey, Geoffrey Brahm. "Liberal Nationalism and the Australian Citizenship Tests." *Citizenship Studies* 18, no. 2 (2013): 175–189.

Maaka, Roger, and Augie Fleras. The Politics of Indigeneity: Challenging the State in Canada and Aotearoa New Zealand. Dunedin, NZ: University of Otago Press, 2005.

Maas, Willem. *Multilevel Citizenship*. Philadelphia: University of Pennsylvania Press, 2013.

Macklin, Audrey. "From Settler Society to Warrior Nation and Back Again." In *Citizenship in a Transnational Perspective*, edited by J. Mann, 285–314. New York: Palgrave Macmillan, 2017.

Macklin, Audrey and Francois Crepeau. "Multiple Citizenship, Identity, and Entitlement in Canada." *IRPP*, June 22, 2010.

Mann, Jatinder. "The Introduction of Multiculturalism in Canada and Australia, 1960s-1970s." *Nations and Nationalism* 18, no. 3 (2012): 483–503.

Mann, Jatinder. *The Search for a New National Identity: The Rise of Multiculturalism in Canada and Australia, 1890s-1970s.* New York: Peter Lang, 2016.

Mann, Jatinder (ed.). *Citizenship in a Transnational Perspective: Canada, Australia, and New Zealand.* New York: Palgrave, 2017.

Marwah, Inder and Triadafilos Triadafilopoulos. "Europeanizing Canada's Citizenship Regime. Commentary. Canada-Europe Transatlantic Dialogue: Seeking Transnational Solutions to 21st Century Problems." *Strategic Knowledge Cluster.* May 2009.

Markus, Andrew. "Australia' Immigrants: Identity and Citizenship." In *Citizenship in a Transnational Perspective,* edited by J. Mann, 225–244. New York: Palgrave Macmillan, 2017.

Markus, Andrew. "Mapping Social Cohesion." *The Scanlon Foundation Surveys 2016.* Melbourne: Monash University, 2016.

McMillan, Kate. "Developing Citizens. Subjects, Aliens, and Citizens in New Zealand since 1840." In *Tangata, Tangata: The Changing Ethnic Contours of New Zealand,* edited by P. Spoonley and C. Macpherson, 267–290.

McMillan, Kate. "National Voting Rights for Permanent Residents: New Zealand's Experience." In *Global Migration: Old Assumptions, New Dynamics,* edited by D. A. Arcarazo and A. Wiesbrock. Santa Barbara: Praeger, 2014.

McMillan, Kate. "Redefining Political Community After Empire. New Zealand and Non-Citizen Voting Rights." Paper Presented to the Citizenship in Transnational Perspective Conference, University of Alberta, Edmonton, July 6–7, 2016.

Menzel, Annie. "Birthright Citizenship and the Racial Contract." *DuBois Review: Social Science Research on Race* 10, no. 1 (2013): 29–58.

Mercer, David. "Citizen Minus? Indigenous Australians and the Citizenship Question." *Citizenship Studies* 7, no. 4 (2003): 421–425.

Millbank, Adrienne. "Dual Citizenship in Australia." *Current Issues Brief* 5 (2000–2001): November 28, 2000.

Monchalin, Lisa. *The Colonial Problem. An Indigenous Perspective on Crime and Injustice in Canada.* Toronto: University of Toronto Press, 2015.

Multiculturalism Policy Index. "Multiculturalism Policies in Contemporary Democracies." Retrieved from http://www.queensu.ca/mcp. June 18, 2016.

Orleck, Annelise. "The Flow of History." *The Problem of Citizenship in the United States.* Retrieved online http://flowofhistory.org/site/the-problem-of-citizenship-in-american-history-2/

Orleck Annelise. "Gender, Race, and Citizenship Rights: New Views of an Ambivalent Historical Evolution." *Feminist Studies* 29, no. 1 (2003).

Papillon, Martin and Gina Consentino. "Lessons From Abroad: Towards a New Social Model for Canada's Aboriginal Peoples." CPRN. *Social Architecture Report* f/40. April 2004.

Paquet, Gilles. "Governance and Emergent Transversal Citizenship: Towards a New Nexus of Moral Contracts." In *From Subjects to Citizens: A Hundred Years of Citizenship in Australian and Canada,* edited by P. Boyer et al., 231–262. Ottawa: University of Ottawa Press, 2004.

Pearson, David. "Rethinking Citizenship in Aotearoa New Zealand." In *Tangata, Tangata: The Changing Ethnic Contours in New Zealand,* edited by P. Spoonley, C. McPherson, and D. Pearson, 294–311. Southbank: Dunmore Press, 2004.

Peterson, Nicolas and Will Sanders (eds.). *Citizenship and Indigenous Australians: Changing Conceptions and Possibilities*. Cambridge: Cambridge University Press, 1998.

Renshon, Stanley. "Reforming Dual Citizenship in the United States." Center for Immigration Studies. October 2005.

Ricatti, Francesco. "A Country Once Great? Asylum Seekers, Historical Imagination, and the Moral Privilege of Whiteness." *Journal of Australian Studies* 40, no. 4 (2016): 478–493.

Rodriguez Cristina. "A Review of Peter Spiro's Beyond Citizenship: American Citizenship After Globalization." Public Law & Legal Theory Research Paper. Working Paper No. 10–35. New York University School of Law, 2010.

Rubenstein, Kim. "From Supra-National to Dual to Alien Citizen: Australia's Ambivalent Journey." In *Citizenship in a Post-National World*, edited by S. Bronitt and K. Rubenstein. 1–15. The Federation Press, 2008.

Sandercock, Leonie. "Planning in the Ethno-Culturally Diverse City: A Comment." *Planning Theory and Practice* 4, no. 3 (2003): 319–323.

Sassen, Saskia. "Towards Post-National and Denationalized Citizenship." In *Handbook of Citizenship Studies*, edited by Engin F. Isin and Bryan S. Turner, 277–292. Sage Publications, 2002.

Schatz, Brian. "This is What Would Happen if We Repealed Birthright Citizenship." *Mother Jones*. August 26, 2015.

Siemiatycki, Meyer. "Diversity Our Strength: the Toronto Experience." *Transitions* (Summer): 11–15 (2006).

Simon-Kumar, Rachel. "Difference and Diversity in Aotearoa/New Zealand: Post-neoliberal Constructions of the Ideal Citizen." *Ethnicities* 14, no. 1 (2014): 136–159.

Smith, David, Janice Wykes, Sanuki Jayarajah, and Taya Fabijanic. "Citizenship in Australia." Paper prepared by the Department of Immigration and Citizenship for OECD seminar on Naturalisation and the Socio-Economic Integration of Immigrants and their Children. October 2010.

Smith, Lamar. "Daily Signal." *Why We Should Have a Debate on Birthright Citizenship*. 2015. Retrieved from http://dailysignal.com.

Smyth, John. "The Australian Case of Education for Citizenship and Social Justice." In *The Palgrave International Handbook of Education for Citizenship and Social Justice*, edited by A. Peterson, R. Hattam, M. Zembylas, and J. Arthur, 307–205. New York:Palgrave Macmillan, 2016.

Soysal, Yasemin Nuhoglu. *Limits of Citizenship*. Chicago: University of Chicago Press, 1994.

Soysal, Yasemin Nuhoglu. "Postnational Citizenship: Reconfiguring the Familiar Terrain." In *The Blackwell Companion to Political Sociology*, edited by Kate Nash and Alan Scott. 333–341. Blackwell, 2004.

Spiro, Peter J. *Beyond Citizenship. American Identity After Globalizations*. New York: Oxford University Press, 2008.

Spoonley, Paul. "Migration and the Reconstruction of Citizenship in Late Twentieth Century Aotearoa." Migration and Citizenship, Aotearoa, APMRN. 1997. Retrieved from http://www.unesco.org.

Spoonley, Paul. "New Diversity, Old Anxieties in New Zealand: the Complex identity Politics and Engagement of a Settler Society." *Ethnic and Racial Studies* 38, no. 4 (2015): 650–661. Originally Published Online, November 19, 2014.

Spoonley, Paul. "Renegotiating Citizenship: Indigeneity and Superdiversity in Contemporary Aotearoa/New Zealand." In *Citizenship in a Transnational Perspective*, edited by J. Mann, 209–224. New York: Palgrave Macmillan, 2017.

Spoonley, Paul and Richard Bedford. *Welcome to our World? Immigration and the Reshaping of New Zealand.* Auckland: Dunmore Publishing, 2012.

Spoonley, Paul, Richard Bedford, and Cluny Macpherson. "Divided Loyalties and Fractured Sovereignty." *Journal of Ethnic and Migration Studies* 29, no. 1 (2003): 27–46.

Stasiulis, Daiva. "Respatializing Social Citizenship and Security Among Dual Citizens in the Lebanese Diaspora." In *Citizenship in a Transnational Perspective: Canada, Australia, and New Zealand*, edited by J. Mann. 49–78. New York: Palgrave, 2017.

Stephens, Mamari. "'A Useful and Self-Respecting Citizenship': Maori as Citizens in the Quest for Welfare in the Modern New Zealand State." In *Citizenship in a Transnational Perspective*, edited by J. Mann, 189–208. New York: Palgrave Macmillan, 2017.

US Department of Citizenship and Immigration. *Policy Manual*, 12, Part D, January 5, 2017.

Voloder, Lejla. "Avenues for Belonging: Civic and Ethnic Dimensions of Multicultural Citizenship in Australia." In *Migration, Citizenship, and Intercultural Relations: Looking Through the Lens of Social Citizenship*, edited by F. Mansouri and M. Lobo, 103–124. Burlington, VT: Ashgate Publishing, 2013.

Waldron, Holly. "Overseas-Born Maori and New Zealand Citizenship: Missing Men." Backround Paper, Institute of Policy Studies. May 2011.

Warr, Deb and Richard Williams. "The Shifting Terrain of Citizenship: A Wayfarers Guide." Scoping Report for the Melbourne Social Equity Institute. University of Melbourne, 2015.

Winter, Elke. "Becoming Canadian: Making Sense of Recent Changes to Citizenship Rules." IRPP Study No 44. January 2014.

Zong, Jie and Jeanne Batalova. "Frequently Requested Statistics on Immigrants and Immigration in the United States." *Migration Policy Institute*. March 8, 2017.

· 4 ·

CITIZENSHIP IN A MULTICULTURAL CANADA

Canada: A Citizenship Poster Child

Oath or Affirmation of Citizenship

I swear (or affirm) that I will be faithful and bear true allegiance to Her Majesty, Queen Elizabeth the Second, Queen of Canada, Her Heirs and Successors, and that I will faithfully observe the laws of Canada and fulfil my duties as a Canadian citizen.

Canadians pride themselves as citizens of a widely admired society with an enviable international reputation (Clarkson, 2014; US News and World Report, 2016). Canada's commitment to actively pursue the naturalization (citizenization) of newcomers is no less unparalleled (Schmidtke, 2017). According to the UNHCR (2016) in their annual global trends report, Canada naturalized 25,900 refugees in 2015 or 81 percent of the world's refugee population who acquired citizenship status in that year. Canada's seemingly seamless acceptance and resettlement of over 40,000 Syrian refugees by the end of 2016 further sealed its lofty status as a global outlier in cementing the "warmth of the welcome". Even widely criticized moves by the Conservative government (2006–2015) to restrict citizenship access hardly put a dent in derailing its appeal to newcomers. Over 262,000 newcomers became citizens of Canada in 2014, a substantial increase over the previous year, despite fears of a downward dip in naturalization rates in light of the governments "harder to get, but easier to lose" mentality (Griffith, 2015b). About 85 percent of all immigrants who permanently settle in Canada eventually take the oath of citizenship, in effect putting Canada at the forefront of the global citizenship sweepstakes. Such an assessment is hardly surprising: A Canadian citizenship entitles its bearer to rights, entitlements, and privileges, often beyond the dreams of those in the applicant's home country. Newcomers to Canada also gain access to membership in what many regard as one of the world's premier places to live.

Popularity aside, questions about Canadian citizenship continue to abound. What is the meaning of citizenship in a diverse and changing Canada? What does it mean to be a citizen of Canada when lived through a local/national/global nexus? What rationale and whose logic prevails in defining who belongs, how they belong, and what belonging entitles? These questions were once ignored, treated with indifference, or dismissed as unproblematic. But current trends—from Canada's growing expatriate community to communication technologies that facilitate transmigrant linkages—put pressure on clarifying the meaning of citizenship, what it means to be a citizen, and what at present constitutes a meaningful citizenship (Environics Institute, 2012)? Yet the centrality of citizenship to Canada-building remains a constant, as pointed out by Senator Ratna Omidvar (cited in Keung, 2017b: A-8):

> Citizenship is one of the most powerful indicators of inclusion and belonging. When we facilitate citizenship for newcomers and protect the fundamental equality among all citizens by birth or naturalization, we are nation-building.

In theory, acquisition of citizenship secured an enviable package of rights, including Charter protection, the right to vote, and possession of a passport for reentry into Canada. (Banulescu-Bogdan, 2012). Citizens were expected to reciprocate by obeying Canada's laws in fulfilment of their duties and obligations. In practice, however, the concept of a good (or ideal) citizen has a more expansive range. Reference to shared citizenship trumpets the ideals of solidarity and co-responsibility with other Canadians, respect for differences, trust in public institutions and willingness to cooperate in creating a coherent Canadian community based on the primacy of individual rights, socioeconomic equity and political equality (Banting et al., 2007; Kymlicka, 2007). For example, a 1996 information brochure distributed by Citizenship and Immigration Canada defined a good Canadian citizen as someone who is loyal to Canada and the Queen, obeys Canadian laws, upholds Canadian ideals such as democracy and tolerance, is protective of Canadian heritage, and respectful of people's rights and private/public property (cited in Labelle and Salee, 2001). The 2011 Discover Canada guide book emphasized the virtues of a Canadian citizen as one who respects Canada's British and military history, rejects barbaric practices such as female genital mutilation, and is employed (Sobel, 2015). A substantially revised guide book in the draft stage focuses on a distinction between voluntary responsibilities (from respect human rights to participating in the political process) and mandatory responsibilities including paying taxes, obeying the law, serving on jury duty, filling out the census, and respecting treaty rights (Levitz, 2017).

Canada-wide polls reinforce many of these ideals and commitments. For example, a 2011 National Survey on Canadians and Citizenship asked a series of questions about what defines good citizens and good citizenship (Environics Institute, 2012). Based on a list of 17 prompted attributes, the concept of a good citizen was synonymous with the equality of gender treatment (95% said it was a critical component of good citizenship). This was followed by obedience to Canadian laws (89% of the respondents), tolerance toward others (82%), voting in elections (82%), and protecting the environment (recycling) (80%). In terms of being a good citizen, Canadians define citizenship as more than the possession of a passport or payment of taxes. Just as important in defining good citizenship based on unprompted responses are social responsibilities such as active participation in a community, assistance to others, and acceptance of differences. More specifically, the unprompted responses to what constitutes a good citizen endorsed the following attributes: Obeys laws (42%), actively participates in the community (33%), embraces Canadian values (17%), works hard (14%), and respects country/loyalty (9%). A follow up survey in 2016 to track changes since 2011 conveyed nearly identical responses (Environics Institute, 2016). However, respondents put more emphasis on obeying laws (up 7% from 2011 to 49%), active participation (up 8% to 41%), shares Canadian values (up 5% to 22%), works hard (up 5% to 19%), and respects/loyalty to Canada (up 9% to 18%) (Environics Institute, 2016). Both surveys also confirmed that Canadians believe anyone regardless of their birthplace can become a good citizen (Stokes, 2017).[1] And while newcomers are expected to make an effort to become good citizens by adopting Canadian customs and traditions, Canada also must play a part in facilitating the process of integration. Finally, both surveys concluded that both the Canadian- and foreign-born share a similar vision about the meaning of citizenship and what it means to be a good citizen.

Clearly, then, Canada is a poster-child in advancing the concept of a progressive citizenship regime (Schmidtke, 2017). Its credentials are secured by guaranteeing a citizenship by birth to a Canadian or to someone resident on Canadian soil (however temporarily), in addition to actively promoting citizenship to all newcomers. Canada is also at the forefront of countries in advancing the once unorthodox notion that citizens do not have to belong or identify in the same way to enjoy the same entitlements. Even Canada's national citizenship with its emphasis on the universal and the unitary acknowledges the salience of diverse identities, practices, and expectations as a precondition for living together. For example, Quebecers may be Canadians citizens; nevertheless, they express their identity and belonging to Canada through their ethnicity as members of the Quebec nation/distinct society. Furthermore, Canada's immigration success story in citizenizing immigrants complies with the principles of an official multiculturalism (Bloemraad, 2015; Kymlicka, 2016). A multicultural agenda allows people to belong, identify, and integrate through their ethnicity, in the process creating "…space for multiple identities and multiple loyalties, for an idea of belonging which is comfortable with contradictions, which shifts humans from their autocratic role as masters of the universe to one more integrated into the place itself" (Saul, 2016).

This chapter takes advantage of these insights, convergences, and developments by framing Canada's commitment to an inclusive citizenship as an unfinished project in progress (Abu-Laban, 2016). Citizenship in Canada as status, discourse, and practice resembles a contested yet jumbled site that yields a range of disagreements over the "who", the "how", and the "why" of identity, membership, and entitlements. A discursive shift in the debates over how we think, talk, and do citizenship is hardly a surprising revelation; after all, references to what citizenship means and what it means to be a Canadian citizen remains slippery and elusive rather than unproblematic or uncontested (Lee, 2016). The chapter begins with a brief history of citizenship as concept and legal status in Canada; examines how Canadian citizenship is subject to controversy over form, function, and process; discusses the transformational shift from a universal citizenship regime to one reflective of Canada's multicultural agenda; and articulates the possibility of a distinctive Canadian citizenship model. Particular attention is devoted to the concept of multicultural citizenship (Kymlicka, 1996, 2016). The customizing of citizenship along diversity lines is shown to align with different patterns of belonging, identity, and entitlements that, in turn, reflect and reinforce the politics of diversity. The chapter concedes the obvious: Canada may well prove one of the world's most progressive citizenship regimes. But it is precisely this vaunted status as a global benchmark that subjects Canada's citizenship model to criticism and calls for adjustments (Bakan, 2016).

An Historical Timeline

Canada's status as a citizenship superpower implies a certain historical scenario: the evolution of its citizenship program in a progressive and expansionist manner. Yet evidence points to a journey that has proven both narrow and sporadic as well as racist and selective—and all too often aligned with the hegemonic and homogenizing logic of the Canadian state but inconsistent with Canada's bona fides as an inclusive and multicultural society (Mahoney, 2008; Winter, 2014). Canada's immigration agenda endorsed those cultural chauvinisms and racist ideologies intent on securing a British Canada as a white colonial outpost (Thobani, 2007). But as a settler society dependent on immigration for economic growth and demographic expansion, reality clashed with supremacist ideals. Canada had little choice except to create a citizenship regime that assured recognition of the foreign born, while removing the most egregious patterns of discrimination based on race, ethnicity, and national origins (Winter, 2015).

According to Elke Winter (2014), four phases inform Canada's history of citizenship legislation and naturalization processes from World War Two onwards (1) creation of a citizenship that differed from the principle of British subjecthood (2) a de-ethnicization of citizenship from mid 1960s to late 1980s (3) a remaking of citizenship within the context of neoliberalism from late 1980s to mid-2000s, and (4) a renationalizing of citizenship from 2006 to 2015 based on reviving Canada's British traditions. The new Liberal government would appear to shifting back toward a more civic oriented model of citizenship (Levitz, 2017). Admittedly, no one is suggesting a linear development from one phase to another; nor is anyone proposing the total domination of a single perspective at one point in time. Rather the point of the exercise is to acknowledge the emergence of new eras that challenged previous phases and capitalized on existing perspectives (also Rouhana and Sabbagh-Khoury, 2015).

Prior to the end of the second world war, residents of Canada possessed no independent status except as British subjects, "aliens" (or immigrants) or

"Indians" as set out in the 1867 Constitution Act (Brodie, 2002). The first federal act was passed in 1868 (Aliens and Naturalization Act) stipulated that any person naturalized in any part of the Dominion possessed the same status in Canada as someone naturalized under the Act. But there was no such thing as a Canadian citizen apart from a Commonwealth context until passage of the *Citizenship Act*. To be sure, the Acts listed below (as well as 1921 Canadian Nationals Act) may have used the term Canadian citizenship, but primarily for descriptive flourish rather than articulating a distinct legal status (Chabot, 2007; Kaplan, 1993). "Canadians" were defined as British subjects who happened to be domiciled in Canada, with a corresponding obligation to conduct themselves accordingly. The 1910 Immigration Act created a separate subset of British subjects who were born, naturalized, or resident in Canada, followed by the 1914 Naturalization Act which specified the particulars of naturalization as British subjects, including 5 years of residency, knowledge of English, and possession of a good character. Male British subjects could transmit their citizenship to their legitimate children, although this right was withheld from female British subjects who married non British subjects. Women assumed the citizenship of their husbands. While a foreign-born woman who married a Canadian acquired his citizenship status (Winter, 2015), Canadian-born women could lose their citizenship and be deemed aliens if they married a foreign-born husband or if their husband's status was downgraded to that of an alien (Griffith, 2016). Finally, the restrictiveness of Canadian citizenship was on display. Both the Immigration Act and the Naturalization Act empowered officials with the authority to preserve the ethnic composition of a white Canada. Racialized immigrant categories were prohibited from settling into Canada because of their origins, social class, occupation, physical condition, moral standards, and potential to assimilate into Canada (Joshee, 2004; Winter, 2015). Nevertheless, the renaming of the Nationalities Branch of the Secretary of State to the Citizenship Branch in 1945 heralded the onset of a discursive shift. The ethnic overtones implied by the term nationality gave way to the more democratic and modern connotations implicit in the expression of citizenship (Winter, 2015).

Passage of the *Citizenship Act* announced that Canadians had acquired autonomous legal status. Canadians, in turn, were no longer simply transplanted British "expats" or a subset of British subjecthood, despite ongoing linkages to the Crown (Bloemraad, 2006; Macklin and Crepeau, 2010; Mann, 2016). (According to Federal Court Decisions (2006), Canada issued two types of passports prior to 1947: blue for British subjects by birth, red for naturalized British subjects). On January 1, 1947, all persons living legally in Canada became Canadian citizens as if they were born in Canada on New Year's

Day, i.e. British subjects resident in Canada were automatically converted to Canadian citizens. With passage of the Citizenship Act, Canada become one of the first Commonwealth countries to enact a national citizenship status independent of British nationality (the Irish Free State passed its own nationality law in 1935), although references to British subjecthood for immigration purposes remained in effect until the late 1970s (Abu-Laban, 2014; Winter, 2013). Key provisions of the Act reinforced the continuing centrality of Britishness, including a five year residency requirement for non-British migrants (only one year for British immigrants) in addition to language and knowledge requirements (but waived for British immigrants) assessed through an interview with a judge (Griffith, 2016). The Act established who was and who could become a Canadian citizen, including provisions for loss of citizenship; for example, Canadians who acquired citizenship in another country (Dual citizenship was not recognized until 1977, although it was tolerated for foreign nationals who applied for Canadian citizenship). Discarding the provision that disenfranchised them upon marriage to a non-Canadian citizens accorded married women full control of their citizenship (Grey and Gill, 2015)—a substantial improvement over their previous classification (for citizenship purposes) with that of minors, lunatics, and idiots (Frith, 2003?).

A new kind of belonging was proposed commensurate with the maturing of Canada on a path to full nationhood while enfranchising those previously excluded (Triadafilopoulos, 2012, but see Chapman, 2015 for anomalies). The Act sought to integrate all Canadians into a single body politic by eliminating nearly all distinctions between Canada-born ("Canadians by birth") and naturalized citizens ("Canadians by choice") (Winter, 2015). Paul Martin Sr., a Liberal Cabinet Minister, issued a statement to this effect in the House of Commons on October 22, 1945:

> Our "new Canadians" bring to this country much that is rich and good, and in Canada they find a new way of life and new hope for the future. They should all be made to feel that they, like the rest of us, are Canadians, citizens of a great country, guardians of a proud tradition, and trusties of all this is best in life for generations of Canadians yet to be. For the national unity of Canada and for the future and greatness of this country it is felt to be of utmost importance that all of us, new Canadians and old, have a consciousness of a common purpose and common interests as Canadians; that all of us are able to say with pride and say with meaning: "I am a Canadian citizen."

The Citizenship Act may have symbolized a landmark in Canadian history that offered a template for other Commonwealth countries. Nevertheless, Canadian citizenship remained exclusionary. Citizenship was defined as a privilege to be conferred on those most qualified, namely, immigrants from US, Europe, and the old Commonwealth countries (Chabot, 2007). Canada's Indigenous peoples continued to be defined as wards of the state under the Indian Act instead of legal persons; as a result, they occupied a liminal status, neither citizens nor subjects. Until 1956 and passage of an amendment to the 1947 Act, Indigenous persons could only become citizens by renouncing their "Indianess" through voluntary disenfranchisement or compulsory enfranchisement. It was not until 1960 that an amendment to the Elections Act granted them full voting rights as part of a Canadian citizenship package (Chabot, 2007). It should be noted that naturalization requirements have varied since 1947 (Griffith, 2016), with residence requirement ranging from three to five years, age of testing from 14 to 64 years, the insertion or removal of an intent to reside clause, age of declaration for retention of citizenship for those Canadians born overseas, and an expansion or contraction of the criteria for revoking citizenship.

The Citizenship Act of 1977 updated the 1947 Act with a more equitable framework that sought to improve access and equal treatment (Winter, 2013; Young, 1998). Passage of the Act also reflected and reinforced a broader Liberal strategy to harness the support of ethnic and immigrant voters (Triadafilopoulos, 2012). The Act specifically stated that a naturalized citizen (Canadians by choice) was entitled to the same rights and privileges a Canadian-born citizen as well as subject to the same duties and obligations. British subjects no longer received special treatment (thus de-ethnicizing the Britishness at the core of Canadian citizenship); dual citizenship was recognized (thus allowing multiple allegiances and different forms of belonging); second generation persons born (or adopted) outside of Canada would relinquish their citizenship without a formal declaration by their 28th birthday (at present, any child born abroad can acquire Canadian citizenship but only if one parent was born in Canada or had naturalized status prior to the child's birth [Macklin and Crepeau, 2010]); and citizenship for all qualified applicants was deemed a right rather than privilege (Winter, 2013; Young, 1998). Under the Act, citizenship was automatically granted to any person 18 years of age or over who applied, was lawfully admitted into Canada for permanent residence, resided in Canada for three of the previous four years prior to the application, possessed an adequate knowledge of Canada and competence in one of the two official languages, and was not subject to a deportation order. The Canadian Charter of Rights and Freedoms which came into effect in 1985 specified the rights and freedoms of all persons living in Canada (Chabot, 2007). Charter rights included legal rights (for example, the right to a fair trial), equality rights (protection against discrimination) and mobility rights (the right to live and work anywhere in Canada), while basic freedoms incorporated freedom of thought, speech, religion, and peaceful assembly. Responsibilities extended to voting in elections, serving on jury duty, obeying Canadian laws, respecting rights and freedoms of others, protecting Canada's heritage and environment, and supporting multiculturalism and equality. But as Richez and Manfredi (2014) point out, the Charter was largely silent about citizenship, with only three citizenship rights explicitly referred to by the Charter—voting and legislative membership rights (eligibility for political office), mobility rights, and access to minority language education rights (receive an education in either official language). Nonetheless in contrast to non citizens or permanent residents, Canadian citizens enjoy additional entitlements including the right to a Canadian passport, free movement in and out of Canada, and preferred access to government jobs.

From the late 1980s to the early 2000s, the citizenship concept was increasingly informed by a neoliberal agenda. A commitment to neoliberalism capitalized on three key planks—more market, less government, and more individual responsibility—that exerted pressure on existing citizenship forms. For example, in 1996, the format of Canada's citizenship test shifted from an oral hearing under the auspices of a citizenship judge to a standardized multiple choice test—presumably as a low cost alternative to time consuming interviews consistent with fiscal cutbacks across all government departments for client based programs (Winter, 2011). The Strengthening Canadian Citizenship Act which came into force in June 2015 was the first comprehensive reform to the Citizenship Act since 1977. The amendments addressed the modern issue of terrorism and citizenship, clarified definitions of residence in Canada, streamlined the citizenship process (from a three-step process with a processing time on average of 2–3 years, to a one-step process concluded in less than a year), and endorsed a "renationalizing" or "re-ethnicizing" of citizenship to reflect Canada's historical status as a loyal member of the British empire (Macklin, 2016; Winter, 2013). The revocation of Canadian citizenship was expanded beyond that of fraud or application misrepresentation (Elgersma, 2014) Grounds for revocation included criminal convictions related to security matters (from terrorism and violations of human rights to war crimes and organized crime) in both Canada and abroad. It should be noted that, with passage of Bill C-6 (Bechard & Elgersma, 2016) which received final approval in the House in May 2017, the Liberal government

(2015- present) has repealed or relaxed residency requirements, grounds for citizenship revocation, and age limitations for language and knowledge tests.

Contesting Canadian Citizenship: The Good, the Bad, the Ugly

Seventy years after the grounding breaking 1947 Act, Canada is loftily perched as a citizenship go-to destination (Schmidtke, 2017). It is widely regarded as having one of the user-friendliest pathways for citizenship acquisition ("naturalization"); the legal and administrative dimensions are accessible and easy to navigate; the principle of jus domicile (citizenship by choice) minimizes barriers to full legal membership in the Canadian community; the availability of dual citizenship bolsters Canada's brand as an attractive immigrant destination; relatively open access to citizenship enhances the integration of newcomers into Canada's social fabric: and new citizens are generally welcomed into the fold either as Canadians-in-the-making or to offset skilled labour shortages, a declining birthrate, and an ageing population (Bloemraad, 2015; Korteweg and Elrick, 2014). Even non-citizens are accorded Charter's equality protection because of a 1985 Supreme Court ruling that accorded Charter benefits to anyone physically present in Canada, so that withholding citizenship rights could be construed as a form of discrimination (Dauvergne, 2014). As proof of Canada's seemingly exalted status, a US News & World Report et al. (2016) asked 16,200 respondents (including political elites, business makers, and ordinary citizens) to rank 60 countries along 65 different categories. Canada not only placed second overall as a best country by brand (Germany was number 1), but it was ranked second in citizenship status (based on respect for property rights, trustworthiness, well-distributed political power, religious freedom, and respect for human rights). That the vast majority (85%) of newcomers to Canada become citizens within ten years of their arrival should come as no surprise.

Kudos aside, however, Canada's generous approach to citizenship is subject to commentary and criticism (Herzog, 2014). For example, Yann Martel on accepting the 2002 Booker prize complimented Canada's progressive stance when acknowledging Canada as the "...greatest hotel on earth. It welcomes people from everywhere". Or put a bit differently, Canada is the kind of place where people enter and leave at their leisure, claiming citizenship as little more than a room key (Brean, 2012). But others disagree with what they see as a thinly veiled insult. Andrew Cohen (2007) and Rudyard Griffiths (2009) challenge this "home-away-from-home" metaphor as inappropriate and unhelpful. They believe little of value can be gained from Canada's reckless recognition of dual citizens. Even less can be gleaned from its postnational embrace of hybrid national identities, diasporic communities, and fragmented allegiances (Sibley, 2015). Jason Kenney the Minister of Immigration and Citizenship (and Multiculturalism) for much of Harper's reign rejected the accuracy of this hotel metaphor. According to Kenney, the Conservative Governments envisioned Canada as a family of patriotic Canadians whose knowledge of and loyalty to Canada contributed to a sense of social cohesiveness, mutual obligations, and civic responsibility (in Brean, 2012; Kenney, 2009).

To banish the image of Canada as the world's premier "bed and breakfast" destination, the Conservative regime reinforced a spatialized sense of national citizenship in which a prospective citizen had to be resident or intend to reside. Instead of envisioning an inclusive Canadian citizenship as a global asset, the government sought to re-nationalize (re-ethnicize) by privileging the more militaristic aspects of Canadian history (Winter, 2014). This "culturalization of citizenship" reflected similar patterns in European countries such as the Netherlands where multicultural models of civic citizenship shifted toward a more mono-cultural and assimilationist definition of belonging and identity. A new citizenship guide placed greater emphasis on military history, British traditions, and the monarchy (Macklin, 2016; Sobel, 2015). It also singled out certain cultures and practices as less desirable or unCanadian in the process accentuating a more distrustful and accusatory tone (Harder and Zhyznomirska, 2012; No One is Illegal, 2015). Finally, in contrast to the past when citizenship status, once acquired, was relatively secure from revocation unless fraudulently obtained, the Act allowed the citizenship of dual citizens to be rescinded for reasons other than fraud, in the process creating a two tier class of citizens based on a decision by a citizenship officer rather than federal court judge as in the past, with no chance of a full hearing or later appeal (Bahrami, 2014). Despite the Liberal government's "sunny ways" approach to governance, included proposals for a more civic-oriented overhaul of the guide to good citizenship (Levitz, 2017), actions do speak louder than words. A total of 236 Canadians were stripped of their citizenship since the Liberal government came into power in November 2015, compared to a ten year total of 115 under the Conservative government (Keung, 2017a).

Many have deplored the decision to make citizenship harder to get but easier to lose, ostensibly justified on the grounds that something is more valued when earned rather than bestowed (Abu-Laban, 2016). The 2015 Strengthening Canadian Citizenship Act reframed citizenship not as right on the path to integration, but as a privilege or reward conditional on good conduct and a successful adaptation (Abu-Laban, 2015; also Puzzo, 2016). The government also raised the processing fee for naturalizing new Canadians from $100 to $530 in 2015, including an additional $100 right of citizenship fee upon approval of the application. Such a steep fee increase may have contributed to a dramatic 50 percent decrease in new citizenship applications (from 111,993 in 2015 (January to September) to 56,446 during the same period in 2016) (Griffith, 2016; Keung, 2017). But Canada's bona fides as principled citizenship society that abides by multicultural principles were put to the test by a proposed banning of full veil face coverings at citizenship ceremonies (Merolli, 2016; Winter, 2014; also Griffith, 2015a).

Insight Post

The Politicization of Citizenship and the Politics of Veiling

The outcome of Canada's 2015 federal election may have hinged on a woman's insistence to remain fully veiled during the citizenship oath ceremonies (Coyne, 2015; Fleras, 2016; Majka, 2015). In 2011, Zunera Ishaq, a 29 year old Pakistani woman who came to Canada in 2008 successfully challenged the government's proposed ban on face coverings during the citizenship swearing-in ceremonies (Southey, 2015). Ms Ishaq had indicated a willingness to confirm her identity by unveiling privately just prior to taking the oath, but the government—long a proponent that all things Muslim must be smeared as security issues [Fisk 2015])—dismissed as unCanadian this seemingly reasonable accommodation. In mid-September 2015, the Federal Court of Appeal again ruled against the government's determination to ban the practice of "oathing while veiling" (Selley, 2015), arguing the ban was unlawful and contravened the Citizenship Act. In what may have amounted to a carefully orchestrated act of political theatre, the government promised to bump the banning of the ban all the way to the Supreme Court by requesting for a stay of the decision, but the Federal Court of Appeal refused to suspend its earlier rulings (Fine, 2015).

The government ostensibly justified its stand on grounds that no person should be allowed to hide their identity or compromise their loyalty at the very moment they commit to join the Canadian family. According to the government, citizenship is a privilege, not a right, and everyone should comply with established protocols as a sign of loyalty. But critics accused the government of a politically expedient attack on individual and minority rights including the right to freedom of religious expression that not only pandered to the lowest common denominator but also diverted attention from more serious political and economic issues (Wente, 2015). The Canadian public appeared to side with the federal government stand (also Valpy, 2017). A government-funded poll of 3,000 adults conducted by Leger on behalf the Privy Council Office in March, 2015 found that 82 percent of respondents, including 93 percent of respondents in Quebec, agreed that women should unveil during the citizenship ceremonies (Levitz, 2015). Another survey in late September 2015 by Forum Research found that 64 percent of the 1,499 respondents opposed fully veiled women from swearing the oath of citizenship (26% support it), including 79 percent in Quebec (Vincent, 2015). The poll also found that 56 percent of respondents believe the niqab oppresses women (29% disagree). These figures reinforce Canadian ambivalence toward an official multiculturalism (Donnelly, 2017)—a commitment that's long on principle but short on practise if the multicultural accommodation of diversity is costly, creates inconvenience, or challenges who's in charge in defining what counts as differences, what differences count (Fleras, 2009).

How unflattering: Canadians may imagine themselves as beacons of multicultural enlightenment, but the politics of veiling picked at the scabs of those phobias and bigotries that lurk beneath our comforting fictions and collective delusions (Chazan et al., 2011; Cohn, 2015; Dedi, 2015). The coded language of a commitment to Canada and its values that framed the niqab debate expresses what might be called "dogwhistle racism". Just as a dogwhistle produces a high pitched sound beyond human reception, so too does dogwhistle racism consist of seemingly innocent speech codes that secretly insult or demonize minorities, and are understood as such for those "in the know". Although the words sound normal to the general public, if challenged by constituents or activists, they can be excused as lacking malice or justified as well intentioned (Lopez, 2015).Not surprisingly, a government that was prone to playing the wedge politics of fear and division thought it had hit the electoral jackpot with its hard-line stand on the niqab—mistakenly as it turned out when it lost the federal election in the fall of 2015).

So what's going on? Is this about an anti-niqab resistance or, more accurately, *opposition to a niqab at a citizenship ceremony*? Does the controversy reflect the growing culturalization (re-ethnicization) of citizenship that is inclined to frame it along monocultural lines rather than inclusively (Moors, 2009)? Is antagonism toward the niqab reflective of high levels of closet bigotry, especially now that the politics of diversity accommodation are increasingly animated by the Muslim question (Dedi, 2015). Or, alternatively, is public opposition more about the niqab as a proxy or code for wider worries over cultural incompatibilities because of social change, disputed values, Islamist extremism, and debates over tolerance and accommodation. Of particular note is the age-old question of whether newcomers should accommodate to Canada or should Canadians be more accommodative of religious and cultural diversities [Wente, 2015]). However controversial these concerns, a sense of perspective is useful. The governance of Canada's diversity relations shouldn't be swayed by polls, fear, or wedge politics. Canada should not be governed by the tyranny of majority rule or through public apprehension but on the rule of law and the principle of individual rights. Unlike assimilationist citizenship models that envision the nation state as culturally homogeneous, Canada's multicultural model promotes a relatively smooth and accommodative path to citizenship regardless of race, ethnicity, or religion (see also Kilic et al., 2008). That makes it abundantly clear: Not only is the niqab ban unlawful (and possibly unconstitutional in violation of Charter rights), but wearing the niqab is also consistent with Canada's multicultural principles since the full face veiling does not break the law, violate individual rights, or contravene core constitutional values. As Andrew Coyne (2015) writes, unless a practice inflicts some identifiable harm rather than simply discomfort or outrage, there is no justification in Canadian law for restricting someone's rights during citizenship protocols.

In October 5th, wearing her full veil, Zunera Ishaq became a Canadian at the swearing in citizenship ceremony. Thirteen days later, the anti-niqab Conservative Government lost the federal election to the Liberal Party which promptly dropped the previous government's Supreme Court appeal of an earlier ruling (Fleras, 2016a).

Minor setbacks, notwithstanding, Canada's commitment to an inclusive citizenship remains largely intact. This commitment ranges from recognition of Canada's Indigenous peoples as citizens-plus (or indigeneity-plus) to the principle of a multicultural citizenship (see below) and the government's acknowledgement of Quebec as distinct nation within a united Canada (Prime Minister Harper's speech, November 22, 2006). The concept of nested identities and multiple belongings continues to inform the parameters of Canadian citizenship. Just as a person can differently belong to Canada through their ethnicity, so too can they join Canada's citizenship community through transnational linkages and diasporic group membership. Inasmuch as individual and group identities are multidimensional and multilayered as well as fluid and flexible, such an endorsement acknowledges the inescapable.[2]

Canada's Multicultural Citizenship Regime

The politics of multiculturalism in Canada represents a key dynamic and core challenge. The challenge of accommodating multicultural identities while advancing social justice through intercultural dialogue assumes an even greater prominence within the context of globalization, international mobility, and global communication networks. Yet reactions are varied and shifting in assessing the costs and benefits associated with multicultural governance. For some a triumph of positive connotations; for others a disaster in the making; for still others something in between these scenarios (Crowder, 2013); for still others, a crisis at best, irrelevant at worst (Latour and Balint, 2013). Many believe a commitment to accommodating multicultural diversities is inherently positive in consolidating a cooperative and cohesive coexistence. The accommodation of diversities under a multiculturalism umbrella fosters minority attachment to and involvement in the broader polity (Bloemraad, 2011). Other contend that such a governance model generates conflicts by eroding a commitment to common humanity, especially since the cross-border dynamics of globalization may intensify identity-linked social cleavages and culturally affiliated friction. Still others point to the ubiquity of globalized communications and international travel in expanding intercultural contacts and connections. A transnational and transmigrant world where notions of belonging and identity are increasingly de-territorialized and pan-national questions the worth of a spatialized governance model for accommodating the complexities of diverse-diversities (Fleras, 2014).

The challenge is now clearly in focus: How to balance the homogenizing logic of a national citizenship with Canada's multicultural commitment to respect cultural diversities and accommodate difference-based disadvantages?

Reference to an official multiculturalism as diversity governance has transformed political debate and public input over the meaning of citizenship as belonging and identity. Controversies swirl around the nature of the relationship between multiculturalism and citizenship, particularly when conventional citizenship models acknowledge a definitive alignment between citizenship rights and territorial boundaries regardless of whether membership reflects an accident of birth or attained through some form of probationary residence or mandatory citizenship test (Mann, 2017). Does multiculturalism undermine common citizenship and all that implies in terms of national unity, identity, and prosperity? Or is it more likely to consolidate a robust commitment to citizenship in that immigrants under the sway of a multicultural agenda are more likely to become citizens, more trustful of political institutions, more inclined to participate in local and national politics, and more attached to a national identity that embraces them as full-fledged members (Bloemraad, 2015). In other words, the link between multiculturalism and citizenship offers a new way of being a Canadian citizen. A model of democratic citizenship, ("citizenization") informed by the principles of a universal personhood and minority rights displaces those state-centric practices formerly organized around unequal layers of group-differentiated entitlements and rights (Kymlicka 2012, 2016).

Canada's citizenship model acknowledges the primacy of universality as a basis for belonging and entitlement (Fleras, 2016a). Defined primarily as legal status that accords identical rights to all members of a polity (Stanford, 2011), a universal citizenship treats all citizens the same, without exception, since everyone is thought to belong in the same way. Each citizen regardless of race, origins, or ethnicity is entitled to the same benefits and rights—and occupies a similar relationship to the state because everyone is equal before the law. Entitlements because of difference are ignored under a universal citizenship. Just as people's differences cannot be used to exclude, so too should their differences not entitle them to special privileges or preferential treatment. A universal citizenship also rejects any type of entitlement rooted in collective rights as contrary to the principle of individual equality before the law. Promotion of group differences on racial or ethnic grounds—even in the spirit of inclusiveness and progress—can only undermine the universal bonds of loyalty, unity, and identity. The boldness of this universalistic commitment cannot be underestimated. In the past when differences invariably invoked notions of inferiority and exclusion, the universality espoused by the *Citizenship Act* broke with precedent by embracing all lawfully residing Canadians as citizens regardless of who they were or where they came from. A universal citizenship proposed that both foreign- and Canadian-born individuals possessed the same rights and entitlements as well as similar duties and obligations.

However enlightened for its time, the concept has come under fire as outdated in a fluid, mobile, and hybridic world of complex diversities and diverse complexities. (Bosniak, 2006; Harty & Murphy, 2005; Kernerman, 2005; Yuval-Davis, 2007). Those universal and undifferentiated citizenship frameworks that once worked in the past no longer resonate with meaning and authority in addressing the highly politicized and collective claims of sub-state national minorities and Indigenous peoples (Fleras, 2016b). The dynamics of globalization and transnational mobilities have disrupted conventional assumptions that prioritized the nation-state monopoly in securing citizenship entitlements (Ang, 2011). Or put more bluntly, in a diasporic world of coming and goings that transcend (rather than simply cross) national boundaries, it no longer make sense to talk about a universal citizenship as a place-specific model of entitlements, especially when peoples' notions of identity and belonging are increasingly realigned across multiple jurisdictions (Stasiulis, 2016). Nor is there much value in promoting a one-size-fits-all citizenship if we aspire to live together in (not just with) diversity. The interplay of globalization with trans-migratory connections and communication technologies fosters the viability of multiple meaningful links through the acceptance of dual or multiple citizen-ships (Fleras, 2016b; Macklin and Crepeau, 2010; Simmons, 2010). In short, a world of transmigration and multiple identities renders the idea of a universal citizenship as unsustainable, although some would argue that, paradoxically, the fragmentary effects of complex diversities, transmigrant mobilities, and cosmopolitan openness, intensifies the importance of a universal citizenship as a precondition for social solidarity and national identity (Motomura, 2006).

The concept of a universal citizenship is under pressure to differentiate. Pressure is mounting to disaggregate citizenship into patterns of belonging and blocks of rights depending on the social category in question (Kym-licka and Norman, 2000). A multicultural citizenship model is advanced, one in which citizenship entitlements and patterns of identity and belong-ing are differentiated (or "customized") along group-specific lines and reali-ties, including the constitutional status of Indigenous peoples, equity rights of racialized migrants and minorities, the cultural considerations of eth-noculturally and faith based groups, and the experiences of transmigrants with multiple affiliations. Entitlements under a differentiated ("multicul-tural") citizenship fall into three categories (Kymlicka and Norman, 2000):

representation rights for disadvantaged groups through measures that alleviate obstacles to full and equal participation in society; multicultural rights for migrants and minorities through exemption from laws or policies that disadvantage them or through initiatives that protect their language, culture, or religions; and self-governing rights through self-determining autonomy for national minorities and Indigenous peoples. A fourth category can be included that acknowledges the centrality of those transnational patterns of identity and belonging that cross (or transcend) national borders. Accordingly, four types of customized citizenship rights and group-differentiated entitlements can be discerned under Canada's multicultural citizenship regime (multicultural used in the broadest sense): *equity, ethnocultural, self-determining,* and *transnational* (Fleras, 2016a).

- *Equity Entitlements*: Historically disadvantaged minorities and migrants may require a different set of entitlements to solidify full citizenship rights. Equity citizenship entitlements are aimed at improving institutional access and societal integration through the removal of discriminatory barriers and the introduction of proactive equity programs.

- *Ethnocultural Entitlements*: Both racialized and cultural minorities may require some degree of official protection of their ethnocultural heritage. Multicultural citizenship goes beyond a demand for cultural rights or acceptance of cultural differences as an option. Rather, it operates on the assumption that membership in a living and lived-in cultural reality provides individuals with meaningful choices to sustain a meaningful existence (Allegritti, 2010; Kymlicka, 1992).

- *Self-Determining Rights and Entitlements*: Another type of citizenship entitlement involves Indigenous peoples and the Québécois/Quebecers. Both Indigenous peoples as the "nations within" and substate nations such as Quebec endorse different group-specific needs, aspirations, status, and experience; as a result, citizenship entitlements must be customized accordingly. In contrast to migrants and minorities who, sociologically speaking, are defined as voluntary minorities anxious to "get in" and benefit from all that Canada offers, Indigenous peoples and substate national minorities are bucking to "get out" out of political arrangements forcibly imposed on them and not working to their advantage or interests (Fleras, 2016a). As peoples or nations, their demands as citizens go beyond the universal entitlements of a settler-centric citizenship. They include claims upon the state for control over land,

culture, language, and identity; the right to self-government and jurisdiction over matters of direct relevance; access to power and resources
that flow from their unique relational status; and the right to belong
indirectly to Canada through membership in their nations rather than
through conventional channels.

- *Transnational (or Transmigratory) Entitlements*: A transnational citizenship refers to the possibility of dual or even multiple citizenships, both
concurrently and without contradiction. In an age of migration where
up to 245 million people may be on the move at any time and connections are a mouse click away, new patterns of belonging and identity may
reflect concurrent loyalty to the home country and the adopted country
(Castles et al., 2013). The concept of a transnational citizenship in a
global era is predicated on three realities: (1) the contesting of state sovereignty as sources of identity and belonging (but not of entitlements);
(2) increased mobility patterns and new communication technology; and
(3) the propensity of migrants to forge and maintain cross-national links
regardless of where they live (Simmons, 2010). Under a transmigratory
entitlement, a person's singular national loyalty to one sovereign state is
replaced with a more global oriented framework that fosters a flexibility
to belong to and identify with multiple nation states (Ong, 1999).

Reaction is mixed to these two ideal-typical citizenship models: universal
and multicultural (or differentiated) (Fleras, 2016a). For some, a universal
citizenship must take precedent since it alone can perform the twin tasks of
protecting Canada's national interests while ensuring protection of the fundamental rights for all Canadians. A citizenship differentiated into "this" and
"that" cannot possibly fulfil its basic integrative function of fostering loyalty and mutual trust, forging common identity, and internalizing patriotic
commitment. Without the shared values of a difference-blind citizenship for
bonding and bridging, the danger of society splintering into a series of fractured communities is all too real. Moreover, the concept of a differentiated
citizenship is dismissed as un-Canadian since (1) some individuals are treated
more equally than others, (2) special group rights are elevated over individual rights, and (3) the legitimacy of the political community at large is compromised by group interests. For others, a rapidly changing and increasingly
diverse Canada that commits to inclusiveness requires a more differentiated
citizenship. A one-size-fits-all citizenship no longer resonates with relevance
within the complex context of Canada's multilayered diversity and deeply
divided difference (Hebert and Wilkinson, 2002). Entitlements and rights

under a universal citizenship may sound good on paper. In reality, however, they not only gloss over systemic exclusions ("inconvenient truths") beneath a veneer of universality ("polite fictions"), but also reinforce the marginality of minorities by sacrificing the particular for the sake of the national (Green, 2016; Stanford 2011).

Clearly, then, a universal citizenship model possesses strengths and weakness. It promises formal equality to all regardless of race or ethnicity, exchanges the particular for a shared commonality through difference-blind laws, and acknowledges the moral worth and equality of each individual. But a one-size-fits-all model also runs the risk of not taking differences that disadvantage into account when necessary to ensure substantive equity. Nor has the extension of universal citizenship rights to previously excluded groups always translated into the realities of a level playing field (Stanford, 2011). As argued by Iris Marion Young (1990), a universal conception of citizenship that purports to be neutral because everyone is held to similar standards and norms is unfair and oppressive, especially when reducing all citizens to disembodied individuals in the abstract rather than as disadvantaged minorities in a lived-world of inequalities and exclusions. Equal treatment as a sameness ideal ignores those lived-differences that might impair people's participation as equals, whereas the key to a substantive inclusiveness resides in group specific entitlements/exemptions that secure equitable outcomes (inclusivity) (Kymlicka, 1996). Finally, Canada can no longer be defined in terms of singularity—one nation, one identity, one culture, or one belonging (Hebert and Wilkinson, 2002). Identities in a globalized world of transnational connections are openly and politically plural, with people belonging to many different groups and defining themselves accordingly without necessarily experiencing contradiction or rejecting commonalities (Karim, 2006; Mawani, 2008).

Is Canada ready for a more inclusive citizenship that is (1) differentiated by way of complexity rather than locked into homogeneity, (2) inclusive of differences yet united in purpose, (3) responsive to both individual and collective group rights, and (4) reflective of a primary affiliation with the whole without disavowing the parts in the process. Should the principle of a universal citizenship predominate to ensure national unity and identity? Or is it time for a more nuanced and multiculturally differentiated citizenship consistent with contemporary dynamics, demands, and divisions? Are multicultural societies capable of accommodating particularist forms of religious, cultural, and social diversities without collapsing into incoherence or compromising a commitment to commonalities (Kymlicka and Norman, 2000; also Harty and Murphy, 2005; Kernerman, 2005)? The challenge lays in conceptualizing a citizenship model that incorporates the strengths of each while discarding respective weaknesses of both. An inclusive citizenship combines the rights of universal citizenship for all with the differentiated claims of Indigenous peoples, sub-state national communities, and racialized migrants and minorities (Harty and Murphy, 2005; Kymlicka, 1996). Citizenship is thus visualized as a rope of interwoven strands: One of these strands emphasizes universal citizenship rights with respect to individual equality and equality before the law. Another strand focuses on those differentiated citizenship entitlements based on the principle of multicultural accommodation and recognition of special minority rights (Stanford, 2011). Admittedly, as Ruth Lister (1997) concludes, the balancing act implicit in fostering a "differentiated universalism" (Squires, 2007) will prove difficult and awkward, since neither is sufficient in its own right but requires the other to complete it:

> [R]ejecting the "false universalism" of traditional citizenship theory does not mean abandoning citizenship as a universalist goal. Instead, we can aspire to a universalism that stands in creative tension to diversity and difference and that challenges the divisions and exclusionary inequalities which can stem from diversity. (p. 66)

The following Insight Post addresses the possibility of a critically informed yet ideal-typical model of Canadian citizenship that aspires to inclusiveness, without relinquishing a commitment to national interests.

Insight Post

Canada's Citizenship Model: A Work in Progress

Does Canada have a citizenship model? It does, although its content will vary with those who see citizenship as model for as inclusion and integration vs those who frame it as hegemonic and controlling, as a mechanism for society building vs one for advancing human rights, and an instrument for advancing justice and equality vs a tool for securing an unequal status quo. Acknowledging the simultaneity of these discursive frames reinforces how Canada's citizenship model may prove progressive and regressive both in intent and by consequences. The following principles provide a starting point in formulating an ideal-typical model:

1. *A Multi-dimensional Citizenship Model: By Birth, by Choice.* Canada commits to different models of citizenship attainment and membership. Canada's citizenship model is predicated on the principle

that individuals can belong to Canada based on birth—both the principle of jus soli (born of the land) and jus sanguinis (born of blood, descent, or ethnicity)—and by choice (jus domicile) through naturalization. Those born in Canada are automatically conferred citizenship regardless of the circumstances or parental status (with the exception of diplomatic corps members). An element of jus sanguinis exists by virtue of automatic citizenship to the first generation of children born abroad to a Canadian parent. The conferral of jus domicili citizenship entails a process of naturalization in which those who are legally resident in Canada can acquire Canadian citizenship by agreeing to its core values and the rule of law. There is a growing acceptance for confering citizenship rights to those without legal status in Canada but who express a commitment to residency and community (jus nexi) (Bauder, 2012).

2. A *Civic-based Citizenship* Canada's citizenship model claims to abide by the principles of a civic citizenship.[3] A civic citizenship model is anchored in protocols and ideals that are principled, that is, based on the rule of law rather than ad hoc and discretionary in stipulating who is eligible, how citizenship is acquired or lost, and what comprises rights and obligations. A civic society—conceptualized as a non-ethnicized community united around the shared values of a political community—facilitates the acquisition of citizenship. For example, migrants and minorities need not renounce their homeland affiliation since ethnicity is largely irrelevant as the basis for belonging since membership in Canada is not conditional on affiliation with the dominant ethnic group (also Voloder, 2013). In other words, individuals can belong to and identify with Canada through their membership in an ethnic community or Indigenous nation.

3. A *Liberal Citizenship* Canada's citizenship model assigns priority to citizenship as a status with rights (see also Stanford, 2011). Citizenship in Canada is largely about protection of individual rights rather than participation in the public domain or political affairs. The formal rights of citizens not only buffer the private sphere from external interference, but also bolster the free pursuit of particular interests. A liberal citizenship is anchored in the principle of liberal universalism, namely, our commonalities as freewheeling and morally autonomous individuals supersede our group-based differences for purposes of citizenship status

and rights. Emphasis is on a citizenship both universal and unitary. Everyone belongs in the same way to the same set of principles; nevertheless, differences may be taken into account when necessary to offset disadvantages. And while ethno cultural differences tend to be framed as superficial, irrelevant, and best restricted to private domains, Canada's citizenship model also acknowledges that "deep" differences such as those pertaining to Indigenous peoples or sub-state national minorities fall under the parameters of a Canadian citizenship.

4. *Immigration as Pathway to Citizenship*. Canada's citizenship model is embedded in Canada's status as an immigration society. Lawful newcomers to Canada constitute permanent residents who are expected to become fully fledged citizens as part of the settlement process and integration program. Generally easy access to citizenship and a relatively thin national identity facilitates the integration of newcomers into Canada, while reinforcing how citizenship is the ultimate prize in the transition from there to here. The fact that, within ten years, about 85 percent of newcomers acquire citizenship is testimony to this commitment.

5. *Citizenship as a Right*. "A Canadian is a Canadian is a Canadian"[3] according to Prime Minister Justin Trudeau in a pre-election debate with the then Prime Minister Stephen Harper. For it to mean anything at all, Trudeau argued, citizenship must be more reliable than a status conferred or revoked for political reasons or reasons of expediency. It must be framed as an inalienable right because, without citizenship, a person loses her right to have or to claim rights, while running the risk of becoming stateless. But while citizenship is widely perceived as a legal right, in reality it's not (Chapman, 2015). In contrast to Americans who can lose their citizenship only by voluntarily renouncing it, Canadians do not possess an absolute right to citizenship, but rather acquire it as a privilege that, in theory, can be revoked by the judiciary or the Prime Minister (Chapman and Cannon, 2017).

6. *Multiculturalism as Citizenization* Canada commits to an official multiculturalism that endorses immigrant acquisition of citizenship (Bloemraad, 2015; Kymlicka, 2016). The logic behind Canada's official multiculturalism is relatively straightforward. The creation of an inclusive Canada by integrating migrants through naturalization into the existing system.

> 7. *Differentiated Universalism as Inclusive Citizenship* The principle of inclusiveness acknowledges the subsets of inclusion (universal) and inclusivity (differentiated). With a differentiated citizenship, no one should be excluded because everyone possess the same rights in addition to different rights depending on their relational status in society. Or differently phrased, the challenge is to treat people the same as matter of course to ensure a substantive (lived) citizenship, but also differently when required through exemptions and accommodations.

Like it or not, approve or disapprove, the making of a postmulticultural Canada will reflect, reinforce, and advance a discursive shift in how we think, talk, and do citizenship (Foran, 2017). That, in turn, raises the question of whether Canada's citizenship model can rise to the challenge of reconceptualizing citizenship in a world of posts, trans, and isms. An era of transnationalism and diasporic dispersion means people may no longer want to identify exclusively with one country preferring, instead multiple identities and intersecting allegiances that transcend national boundaries (Dijkstra et al., 2001; Fleras, 2016a; Satzewich and Wong, 2006). This acknowledgement serves to remind that now is *not* the time to impose the modernist notion of a national Canadian citizenship, with a dash of multicultural colour thrown in for good measure. Rather, Canada must acknowledge the reality of comings and goings if it wants to attract the brightest and the best. A one-size-fits-all citizenship is unlikely to appeal in a deeply divided and multilayered Canada where some are banging on the door to "get in" while others are breaking down the door to "get out." Nevertheless, the postmulticultural goal of belonging differently together without drifting apart is contingent on addressing a seeming paradox. That true equality and inclusiveness derives from treating people equally (similarly) as a matter of course but treating them as equals (differently) when the situation calls for system adjustments. Such a nuanced interpretation raises the question: is Canada ready for postmulticultural citizenship? The next chapter offers some answers.

Notes

1. A Pew Research Center on national identity (Stokes, 2017) based on 14,500 respondents from 14 countries found that being born in a particular country was not deemed to be critical to national identity (i.e., to be truly one of us). Data disaggregated for Canada ($n = 1,020$) indicated the following as being important for being truly Canadian (i.e. Canadian identity).

> 90% believe that sharing Canadian customs and traditions is very (54%) or somewhat important
> 88% believe that being able to speak English or French is very (59%) or somewhat important
> 43% believe that being born in Canada is very (21%) or somewhat important
> 34% believe that being a Christian is very (15%) or somewhat important

Responses varied on the basis of the age of respondents, political sympathies, and levels of education.

2. Survey data bear this out: For example, most Canadian Muslims possess multiple identities according to studies by the prominent pollster Michael Adams (2007). They identify first as Muslim (56%), second as Canadian (23% +17% both), while their pride in being Canadian matches the national average (94% vs 93%). The General Social Survey on Social Identity based on 2013 data (Ahsan, 2015) arrived at a similar conclusion: 63% of Muslim Canadians possessed a very strong sense of belonging to Canada (also Statistics Canada, 2015), 45 % identified with the province of residence, 32 % with the local community Compare these figures for Quebecers: 44 % identified primarily with Canada while 52 % identified with Quebec.

3. Canada claims to abide by the principles of a civic citizenship in which all individuals are welcome as long as they obey the laws and commit to Canada. But the concept of ethnic citizenship continues to intrude as an inconvenient truth. For example, a person born to a Canadian citizen (by descent) outside of Canada is entitled to Canadian citizenship for one generation only, provided they acquire a Canadian citizenship certificate as proof of birth. Or consider how the denial of both entry admission and access to naturalization for groups such as unskilled or temporary foreign workers serves to fortify an ethnic version of citizenship—a scenario reinforced with initiatives by the Harper Government to renationalize Canadian citizenship along British lines (Winter, 2014). This inconvenient truth conceals a polite fiction: to one side, the foundational ideals of Canada that commits to openness, inclusion, equality, and opportunity for those interested in participating in its endeavor (see Rodriguez, 2010 for the USA); to the other side, a Canada that continues to extol an ethnic citizenship by prioritizing the primacy of, and proximity to, Anglo-American values and norms.

References

Abu-Laban, Yasmeen. "Rethinking Canadian Citizenship: The Politics of Social Exclusion in the Age of Security and Suppression." In *Liberating Temporariness?*, edited by Leah Vosko, Valerie Preston, and Robert Latham, 38–59. Montreal and Kingston: McGill-Queens University Press, 2014.

Abu-Laban, Yasmeen. "Transforming Citizenship: Power, Policy, and Identity." *Canadian Ethnic Studies* 47, 1 (2015): 1–10

Abu-Laban, Yasmeen. "Building a New Regime? Canadian Citizenship in the New Century." Paper presented to the Citizenship in Transnational Perspective Conference, University of Alberta, Edmonton, July 6–7, 2016.

Adams, Michael. "Muslims in Canada: Findings from the 2007 Envirionics Survey." *Policy Horizons Canada*, Government of Canada, 2007.

Ahsan, Sadaf. "We're Canadians First, Identity Survey Finds." *National Post*. July 9, 2015.

Allegritti, Inta. "Multiculturalism and Cultural Citizenship." In *Cultural Citizenship and the Challenges of Globalization*, edited by W. Ommundsen et al. Cresskill, NJ: Hampton Press, 2010.

Ang, Ien. "Navigating Complexity: From Cultural Critique to Cultural Intelligence." *Continuum: Journal of Media & Cultural Studies* 25, no. 6 (2011): 779–794.

Bahrami, S. "Critical Review of the New Canadian Citizenship Law Bill C-24." Faculty of Education. Centre for Education, Law, and Society. Simon Fraser University. December, 2014.

Bakan, Abigail B. "Multiculturalism and its Contradiction: Education for Citizenship and Social Justice in Canada." In *The Palgrave International Handbook of Education for Citizenship and Social Justice*, edited by A. Peterson, R. Hattam, M. Zembylas, and J. Arthur, 347–368. New York: Palgrave Macmillan, 2016.

Banting, Keith, Thomas J. Courchene, and F. Leslie Seidle. "Conclusion: Diversity, Belonging, and Shared Citizenship." In *Belonging? Diversity, Recognition, and Shared Citizenship in Canada*. Montreal/Kingston: McGill-Queens University Press, 2007.

Banulescu-Bogdan, Natalia. "Shaping Citizenship Policies to Strengthen Immigrant Integration." MPI, August 2, 2012.

Barbrook, Richard. "Digital Citizenship: From Liberal Privilege to Democratic Emancipation." *Open Democracy*, March 24, 2015.

Bauder, Harald. "Jus Domicile: In Pursuit of a Citizenship of Equality and Social Justice." *Journal of International Political Theory* 8, no. 1–2 (2012): 184–196.

Bechard, Julie and Sandra Elgersma. "Legislative Summary of Bill C-6: An Act to Amend the Citizenship Act and to Make Consequential Amendments to Another Act." Ottawa Library of Parliament Research Publications. May 5, 2016.

Bloemraad, Irene. "Citizenship in the United States and Canada." *Canadian Diversity* Fall (2006): 129–133.

Bloemraad, Irene. "Multiculturalism and Citizenship Are Complements, Not Opposites. Equity Matters." *Federation for Humanities and Social Sciences*. March 11, 2011.

Bloemraad, Irene. "Theorizing and Analyzing Citizenship in Multicultural Societies." *The Sociological Quarterly* 56, no. 4 (2015): 591–606.

Bosniak, Linda. *The Citizen and the Alien*. Princeton, NJ: Princeton University Press, 2006.

Brean, Joseph. "The Changing Meaning of Citizenship in Canada." *National Post*, March 16, 2012.

Brodie, Janine. "Citizenship and Solidarity: Reflections on the Canadian Way." *Citizenship Studies* 6, no. 4 (2002): 377–394.

Castles, Stephen, Hein de Haas, and Marvin Miller. *The Age of Migration*. 5/e. New York: Palgrave, 2013.

Chabot, Lynn. "The Concept of Citizenship in Western Liberal Democracies and in First Nations: A Research Paper." Prepared for the Governance Policy Directorate, Lands and Trusts Services. INAC, March 2007.

Chapman, Don. *The Lost Canadians: A Struggle for Citizenship Rights, Equality, and Identity*, Kobo Ebook, 2015.

Chapman, Don and Chris Cannon. "Canadian Citizenship Must Be a Constitutional Right." *Globe and Mail*. February 25, 2017.

Chazan, May, Lisa Helps, Anna Stanley, and Sonali Thakkar. "Introduction." In *Home and Native Land: Unsettling Multiculturalism in Canada*, edited by May Chazan et al., 1–14. Toronto: Between the Lines, 2011.

CIC News. *Government of Canada Aims to Pass Changes to Canadian Citizenship Act Into Law by July 1*. May 2016, Retrieved from http://www.cicnews.com.

Clarkson, Adrienne. *Belonging: The Paradox of Citizenship*. Toronto: Penguin, 2014.

Cohen, Andrew. *The Unfinished Canadian: The People We Are*. Toronto: McClelland & Stewart, 2007.

Cohn, Martin Regg. "Smear and Goading: How Harper Lifted the Veil on Our Phobias." *Toronto Star*, October 4, 2015.

Crowder, George. *Theories of Multiculturalism*. Malden MA: Polity Press, 2013.

Dauvergne, Catherine. "Non-Citizens and the Charter of Rights and Freedoms." *In Due Course: A Canadian Public Affairs Blog*. Posted March 14, 2014.

Dedi, Barb. "Muslim Village." *Canada: Anti-Muslim Bigotry on Rise*. 2015. Retrieved from http://muslimvillage.com

DeVoretz, Don J. "Immigration Circulation and Citizenship: Hotel Canada?" IZA Discussion Paper No 4312, Bonn Germany, 2009.

Dijkstra, S., K. Geutjen, and A. De Ruijter. "Multiculturalism and Social Integration in Europe." *International Political Science Review*, 22, no. 1 (2001): 55–84.

Donnelly, Michael J. *Canadian Exceptionalism. Are We Good or Are We Lucky? A Survey of Canadian Attitudes in Comparative Perspective*. Montreal: McGill Institute for the Study of Canada, 2017.

Elgersma, Sandra. "Canada's Changed Citizenship Law—An International Comparison." Prepared for the Legal and Social Affairs Division. October 15, 2014. Retrieved from https://hillnotes.wordpress.com.

Environics Institute (in partnership with Institute for Canadian Citizenship, Maytree Foundation, CBC News, and RBC). "Canadians on Citizenship Final Report," February, 2012.

Environics Institute, in Partnership with Institute on Governance 2016. "Canadian Public Opinion on Governance." Final Report, June 2016.

Federal Court Decisions. "Taylor v. Canada (Minister of Citizenship and Immigration)." September 1, 2006. Retrieved from http://decisions.fct-cf.gc.ca.

Fine, Sean. "Court Backs Wearing Niqab in Citizenship Ceremony." *Globe and Mail* October 6, 2015.

Fisk, Robert. "Niqab Row: Canada's Government Challenges Ruling Zunera Ishaq Can Wear Veil While Taking Oath of Citizenship." *The Independent* September 30, 2015.

Fleras, Augie. *The Politics of Multiculturalism: Multicultural Governances in Comparative Perspectives*. New York: Palgrave Macmillan, 2009.

Fleras, Augie. *Immigration Canada*. Vancouver: UBC Press, 2014.

Fleras, Augie. *Unequal Relations*. 8/e. Toronto: Pearson, 2016a.

Fleras, Augie. "Re-imagining Citizenship in Canada, New Zealand, and Australia: Transnational Dynamics, Postnational Complexities, Postcitizenship Possibilities." Plenary Paper, Citizenship in a Transnational Context, University of Alberta, Edmonton, July 6–7, 2016b.

Fleras, Augie. *Inequality Matters*. Toronto: Oxford University Press, 2017.

Foran, Charles. "The Canada Experiment: Is This the World's First 'Postnational' Country?" *The Guardian*, January 4, 2017.

Frith, Rosaline. "Citizenship of Canada Act. Strengthening the Value of our Citizenship." *Canadian Diversity?* 2, 1 (2003): 126–131.

Green, Joyce. "The Impossibility of Citizenship Liberation for Indigenous Peoples." Paper presented to the Citizenship in Transnational Perspective Conference, University of Alberta, Edmonton, 6–7 July, 2016.

Grey, Julius H. and John Gill. "The Canadian Encyclopedia." *Citizenship* (2015).

Griffith, Andrew. "Multicultural Meanderings." *Multiculturalism in Canada: Evidence and Anecdote*. 2015a.

Griffith, Andrew. "Multicultural Meanderings." *Canada Faces Dramatic Drop in Citizenship, Prompting Concerns About Disengaged Immigrants*. March 24, 2015b.

Griffith, Andrew. "The Evolution of Citizenship: Policy, Programs, and Operations." *Canadian Immigration Historical Society* #78, September 2016.

Griffiths, Rudyard. *Who We Are: A Citizen's Manifesto*. Vancouver: Douglas & McIntyre, 2009.

Harder, Lois and Lyubov Zhyznomirska. *"Claims of Belonging: Recent Tales of Trouble in Canadian Citizenship."* Ethnicities 12, 3 (2012):293–316

Harty, Siobhan and Michael Murphy. *In Defence of Multinational Citizenship*. Vancouver: UBC Press, 2005.

Hebert, Yvonne M. (ed.). *Citizenship in Transformation in Canada*. Toronto: University of Toronto Press, 2002.

Hebert, Yvonne M. and Lori Wilkinson. "The Citizenship Debates: Conceptual, Policy, Experiential, and Educational Issues." In *Citizenship in Transformation in Canada*. edited by Y.M Hebert, 3–36. Toronto: University of Toronto Press, 2002

Herzog, Ben. "Being Canadian: Dual Citizenship in Historical Perspective." *American Review of Canadian Studies* 44, 4 (2014):448–466.

Joshee, R. "Citizenship and Multicultural Education in Canada: From Assimilation to Social Cohesion." In *Diversity and Citizenship Education: A Global Perspective*, edited by J. A. Banks. 127–156. San Francisco, CA: John Wiley, 2004.

Kaplan, William (ed.). *Belonging: Essays on the Meaning and Future of Canadian Citizenship*. Montreal/Kingston: McGill-Queen's University Press, 1993.

Karim, Karim. "American Media's Coverage of Muslims: The Historical Roots of Contemporary Portrayals." In *Muslims and the News Media*, edited by E. Poole. 116–127. I.B. Tauris, 2006.

Kenney, Jason. "CIC News." *Speaking Notes*. 2009, Retrieved from http://www.cic.gc.ca

Kernerman, Gerald. *Multicultural Nationalism: Civilizing Difference, Constituting Community*. Vancouver: UBC Press, 2005.

Keung, Nicholas. "Citizenship Applications Plummet by 50 Per Cent." *Toronto Star*, February 24, 2017a.

Keung, Nicholas. "Ottawa Moves to End 'Second-Class Citizens". *Toronto Star*, A-8. June 23, 2017b.

Kilic, S., S. Saharso, and B. Sauer. "The Veil: Debating Citizenship, Gender, and Religious Diversity." *Social Politics: International Studies in Gender, State, and Society* 15, no. 4 (2008).

Korteweg, Anna and Jennifer Elrick. "Citizenship Research Synthesis 2009–2013 A CERIS Report Submitted to Citizenship and Immigration Canada." Ottawa, 2014.

Kymlicka, Will. "The Rights of Minority Cultures: Reply to Kukathas." *Political Theory* 20 (1992): 140–145.

Kymlicka, Will. *Multicultural Citizenship: A Liberal Theory of Minority Rights*. Toronto: Oxford University Press, 1996.

Kymlicka, Will. *Politics in the Vernacular. Nationalism, Multiculturalism, and Citizenship*. Toronto: Oxford University Press, 2001.

Kymlicka, Will. *Multicultural Odysseys: Navigating the New International Politics of Diversity*. Toronto: Oxford University Press, 2007.

Kymlicka, Will. "Prospects for a Multicultural Citizenship." Pluralism Forum—Reframing Europe's "Multicultural Debates." *Global Centre for Pluralism*. April 2012.

Kymlicka, Will. "Trajectories of Multicultural Citizenship." In *Representation and Citizenship*, edited by R. Marback, 52–78. Detroit: Wayne State University Press, 2016.

Kymlicka, Will and Wayne Norman (ed.). *Citizenship in Diverse Societies*. New York: Oxford University Press, 2000.

Labelle, Micheline and Daniel Salee. "Immigrant and Minority Representations of Citizenship in Quebec." In *Citizenship Today: Global Perspectives and Practices*, edited by T. A. Aleinikoff and D. B. Klusmeyer, 278–315. Washington: Brookings Institute Press, 2001.

Latour, Sophie Guerard de and Peter Balint. "The Fair Terms of Integration: Liberal Multiculturalism Reconsidered." In *Liberal Multiculturalism and the Fair Terms of Integration*, edited by P. Balint and S. Latour, 1–16. New York: Palgrave, 2013.

Lee, Yaniya. "Anxious Territory: the Politics of Neutral Citizenship in Canadian Art Criticism." *C Magazine* Issue 128, Winter 2016.

Levitz, Stephanie. "Canadians' Hearts toward Immigrants Are Hardening." *Waterloo Region Record*, October 31, 2012.

Levitz, Stephanie. "Feds Release New Poll Data on Niqab Ban". *Canadian Press*. September 24, 2015.

Levitz, Stephanie. "Pay Your Taxes: It's Being Canadian." *Canadian Press*, Reprinted in *Waterloo Region Record*, July 24, 2017.

Lister, Ruth. "Dialectics of Citizenship." *Hypatia* 12, no. 4 (1997): 6–26.

Lopez, Ian Haney. *Dog Whistle Politics: How Coded Racial Appeals Have Reinvented Racism and Wrecked the Middle Class*. Reprint Edition. New York: Oxford University Press, 2015.

Macklin, Audrey and Francois Crepeau. "Multiple Citizenship, Identity, and Entitlement in Canada." *IRPP*, June 22, 2010.

Macklin, Audrey. Strenthening Citizenship, Weakening Citizens. Paper presented to the Citizenship in Transnational Perspective Conference, University of Alberta, Edmonton, 6–7 July, 2016.

Mahoney, Kathleen. "Evolving Citizenship: What Difference Has 400 Years Made?" *Policy Options*. July 1, 2008.

Majka, Christopher. *Niqab? Radical Feminism or Female Subjugation*. Rabble.ca September 30, 2015.

Mann, Jatinder. *The Search for a New National Identity. The Rise of Multiculturalism in Canada and Australia, 1890s-1970s*. New York: Peter Lang, 2016.

Mann, Jatinder. "Introduction." In *Citizenship in a Transnational Perspective*, edited by J. Mann, 1–14. New York: Palgrave Macmillan, 2017.

Mawani, Aysha. *"Transnationalism: A Modern Day Challenge to Canadian Multiculturalism."* Paper presented at the Annual Meeting of the International Communication Association, Montreal, May 22, 2008. Available online at http://www.allacademic.com

Merolli, Jessica L. "Manufacturing Desire and Producing (Non) Citizens: Integration Exams in Canada, the UK and Netherlands." *Citizenship Studies* 1–16. Published online, September 16, 2016.

Moors, Annelies. "The Dutch and the Face-Veil: The Politics of Discomfort." *Social Anthropology* 17, no. 4 (2009): 393–408.

Motomura, Hiroshi. *Americans in Waiting. The Lost Story of Immigration and Citizenship in the United States*. New York: Oxford University Press, 2006.

No One is Illegal. "Never Home. Legislating Discrimination in Canadian Immigration." Retrieved from http://www.neverhome.ca.

Ong, A. *Flexible Citizenship. The Cultural Logics of Transnationality*. Durham NC: Duke University Press, 1999.

Puzzo, Catherine. "UK Citizenship in the Early 21st Century: Earning and Losing the Right to Stay." *French Journal of British Studies* xxi, ij (2016):1–12

Richez, Emmanuelle and Christopher P. Manfredi. "Citizenship and the Canadian Charter." In *Migration, Regionalization, Citizenship*. Part of the series, *Politikwissenschaftliche Paperbacks*. Springer Link, 2014.

Rodriguez, Cristina M. "Review: Beyond Citizenship: American Citizenship after Globalization." Peter Kivisto, New York University School of Law. Working Paper no 10–35, July 2010.

Rouhana, N.N. and A. Sabbagh-Khoury "Settler-Colonial Relationship: Conceptualizing the Relationship Between Israel and Palestine." *Settler Colonial Studies* 5, 3 (2015):205–225

Satzewich, Vic, and Lloyd Wong, (eds.). *Transnational Identities and Practices in Canada*. Vancouver: University of British Columbia Press, 2006.

Saul, John Ralston. "A Circle, Edging Ever Outward." *Globe and Mail* April, 23, 2016.

Schmidtke, Oliver. "Migration and Citizenship Policies in Canada and Europe." In *Canada and Europe Face 21st Century Policy Challenges: Convergence or Divergence? Canada-Europe: Transatlantic Dialogue*, edited by Joan DeBardeleben. Ottawa: Carleton University, March 2017.

Selley, Chris. "On Niqabs and 'Canadian Values.'" *National Post*, October 1, 2015.

Sibley, Robert. "How Many? From Where? The Immigration Debate We're Not Having." *Ottawa Citizen*, October 9, 2015.

Simmons, Alan. *Immigration and Canada. Global and Transnational Perspectives.* Toronto: Canadian Scholars' Press, 2010.

Sobel, Nora. "A Typology of the Changing Narratives of Canadian Citizenship Through Time." *Canadian Ethnic Studies* 47, no. 1 (2015): 77–89.

Southey, Tabatha. "Inspired by the Veiled Threat: Give Up a Right Day." *Globe and Mail,* September 19, 2015.

Squires, Judith. *Negotiating Equality and Diversity in Britain. Towards a Differentiated Citizenship.* Philadelphia: Taylor and Francis, 2007.

Stanford. "Stanford Encyclopedia of Philosophy." *Citizenship,* August 1, 2011, Retrieved from http://plato.stanford.edu.

Stasiulis, Daiva. "Respatializing Social Citizenship and Security Among Dual Citizens in the Lebanese Diaspora." Paper presented to the Citizenship in Transnational Perspective Conference. University of Alberta, 6–7 July, 2016.

Stokes, Bruce. "What it Takes to Truly Be 'One of Us.'" Pew Research Center, February 1, 2017.

Thobani, Sunera. *Exalted Subjects.* Vancouver: UBC Press, 2007.

Triadafilopoulos, Triadafilos. *Becoming Multicultural. Immigration and the Politics of Membership in Canada and Germany.* Vancouver: UBC Press, 2012.

UNHCR. Global Trends. Forced Displacement in 2016. Retrieved from www.unhcr.org/global-trends2016.

US News & World Report. "The Best Countries Report." 2016. Retrieved from http://www.usnews.com.

Vincent, Donovan. "Niqab Issue Bolsters Tory Support." *Toronto Star,* October 1, 2015.

Voloder, Lejla. "Avenues for Belonging: Civic and Ethnic Dimensions of Multicultural Citizenship in Australia." In *Migration, Citizenship, and Intercultural Relations: Looking Through the Lens of Social Citizenship,* edited by F. Mansouri and M. Lobo. 103–124. Burlington, VT: Ashgate Publishing, 2013.

Wente, Margaret. "Why the Niqab Matters, Now and In Future." *Globe and Mail,* September 29, 2015.

Winter, Elke. "Becoming Canadian: Making Sense of Recent Changes to Citizenship Rules." IRPP, Study No 44. January 2014.

Winter, Elke. "Descent, Terrritory, and Common Values: Redefining Citizenship in Canada." In *Naturalization Policies, Education, and Citizenship,* edited by D. Kiwan, 95–122. New York: Palgrave Macmillan, 2013.

Winter, Elke. "Report on Citizenship Law: Canada." European University Institute, Florence, Robert Schuman Centre, 2015.

Young, Iris Marion. *Inclusion and Democracy.* New York: OUP, 1990,

Young, Margaret. "Canadian Citizenship Act and Current Issues." Law and Government Division, BP—445E, 1998.

Yuval-Davis, Nira. "Intersectionality, Citizenship and Contemporary Politics of Belonging." *Critical Review of International Social and Political Philosophy,* 10, no. 4 (2007): 561–574.

· 5 ·

CANADA'S CITIZENSHIP/IMMIGRATION/ MULTICULTURALISM NEXUS

Introduction: Conceptualizing Citizenship Through a Diversity Lens

Canada remains a global frontrunner when it comes to the principles and practice of accommodating diversity. Canada's accommodation model is predicated on the need to simultaneously incorporate three major Ethnicities, namely: Indigenous peoples, Quebecers as a sub-state national minority, and racialized minorities and migrants (Fleras, 2016a). There is much to commend in Canada's pace-setting status as an accommodative society (Schmidtke, 2014), including a robust immigration program, an official multiculturalism policy, inclusiveness as a preferred governance model, and an extremely accessible citizenization process (Drew, 2017; O'Doherty, 2017). The working relationship between immigration and immigrants is no less worthy of note. Canada's success as a society of immigrants is contingent on its relatively unique status as an immigration society (or regime), while its credentials as an immigration regime (or society) actively promotes newcomer admission and their integration through citizenship attainment ("citizenization") (Fleras, 2014a; Hiebert, 2016). But Canada's exceptionalism as an accommodative society really sparkles in the mutually constitutive interplay of a citizenship/immigration/multiculturalism nexus. For, in the final analysis, it's not simply the case that Canada is a multicultural society or an immigration society or a citizenship-friendly society. Rather, its distinctiveness arises from the intersection of multiculturalism and immigration in reinforcing the viability of Canada's citizenship regime. In turn, one of the world's most foremost citizenship regimes solidifies the worth of both an official multiculturalism and an immigration program as attractive options for Canadian society. Put a bit differently, Canada's status as an immigration regime fosters an inclusive governance framework that transforms both an official multiculturalism and a multicultural citizenship regime into socially acceptable interventions for living together differently. Meanwhile, widespread support for the principles of multiculturalism and relatively easy access to a naturalized citizenship status shield the immigration program from criticism and makes it a safe bet for Canada-building.

However commendable and noteworthy, even Canada's seemingly progressive citizenship regime is hardly immune to disputes. Major changes in the nature of immigration (including more circular, return, and temporary patterns) as well as in immigrant aspirations, diversities, and politics put pressure on the viability of Canada's citizenship agenda (see Castles, 2016 for similar comments on Australia). An increasingly unbound world of mobility, translocality, and globalization, raises concerns over the legitimacy of defending a territorially-bounded citizenship program, especially when migrant notions of membership, integration, and identity are uncoupled by cosmopolitan yearnings and despatialized by transnational dynamics (Carruthers, 2013; Walton-Roberts, 2011). Of particular note are growing debates over the utility of Canada's official multiculturalism in a rapidly emerging postmulticultural world of discourses and practices (Fleras, 2015). The governance dilemma is sharply etched around a core paradox: Too much of what passes for contemporary citizenship as belonging and identity is grounded in the metaphorical equivalent of a "multi cul de sac" multiculturalism (see Rohinton Mistry, 1995), including concomitant notions of a fixed and homogenous mosaic of ethnocultures within the territorially bounded nation-state (Beck, 2011). A postmulticultural model that builds on yet moves positively beyond an official multiculturalism is proposed as a basis for living together with/in/through our diverse differences, including a framework for differently accommodating more complex citizenships in a postcitizenship world of posts, trans, and isms (Fleras, 2016b, 2017b). These emergent yet clashing dynamics generate yet more disagreements over the relevance of an immigration/multiculturalism/

citizenship nexus within the seemingly opposed contexts of an inhospitable national yet the uninhabitable transnational (Ang, 2009; Karim, 2007; Vertovec and Wessendorf, 2004).

This chapter capitalizes on these developments and disruptions by analyzing the politics of citizenship against the backdrop of an official multiculturalism, the realities of Canada as a normative immigration regime, and the discursive drift toward postmulticulturalism as reality, discourse, and practice. The chapter recognizes the importance of situating citizenship within the framework of Canada's immigration regime and its official multiculturalism; in turn, both immigration and multiculturalism acquire a different reading when refracted through the prism of a citizenship lens. In addition, while Canada's immigration program serves to attract potential citizens for Canada-building, the citizenization logic of an official multiculturalism accelerates the naturalization of new Canadians. Conversely, a robust citizenship program could hardly hope to flourish outside the context of an immigration regime that abides the principles of multiculturalism. In other words, citizenship "works" in Canada (if measured in terms of high naturalization rates and newcomer pride, sense of belonging, and national identification) because both immigration and an official multiculturalism "work" (Bloemraad, 2015). As well, both official multiculturalism and Canada's immigration program "work" because citizenship "works" in naturalizing new Canadians. Even so, the mutually reciprocating arrangement around an immigration/multiculturalism/ citizenship nexus may be slowly unravelling in a Canada that is rapidly changing, increasingly diverse, and more globally connected than ever, yet also more contested and confused.

The chapter begins by looking at Canada as a society of immigrants as well as an immigration society whose principles and practices embody a commitment to citizenization ("the process of naturalizing newcomers"). This is followed by a discussion of official multiculturalism as a diversity governance model that expedites the naturalization and integration of new Canadians along more inclusive lines. Canada's multiculturalism model is shown to advance citizenship pathways despite the difficulties in formulating such a model from a range of clashing issues and complex interpretations (Kymlicka, 2016). A world of complex diversities and diverse complexities not only exposes the growing irrelevance of an official multiculturalism as policy and program. It also establishes a platform for rethinking multiculturalism along postmulticultural lines in advancing the concept of a "multiversal" citizenship (Fleras, 2015; Latham, 2014). The chapter concludes on a visionary note: Canada is no longer a multicultural society if defined and imagined by the static and essentializing images of a mosaic metaphor. More accurately, Canada is better described as an increasingly postmulticultural society thanks to the kaleidoscope of new realities, discourses, and practices, one that proposes to build on yet move positively beyond multiculturalism for differently accommodating a more complex citizenship reality.

An Immigration Society, A Society of Immigrants

Canada has long self-defined itself as a society of immigrants. Immigrants constitute just over 20 percent of Canada's population in light of its robust immigration program—a percentage that's expected to increase, in part to offset a declining birth rate and an ageing demographic, in part to take advantage of what immigrants have to offer. Immigrants from around the world have made significant contributions to Canada-building in the past and at present, and will continue to do so in the networked world of the foreseeable future. But while many countries now see themselves as societies in desperate need of immigrants or overwhelmed by them, Canada represents an immigration society (or regime) with a plan in place to regulate a steady intake of newcomers. Reference to Canada as an immigration regime reflects several levels of meaning, that is, immigration as a sociological *fact* in association with a set of ideas and ideals ("*ideology*") that are expressed as government *policy* and reflected in *practices* both political and economic as well as social and cultural. The concept of an immigration regime also embraces five normative principles (Fleras, 2014b; Reitz, 2012a):

1. a principled framework that regulates admission to ensure newcomers are "legal", "liberal", and "labour-ready"
2. perception of documented newcomers as valued assets for economic prosperity and positive nation-building;
3. the centrality of immigrants and immigration to national identity;
4. newcomer entitlement to all rights of permanent residency including pathways to citizenship acquisition;
5. interventions and programs ("multiculturalism") to facilitate newcomer inclusion (i.e. integration and citizenship)

Canada's immigration agenda clearly subscribes to each of these attributes, at least in principle if not always in practice. Its immigration policy provides a rules-based framework both transparent and colour-blind in defining who gets in, how, and why (Fleras, 2014b; Cavanagh and Mulley, 2013). In 2015, a total of 271,845 newcomers were admitted into Canada: 62.7 percent gained entry through the economic category (including partners and dependents), 24.1 percent through family reunification, and 13.2 percent through the humanitarian category (including nearly 25,000 Syrian refugees, but over 40,000 by the end of 2016). The top five source countries for admission of permanent residents were the Philippines (18.7% of all admissions), India (14.5%), People's Republic of China (7.2%), Iran (4.3%) and Pakistan (4.2%) (Government of Canada 2016).

Canada's status as an immigration regime endorses a core society-building axiom. National economies thrive on a continuous supply of newcomers as valued permanent residents instead of relying on a short-term contingent of rotated temporary workers (OECD, 2014). Surveys repeatedly indicate that Canadians see immigration as beneficial to Canadian society and its economy (but see Donnelly, 2017), especially when admission programs are tied to improving demographic outputs and economic outcomes (Hiebert, 2016). Not surprisingly, the presence and vitality of immigrants is deeply ingrained in Canada's collective consciousness and national identity. Canada as an immigration society assigns considerable importance to integrating newcomers. Substantial amounts of energy and expertise are directed at commandeering their allegiance and loyalty to Canada, facilitating an emotional tie to the core values and shared principles that define Canada and what being Canadian means, and fostering a greater appreciation of the benefits and privileges associated with Canadian citizenship (Labelle and Salee, 2001).

Canada's transition from a society of immigrants to an immigration society has proven transformative (Fleras, 2017c). Alan Simmons (2010) captures a sense of this dynamic by demonstrating how Canada's immigration program (and by implication, its citizenship regime) reflect, reinforce, and advance prevailing images of Canada. A predominantly white British/European nation in the Americas eventually abandoned a White Canada project by the late 1950s in favour of a re-imagined Canada as a multicultural industrial nation. More recently, Canada is being rebranded as a cosmopolitan and postmulticultural player in competing for highly skilled immigrants in a competitive global economy. The reshaping of Canada along more inclusive lines establishes a social climate that extols the virtues of tolerance, abhors the expression of overt forms of prejudice and racism, exerts pressures on institutions to accommodate, and promotes Canada's competitive advantage both abroad and at home through labour market participation—thus confirming Randall

Hansen's prescient notion at a 2009 conference at the University of Augsburg in Germany, "immigration works when immigrants work". This commitment to accommodate the foreign born reflects an adherence to (a) principles (rule of law) rather than ancestry (blood or descent), (b) an inclusive multiculturalism that respects differences while removing discriminatory barriers, (c) a fluid and accommodative national identity, and (d) relatively easy path to naturalization, including the right to multiple citizenships (Kymlicka, 2016).

Admittedly, Canada is not immune to debates over immigrants and immigration. Controversies and criticisms continue to swirl around the questions of "what for", "how many", "what kind", and "where from"; accordingly, Canada's bona fides as an immigrant society of immigration are far from assured. Also open to dispute are issues as disparate as the ability of any single nation-state to control its borders and the boundaries of citizenship (also Noonan and Nadkarni, 2016); the limits of integration as basis for living together with differences; and the centrality of multiculturalism in coaxing a cooperative coexistence (Bloemraad, 2015; Hampshire, 2013; also Pearson, 2010 for New Zealand and Australia). Nevertheless, all signs point to a robust immigration domain as a Canadian exceptionalism in advancing Canada's status as a society of citizens as well as a citizenship society (Fleras, 2017c).

Citizenship Promises, Citizen Disappointments

That Canada remains a destination of choice for international immigrants is hardly an issue (Fleras, 2014b). The Immigration Public Opinion Survey by Washington-based Transatlantic Trends 2010 concluded that Canada may be the world's most welcoming society for newcomers (also Banting and Kymlicka, 2010). An 80 country survey by the US News and World Report in July 2017 ranked Canada as the world's second best country (Sweden was first) to be an immigrant (O'Doherty, 2017). An earlier survey also by US News placed Canada in the second best category overall (after Switzerland) (Drew, 2017). The 2015 Annual Social Progress Index report (comprised of representatives from Harvard Business School, Oxford University, and the Economist) ranked Canada first among 133 countries in the opportunities accorded to newcomers—from access to advanced education to personal freedom and choice, but especially tolerance and inclusion. No less effusive in praise was an international survey commissioned by the Historica-Dominion Institute, in partnership with the Munk School of Global Affairs and Aurea Foundation. Entitled, "What the World Thinks of Canada: Canada and the

World in 2010. Immigration & Diversity", the survey pointed out that, of the 18,600 adult respondents from the 24 leading economies, more than 53 percent said they would abandon their homes and move to Canada if they could, including 77 percent of Chinese respondents and 71 percent of Mexicans. Clearly, then, Canada's success in integrating newcomers through the citizenship channel is of sufficient merit to consolidate its claim as a global outlier *par excellence* (Reitz, 2012a).

Most immigrants appear to be relatively satisfied with their decision to come to Canada. Even the spectre of uneven economic prospects and the demeaning bigotry of sometimes unwelcoming sectors have not dulled their level of satisfaction (Adams, 2007). Newcomers trust that Canada will secure a space where they can settle down, fit in, move up, and get on with the business of making a go of it in their adopted country (Fleras, 2016a). They appreciate the opportunities and services available to them and their children such as access to quality education and healthcare; safe neighbourhoods and primacy of the rule of law; guaranteed rights to personal freedoms; and the presence of market transparency to improve chances of economic success (see also Lewin et al., 2011; Raleigh and Kao, 2010). According to the Longitudinal Survey of Immigrants to Canada (Jedwab, 2012), 84 percent of immigrants within four years of admission into Canada said they would make the same decision to migrate. A similar study by Statistics Canada in 2005 (Jedwab, 2012) revealed that three quarters of recently arrived immigrants were satisfied with life in Canada; four years later, two thirds of the participants said their expectations were met or exceeded. A more recent study confirmed these findings. Newcomers to Canada are generally happy with their lives here, with most immigrant groups displaying higher levels of life satisfaction than their source-country populations and at levels comparable to the Canadian-born (Frank, Hou, & Schellenberg, 2014).

How do positive assessments stack up to reality if immigrant experiences are filtered through the prism of a citizenship lens and the provisions of the Citizenship Act (Kazemipur, 2014)? Is Canada as integrative of immigrants as surveys suggest (Reitz, 2012b; Andrew et al., 2013) or do some well-thumbed polite fictions cloud over uncomfortable truths? Are immigrant experiences consistent with Canada's reputation as a progressive and principled immigration society? A fundamental tension prevails in responding to these questions: Canada's Citizenship Act may guarantee naturalized Canadians the same rights as the Canadian born, namely, fundamental freedoms, democratic rights, mobility rights, legal rights, and equality rights. Yet there is no guarantee of their application or enforcement; as a result, equal rights before the law do not necessarily translate into equitable treatment or outcomes, especially when newcomers must exercise these rights and attain success in a socioeconomic context neither reflective of their lived-realities nor conducive to their interests or expectations (Fleras, 2017a).

In short, Canada may have emerged as a "go-to" destination for attracting the brightest and the best in the global talent wars (Biles and Frideres, 2012), although many concede that Canada is better adept at attracting immigrants than at utilizing their skills (Economist, 2016). Slippages in the Canadian model reinforce a gap between citizenship ideals and citizen realities, in effect exposing how immigrants who look good on paper are not necessarily those in demand (Biles et al., 2012; Economist, 2016). Notwithstanding Canada's commitment to the multicultural principles of tolerance and respect for differences, a conformity model rooted in a monocultural framework tends to dismiss newcomer diversities and lived realities, particularly when they stray outside mainstream norms or entail adjustments that impose cost or inconvenience (Li, 2003). Immigrants are welcome as potential citizens and positively received as a solution rather than a problem, but only if they adopt Canadian values, obey its laws, and seamlessly blend (Donnelly, 2017). In short, Canada may need immigrants but, paradoxically, Canadians may not necessarily want them.

Racism remains a problem in solidifying citizenship commitments. Canada may not be overtly prejudiced or discriminatory; nevertheless, it endorses a gentler version of benevolent racism that combines passive-aggressive tolerance with a politely coded biases (Fleras, 2014a; Henry and Tator, 2009). Not surprisingly, racialized immigrants may be less integrated than white newcomers based on criteria such as "sense of belonging" trust in others', "feeling Canadian" "becoming a citizen" participating in voluntary activities, "voting in Canadian elections" and "life satisfaction" (Reitz, 2012c; but see Banerjee 2012; Wu et al., 2012). Economic prospects related to income and employment levels have proven disappointing (Economist, 2016; Jedwab, 2012). Immigrants in general earn less than the Canadian born, have lower employment rates, and are not compensated for foreign education or credentials (Javdani, Jacks, and Pendakur, 2012, but see Jedwab and Satzewich, 2015). Newcomers continue to experience barriers that deny or exclude, not because they are second-class citizens under the law, but because they must survive and succeed in a society structurally organized along Euro-systemic lines (Fleras, 2016a). They must enter a labour market system that may penalize them for reasons largely beyond their control, especially when overseas credentials and international experiences are discounted (Bonikowska et al., 2011; Foster, 2011; Frank, 2013; Picot and Sweetman, 2012). A Catch 22 looms that many perceive as a proxy for dormant biases (Sakamoto et al., 2013). A newcomer needs Canadian experience to get a job, but cannot acquire this experience without a job in Canada. A gender divide also underscores the challenges of citizenship and integration (Fleras, 2017a). Immigrant males may have a hard time in adjusting to the new environment, including finding work; working at survival jobs that reflect less prestige and lower income than employment in the homeland; and a loss of face both in society at large and in their households. But the position of immigrant women is equally complex and contradictory (Handa, 2003). Many are literally caught between the old world of male dominated submissiveness and a new world of independence, assertiveness, and opportunities. Yet foreign born women may lack the resources, skills, or support to navigate the tricky shoals in transitioning from an "over there" to an "over here". Not surprisingly, thousands of immigrant and refugee women are mired in desperation and depression, suffering in silence from social alienation, financial pressure, family turmoil, and cultural values that foreclose avenues of help (Reinhart and Rusk, 2006).

In sum, Canada may define itself as the paragon of a post-racial ("colourblind") and pro-multicultural society. This image is bolstered by Canada's commitment to remove discriminatory barriers, banish racism into the socially taboo category, and introduce positive measures for levelling an unlevel playing field. But reality is not nearly as accommodating as fiction (Collett, 2010; Mudde, 2012). A paradox is unmistakable: Canada may be one of the world's premier immigration societies based on global surveys (O'Doherty, 2017). Nevertheless, concern is mounting over the growing gap between what Canada says in advancing a friendly welcome ("polite fictions") and what it really does in pulling the welcome mat from under their feet ("uncomfortable truths") (Sakamoto et al., 2013). The resulting gap between citizenship promises and citizenship disappointments—the much-hyped reference to Canada as a land of opportunity ("comforting fiction") versus the inconvenient truth that many immigrants can't find work in their chosen profession—is both counterproductive and counter intuitive. Immigrants are robbed of what they can offer to Canada while Canadians are shortchanged of their talents, optimism, creativity, entrepreneurship, and international connections (Deloitte, 2011). This lose-lose situation is surely a scathing indictment of a multicultural Canada that commits to the principles of an official multiculturalism.

Canada's Official Multiculturalism: Facilitating Citizenization

Canada is widely admired as a multicultural success story. It represents one of a few liberal democratic societies that officially embraces multicultural principles as a principled basis for living together differently (Fleras, 2009; Griffith, 2015; Kymlicka, 2007; Reitz, 2009). Despite changes in tone and direction, the multicultural governance challenge has never wavered from its central mission: *transforming a disparate array of migrants and minorities into a cohesive community of like-minded citizens, with a corresponding sense of commitment, conviction, and consensus* (Fleras, 2015)? That Canada has managed to pull off the seemingly impossible by doing the wildly implausible in achieving the nearly improbable is quite astonishing: forging a working unity from its disparate parts without compromising either national integrity/unity or ethnic identity/ particularity. To be sure, until recently, Canada displayed little inclination for multiculturally managing diversity (Bloemraad, 2015). Laws and practices were in place that deterred many non whites (from Jews to Asians) from migrating to Canada (Atkinson, 2016). Those who managed to make it into Canada rarely found it a hospitable or accommodating destination (Fleras, 2017b). For example, in 1947, Prime Minister William Lyon Mackenzie King insisted on limiting the intake of "Orientals" (his words) for fear they could irretrievably mar the character of Canada's population.

Canada's white national identity was eventually displaced by a new multicultural vision of Canada. The shift could be attributed to host of different factors: to rebrand Canada as different from the U.S; to defuse Quebecois and Indigenous nationalism; to capitalize on the immigrant vote in urban areas; and to pacify European-based ethnic groups over their exclusion from the national project (Bloemraad, 2015). Multiculturalism emerged as part of a broader human rights agenda for shoring up individual minority rights, in large part by abolishing (a) inherited forms of inequality because of prejudicial discrimination, (b) the tyranny of French-English nationalism, and (c) capricious patterns of exclusion rooted in Canada's longstanding self-image as a "white man's country" (Atkinson, 2016). In seeking to neutralize the national unity crisis (Jaworsky, 1979) without disrupting the prevailing distribution of power, multiculturalism as government policy and diversity governance model originated as a political ploy to achieve the political goal of harmonizing competing ethnicities while retaining control of the overall agenda (Duchastel, 2009; Peter, 1978). In that it was conceived as a response to nationalist movements in Quebec and in "Indian" country, an official multiculturalism is inescapably political and politicized (Clarke, 2009). That Canada's official multiculturalism persists for similar reasons speaks volumes of the politics in play in pursuing a raft of political, ideological, and economic goals involving state functions, private interests, policy tradeoffs, and electoral survival.

Reactions are mixed to what many perceive as a double edged instrument of progress and/or regress (Fleras, 2014b). For some an official multiculturalism is endorsed as progressive in fostering the integration of new Canadians. For others, an official multiculturalism is criticized as regressive and disintegrative because of a divisive inherent logic. Still, others denounce it as sociopolitical fiction and a false consciousness, both hegemonic and controlling, and largely disconnected from the everyday realities of racialized migrants and minorities (Salee, 2009). Reactions range from criticism of an official multiculturalism as Canada's "biggest mistake" in eroding a common citizenship (Hitchens, 2010) or a white Canada (Duchesne, 2016), to its "triumphalization" as a "quiet revolution" equivalent in status and stature to three other societal transformations—the French, American, and Russian revolutions (Sandercock, 2006). Tyler Cowen (1999) concludes as much in this glowing assessment:

> Based on the dual ideals of peace and *multiculturalism*, Canada is one of mankind's greatest achievements. It is comparable to the notable civilizations of the past, and indeed exceeds most of them in terms of stability, living standards, and civil liberties. (emphasis added)

Others are more ambivalent: Canadians may be positive about an official multiculturalism at a theoretical level, according to a Leger Marketing Study in 2013 for the Canadian Race Relations Foundation. Yet they also express deep concerns over its practice in tolerating cultural and religious practices at odds with Canadian values (Donnelly, 2017). Still others prefer to frame an official multiculturalism as a clever exercise in state hegemony—an opiate for the masses—that distracts by manipulating the illusion of inclusion in securing the realities of exclusion (Chazan et al., 2011; Walcott, 2009).

Various reactions aside, an official multiculturalism has never wavered from its foundational logic: The creation of an inclusive Canada through the integration of migrants and minorities *as citizens* into the existing framework. Or phrased differently, an official multiculturalism originated and continues to persist as a political acceptable tool for depoliticizing diversities by delivering on the promise of newcomer citizenship. An official multiculturalism aspires to construct a positive social climate and political goodwill that encourages the naturalization of new Canadians and the expression of full citizenship rights as a precondition for living together differently (Kymlicka, 2016; Reitz, 2013). It emphasized (and continues to emphasize) a multi-pronged approach that embraced three core citizenship values: *Canadian identity* (all persons should feel a sense of belonging to Canada); *civic participation* (all Canadians must be actively involved in shaping the future of Canada and their community); *and social justice* (both individuals and institutions must work toward a society that is respectful, equitable and inclusive of all Canadians (Labelle and Salee, 2001).

Despite its centrality to Canada (-building), references to multiculturalism rarely yield a singular meaning. Multiculturalism represents a slippery and elusive concept with a tendency to skitter off in different directions when examined too closely, in the process becoming a conceptual grab bag of spongy associations and infuriating misconceptions (Lentin and Titley, 2011a, b; Murphy, 2012). Answers to the question, "Is Canada a multicultural society?" invite a range of responses, depending on the proposed frame of reference or preferred level of meaning. They include: multiculturalism as *fact*—the reality of diversities in Canada; as *ideology*—beliefs, values, and norms that support the principles of living together with difference; as *policy*—official programs and formal initiatives for accommodating diversities and valuing differences without sacrificing equality or unity; and as *practice*—application of multicultural principles for practical reasons from everyday interaction to political goals (Fleras, 2009). Failure to acknowledge the different semantic levels implicit in references to multiculturalism—*as demographic fact, as a normative ideology, as official policy and program, and as practice*—often generate confusion and foster miscommunication (Fleras, 2016a).

An Official Multiculturalism: Policy and Model

Canada's multiculturalism is expressed at official levels through state policy and federal programs (Bloemraad, 2015). Widely applauded yet prone to criticism regardless of what it does or doesn't do, Canada's multiculturalism policy originated as an all-party agreement in 1971; was subsequently entrenched in the 1982 Constitution Act as an interpretive principle (i.e. Nothing in the Charter of Rights and Freedoms will be interpreted in a manner that detracts from the enhancement and preservation of Canada's multicultural character); and finally accorded statutory standing with passage of the Multiculturalism Act in 1988. That Canada remains the world's only official multiculturalism (in statutory and constitutional terms) speaks volumes of its commitment and convictions. But just as Canada evolved during the multiculturalism era, so too did the multiculturalism agenda in response to shifting realities and emergent challenges as well as social changes and political expediencies. Four overlapping governance stages can be discerned in describing an evolving multiculturalism framework: *ethnicity, equity, civic, and integrative* (Fleras, 2016a). Ethnicity-based solutions have given way to equity-grounded reforms, followed by the promotion of civic belonging and participation, and, most recently, an integrative focus through shared values, social cohesion, and common citizenship (see Castles, 2016 for Australia). A careful analysis of this multiculturalism governance trajectory by reading between the lines of policy and practices yields insights into a Canadian multiculturalism model. This model is predicated on the principle that what an official multiculturalism promises to do deviates from what it really does in practice or what it really intends to do, and it's precisely this reality gap between rhetoric and reality that secures the discursive space for constructing a working model. The following constituents seem pivotal to any reading of Canada's model of multiculturalism.

Multiculturalism as Canada-building Canada's multiculturalism model originated as a political act to achieve political goals in a politically acceptable manner, namely, to create an inclusive Canada by fostering citizenship and integrating newcomers into the existing framework through removal of prejudicial inclinations and discriminatory barriers.

Multiculturalism as Managed Inclusion. Canada's multiculturalism model is focused on the governance ("management") of diversity rather than its promotion or celebration. A commitment to a multiculturalism governance aims at constructing an inclusive Canada through the formulation and implementation of diversity programs so that no one is excluded from full, equal, and active participation in Canadian society for reasons related to race, ethnicity, and nationality (Hyman et al., 2011; Ley, 2007).

Multiculturalism as Liberal Universalism. Canada's multiculturalism model is predicated on the principles of a liberal universalism. According to a liberal universalism, our commonalities as rights bearing *individuals* supersede the relevance of racially-based group differences as basis for recognition and reward. And because everyone is equal before the law under a liberal universalism, equal treatment regardless of race or ethnicity is expected as a matter of course, although exceptions and exemptions may be tolerated.

Multiculturalism as Limits. Canada's official multiculturalism does not condone or celebrate diversity. More accurately it's about respecting an individual's right to be different (within limits), while ensuring these differences provide a springboard for identifying with and belonging to Canada. Differences are tolerated but only to the extent they do not break the law, violate individual rights, contravene constitutional principles such as gender equity, and recognize Canada's sovereign right in defining where to draw the line. Clearly, then, Canada's multiculturalism model rejects an anything-goes mentality or multicultural free-for-all zone that frames all cultural differences as relative, equally valid, or impervious to criticism. Or to put it bluntly, one can be a Lithuanian and Canadian under a Canadian multiculturalism but one is always a Lithuanian *in* Canada.

Multiculturalism as Depoliticizing Diversity Canada's model of multiculturalism is not about incorporating diversity into the public domain but about removing it from the commons. The goal of accommodation under an official multiculturalism is to render the public domain as neutral a site as possible to avoid messy ethnic entanglements. By channelling it into acceptable outlets such as folk festivals and food courts, the threat of ethnic conflict is diminished by defusing the potency and politicization of diversity.

Multiculturalism as Equality. Canada's multiculturalism model prioritizes the primacy of disadvantage over the principle of diversity. A commitment to redistribution over recognition embraces a social justice ideal aimed at addressing the needs of those whose differences have proven disadvantaging (Fries and Gingrich, 2009; Kymlicka, 2012). With multiculturalism, references to cultural differences are transformed into a discourse about *social inequalities* related to citizenship rights.

Multiculturalism as Managing the Mainstream. However counter-intuitive it might appear, Canada's multiculturalism is focused on reforming the mainstream. Think about it: if the goal of an official multiculturalism is an inclusive Canada by integrating newcomers, it stands to reason that mainstream mindsets and institutions are the targets that must be managed to create accommodative space. In other words, the logic behind Canada's multiculturalism model is as much about managing the mainstream through the removal of prejudicial and discriminatory barriers as it's about managing the "other" by facilitating newcomer settlement, integration, and citizenization. This multicultural commitment as a two way process of mutual accommodation is conveyed by the maxim: You adjust, we adapt; We adjust, you adopt.

Multiculturalism as Citizenization. Canada's multiculturalism model extols the importance of welcoming newcomers into the citizenship fold (Kymlicka, 2012, 2016). A commitment to citizenization under a multiculturalism model is informed by the human rights ideals of belonging, participation, and contribution. The citizenization principle is also commensurate with the multicultural commitment to an inclusive Canada of integrated newcomers. The multiculturalism/citizenship nexus points to a new way of being a Canadian citizen, one that identifies with and belongs to Canada through a person's ethnicity.

Not everyone will agree with the specifics of this Canadian multiculturalism model. Much depends on how society is framed, the corresponding status of multiculturalism and its role in Canada-building. Those who see an official multiculturalism as progressive in advancing an inclusive Canada will differ in points of emphasis from those who believe multiculturalism is essentially regressive in fostering divisiveness and confusion. Yet a different frame of reference may be proposed by critics of capitalism who define a state multiculturalism as hegemonic and controlling. The next chapter will delve a bit more deeply into this assessment.

Multiculturalism Positives, Multiculturalism Negatives

To their credit, an official multiculturalism and Canada's multicultural model offer a lot in advancing an inclusive Canada (Perin, 2009). They provide a universalistic promise of inclusion and social justice through removal of discriminatory and prejudicial barriers, access to full and equal participation by promoting a receptive social climate and respect for cultural differences, the right to identify with and belong to Canada through a person's ethnicity without fear of penalty, the promise and benefits of a democratic citizenship, and recognition of the equal moral worth of all individual citizens according to the principles of fundamental justice (Lister, 1997, 2007; Nagel and Hopkins, 2010). A multicultural model of citizenship emphasizes political participation and economic opportunity over cultural recognition per se; priority of human rights over cultural traditions; a commitment to inclusiveness and common national identity over ancestral identities; and assertion of cultural fluidity and hybridic mixing over the reification of static cultural differences (Kymlicka, 2016). Under an official multiculturalism, Canada is deemed to be a better and more productive place to live; preferred over those monocultural systems that endorse uniformity at the expense of creativity and change; and more likely to generate positive commitments to Canada when differences are respected.

But multiculturalism's flaws are too well known to require extensive comment (Fleras, 2009). However progressive for its time, an official multiculturalism has drawn criticism because of the changing nature of global migration, evolving social formations across nation-states, a mounting backlash based on fears from extremism to social breakdown, and the relatively poor socioeconomic performance of newcomers and racialized minorities (Putnam, 2007; Vertovec, 2010). In addition to being blamed for a host of social ills from ghettoization to fragmentation (Mansur, 2011), an official multiculturalism is no longer positioned to differently accommodate a complex Canada of diverse-diversities, nor is it in a position to acknowledge how ethnicity intersects with other devalued identities such as race, class, gender, and sexuality to amplify exclusions (Fleras, 2017a). An official multiculturalism remains foundationally grounded within the constitutional order of a monocultural state that tends to frame diversity as a problem, a challenge, or pragmatic means to an end such as Canada-building or global competition, endorses a belief in liberal universalism that privileges sameness over diversity, and commits to a "pretend pluralism" by eliminating its salience in the public domain. Such a state-centric multicultural model is commensurate with a systemic white Canada as the unmarked norm and tacitly assumed standard that establishes an exclusionary hierarchy that prejudges others and ranks them accordingly (Fleras, 2014a). Moves to manage diversities under the homogenizing and hegemonic logic of an official multiculturalism tend to paper over differences at the expense of those who want their differences valued as an end itself rather than leveraged as a tool for Canada-building (also Pinder, 2010). Or alternatively, an official multiculturalism may pay lip service by promoting a mosaic of differences, but primarily for controlling purposes of divide and rule, in part by deploying discourses of diversity to justify and rationalize state power (Jin, 2012). Not surprisingly, in light of such criticisms, a growing chorus of calls is questioning the utility of an official multiculturalism in the 21st century.

Beyond Multiculturalism: Toward Postmulticulturalism

Recognizing these multiple vectors of difference not only underscores the limits of multiculturalism as a way to frame difference in Canada, it also opens the way toward a post-multicultural framing we might label multiversalism.
(Latham, 2009: 28)

As the saying goes, we do live in interesting times—no more so than in the identity crisis and a crisis of confidence that confront an official multiculturalism as public policy, political discourse, and citizenship construct. To one side, a legitimacy crisis looms that puts pressure to rethink the multiculturalism/citizenship nexus around the following questions: (a) How relevant are place-based governance frameworks such as national citizenship models in a transmigrant and diasporic world of here, there, and in between; (b) What are the chance of belonging together under a bounded multiculturalism when people's notions of identity and belonging as citizens are increasingly diffuse ("unbounded");

and (c) How useful as a national bulwark is a universal citizenship framework against the backdrop of splintered loyalties, multiple identities, and fragmented affiliations (also Motomura, 2006)? To the other side, an official multiculturalism may prove irrelevant or counterproductive in a world of complex diversities and diverse complexities. Migrants and minorities no longer endorse the idea they possess similar experiences and realities—a kind of essentializing that obscures historical, cultural, socioeconomic differences between and within groups. Individuals with minority backgrounds want to be treated as full-fledged citizens rather than being boxed in as passive members of a group under unelected community leaders or deeply conservative spokespersons (Malik, 2011). Their lives and life chances as well as identities and belongings can no longer be squeezed into national citizenship frameworks, ethnic tick boxes, or generic (one-size-fits-all) policies of accommodation (Hiebert, 2011; Malik, 2013). A growing awareness that we live in a world of diverse diversities puts pressure on innovative governance models that differently accommodate this complexity (Fleras, 2015). The challenge is captured by the following aphorism: while an official multiculturalism sought to make Canada safe from diversity yet safe for diversity, a new governance frame points to the possibility of making complex diversities safe from Canada yet safe for Canada.

A multiversal turn in a rapidly changing world of diversifying social realities is unmistakable (Fleras, 2015; Latham, 2008, 2009; Vertovec, 2013). References to multiversal (known also as superdiversity or hyperdiversity) as a theoretical lens and analytical tool possess heuristic value by drawing attention to the growing irrelevance as basis for policy making of existing governance concepts, static categories, and essentialistic identities (Berg and Sigona, 2013). New mobilities are emerging that challenge conventional notions of identities and territorially based political allegiances (Hiebert, 2011). Ethno-cultural communities no longer exist (if they ever did) as discreet, bounded, and enduring groups. More accurately they consist of contexts, categories, idioms, and routines that are processual, hybridic, and fragmented as well as fluid, relational and global in nature (Brubaker, 2005). But governments have been slow in coming around to the fluidity and fragmentation of population changes arising from the impact of transmigration and the hyperdiversity turn. A tendency prevails to rely on old maps as an interpretative blueprint in a world that, paradoxically, lacks a language for conceptualizing multiversal patterns of hyperdiversity (Beck, 2011). That new policy responses to these governance puzzles are slow to materialize is consequential: Ulrich Beck (2011: 53) writes of the dangers that await those foolish enough to pour new diversity wine into old governance skins:

> ...[O]ver the last decades the cultural, social, and political landscapes of diversity are changing radically, but we still use old maps to orient ourselves. In other words, my main thesis is: *we do not even have the language through which contemporary superdiversity in the world can be described, conceptualized, understood, explained, and researched.* (italics in original)

Most countries lack a new normative framework for managing complex diversities or differently accommodating a world of diverse complexities. The prevalance of a multicultural governance tends to lock diversity into ethnic boxes that are fixed and bounded as well as uniform, predictable, and deterministic of people's lives and life chances (Malik, 2013). Existing multicultural policies gloss over the proliferation of newer, smaller, and less organized groups, an intensification of diversities-within-diversities within regions and across borders groups, and the growing presence of non citizen immigrant groups who are radically transforming how we think, talk, and do citizenship (see Vertovec, 2012, 2013). And just as Canadians no longer live in a multicultural world but in a multiversal world of diverse differences and differential accommodation, so too are we moving beyond a citizenship world and into a world more postcitizenship in principle and practices. Such a citizenship challenge puts the onus on refracting the worth of an official multiculturalism through the prism of a postmulticulturalism lens. Or differently phrased, *in a hyperdiverse world of transmigration and multiversality, the challenge of accommodating complex diversities suggests the utility of a postmulticultural governance model for rethinking citizenship along postcitizenship lines.* A "multiversal" multiculturalism project known as postmulticulturalism acknowledges the reality of these cultural comings and goings, while simultaneously coping with the complexities of their transnational identities and belongings beyond the pale of fixed boundaries and permanent locales (Carruthers, 2013; Fleras, 2015).

Clearly, then, diversity no longer occupies a singular universe of differences but rather a multiverse of diverse differences. There is little doubt that multiversal as a concept possesses heuristic value in shedding light on a rapidly changing and increasingly diverse world that existing concepts and categories such as multiculturalism are seemingly incapable of capturing. The concept of multiversal as reality, discourse, and practice provides a helpful perspective from which to interpret a society that is more complex, composite, layered and unequal, whilst simultaneously alerting us to to the interplay of race, gender, generations, and class in defining who gets left out (Berg and Sigona, 2013). According to the Robert Latham (2007/08), the word multiverse conveys the idea of multiple social universes, with a corresponding set of diverse perspectives and lived realities. Differences in a multiverse don't just exist in one universe; more to the point, they prevail within and across many overlapping and intersecting multi-universes, resulting in a proliferation of *fissions, fissures and fusions* (Fleras, 2016a). *Fissions* within migrant and minority communities are increasingly compounded and crosscut by new axes of differentiation, distinction, and demands related to legal status, religion, gender age, nationality, class, and so on (Vertovec and Wessendorf, 2004). *Fissures* within these communities reflect social cleavages, both of a temporary and permanent nature, due to internal politics, conflicting agendas, and variable socioeconomic statuses. *Fusions* reinforce how Canada's urban centres are outgrowing both the traditional model of multiculturalism and the language once used to describe their lived-realities (Habacan, 2007; Sandercock, 2003, 2006). Canadian cities now exhibit the dynamics of hybridity, concludes Daniel Hiebert (2011), including a world of conjoined complexities that point to complicated entanglements rather than a fixed identity, togetherness-in-differences rather than separateness or segregation, and diverse diversities rather than a hegemonic plane of sameness and homogeneity (Ang, 2001). This robust *fusion* of cultures, religions, homeland linkages, and sexual orientation is re-ordering society in unprecedented ways as people renegotiate the citizenship of their multiple differences through the reality of everyday experiences (Wessendorf, 2014). In other words, Canada has moved beyond being multicultural—that is, a juxtaposition of diverse ethnocultural groups as first implied in the early years of multiculturalism—but rather a hybridized dynamic of interpenetrating lifestyles (Saul, 2008; Salee, 2009). The challenge is no longer that of living together with differences but of living together in differences (Ang, 2011).

Societies such as Canada are no longer simply diverse societies. Rather they are diversifyingly complex and complexly diverse owing to an array of demographic changes, mobility movements, immigration patterns, multi-tiered attachments, identity politics, and socioeconomic profiles. The emergent hyperdiversity of a multiversal Canada creates a raft of governance dilemmas when applied to Canada's official multiculturalism and the concept of a single undifferentiated citizenship model (Fleras, 2015). Unlike the "multi cul de sac-ism" of a mosaic multiculturalism model (a turn of phrase borrowed from Rohinton Mistry, 1995) that shackles people around their ethnicity and ancestry regardless of their important to a person's identity, a multiversal model frames ethnicity as but one component of a multidimensional identity (Ang, 2011; Habacan, 2007).Yes, ethnicity may inform peoples' complex and dynamic identities across multiple cultural spaces. Yet it should neither define who they are in terms of national citizenship nor box them into an ethnic straitjacket (Wong, 2007/08; Malik, 2013). This passage is instructive of an emerging multiversal experience that neither severs ties with the home country nor passively assimilates into the host country but flourishes in the positives of a postmulticulturalism.

> **My Name is Sophie and I am Canadian**. And what does that mean? According to Canadian census, it means: I am third generation Canadian on my mother's side and second generation Canadian on my father's side. My maternal grandparents are Canadian and British. My paternal grandparents are Senegalese. My aunts and uncles come from Canada, Thailand, Senegal, and the Ivory Coast. I am Muslim by birth, my father is Muslim, and my mother is Roman Catholic. Our family celebrates Aid El-Fitr and Eid Al-Adha, as well as, Christmas and Easter. I have multiple citizenships: British, Canadian, and Senegalese. I attend French primary and secondary schools and then went to university in English and French. At home I speak English with my mother and French with my father. I don't remember which language I learned first…At the moment…I divide my time living between Abbotsford and Dubai, while working for three companies headquartered in Hong Kong, South Africa, and Guatemala. My taxes are paid on the amount of time I spend in each of my residences (Gaye, 2011).

A commitment to postmulticulturalism as reality, discourse, and practice acknowledges that Canada is less a multicultural social formation but more of a multiversal kaleidoscope of diverse-diversities. Canada's multiculturality is increasingly aligned along the cross-cutting lines of multiracial, multiclass, multigendered, multisexual, multilingual, multireligious, multigenerational, multihistorical, multicitizenships, and so on (Latham, 2008, 2009). The complexities of this coexistence reflects a dizzying range of differences and entitlements, not only between identifiable groups and communities, but also *within* groups and *across* spaces and borders. A multiversal world points to a multitude of racial, ethnic, religious, and linguistic people from diverse locations who are migrating, seeking asylum or adventure, emigrating and leading lives heretofore unheard of, and establishing diasporic linkages between host- and home lands (Carr, 2008; Chodos, n.d.; Roy, 2013). This new and largely unbounded reality puts pressure on shifting the governance framework from a managing-the-mosaic model of multiculturalism to a postmulticultural model which engages with patterns of identity and belonging that are multidimensional, often free-floating and flexible, and consistent with a multiversal world of change, uncertainty, and contradiction (Fleras, 2014b). The logic behind a proposed postmulticultural governance not only recognizes the reality of differences-within-differences, but also exerts pressure for differently accommodating these diverse-diversities.

A multiversal-based postmulticulturalism as diversity governance advances a new discourse and imaginary for how we think, talk, and do citizenship. It also possesses the potential to address the diverse complexities of new (trans) migrants and (hyper)minorities by acknowledging the lived-reality of their translocal identities and belongings beyond fixed boundaries and permanent locales (Carruthers, 2013). Admittedly, a commitment to postmulticulturalism does not spell the end of multiculturalism, despite awareness that we no longer live in a world of multicultural diversity but rather in a fluid network of multiversal diversities based on more nuanced forms of belonging and identity (Fleras, 2015; Latham, 2007/08; also Blommaert, 2013). A new postmulticultural governance model is proposed for differently accommodating a diversity of diversities that complements rather than repudiates an official multiculturalism (Fleras, 2015). There is no need to throw the multicultural baby out with the postmulticultural bathwater; after all, an official multiculturalism and Canada's multicultural model have proven their worth in advancing an inclusive Canada-building while facilitating the settlement, integration and citizenization of migrants and minorities (Fleras, 2016a; Perin, 2009). The value of benefits under an official multiculturalism, notwithstanding, the hyperdiverse realities of an emergent postmulticultural Canada demand a rethink and an upgrade. The postmulticultural challenge involves creating a diversity governance framework that permits complex forms of identity and belonging at both individual and group levels and across a local/national/global nexus without discarding a unifying multicultural framework of social inclusion, equal participation, and full citizenship rights. David Ley (2005: 15) writes of the creative tension in balancing the principle of multiculturalism with the realities of a postmulticulturalism turn:

> …[A] post-multiculturalism is not a rejection of multiculturalism as much as it is a recognition that renewed energies are needed to create a global understanding of diversity across multiple contexts and locales that can be an asset, and not simply a set of problems in need of better judgement.

In short, the universalism of an official multiculturalism and the multiversalism of a postmulticulturalism lens should not be framed as mutually exclusive models for citizenship-making. More accurately, they deserve to be acknowledged as starting points for initiating a constructive dialogue in establishing a postmulticultural basis for belonging together in/with/through our diverse diversities.

References

Adams, Michael. "Muslims in Canada: Findings from the 2007 Environics Survey." Policy Horizons Canada. Government of Canada, 2007.

Andrew, Caroline, John Biles, Meyer Burstein, Victoria M. Esses, and Erin Tolley (eds.). *Immigration, Integration, and Inclusion in Ontario Cities*. Montreal/Kingston: McGill-Queen's University Press, 2013.

Ang, Ien. "Intertwining Histories: Heritage and Diversity." NSW History Council Lecture. Government House. Sydney, September 24, 2001.

Ang, Ien. "Provocation: Beyond Multiculturalism: A Journey to Nowhere." *Humanities Research* (2009).

Ang, Ien. "Navigating Complexity: From Cultural Critique to Cultural Intelligence." *Continuum: Journal of Media & Cultural Studies* 25, no. 6 (2011): 779–794.

Atkinson, David. *The Burden of White Supremacy: Containing Asian Migration in the British Empire and the United States*. Chapel Hill: University of North Carolina Press, 2016.

Banerjee, Rupa. "Perceptions of Workplace Discrimination among Canadian Visible Minorities." *Canadian Diversity* 9, 1 (2012): 29–33.

Banting, Keith and Will Kymlicka. "Canadian Multiculturalism: Global Anxieties and Local Debates." *British Journal of Canadian Studies* 23, no. 1 (2010): 43–72.

Beck, U. "Multiculturalism or Cosmpolitanism: How Can We Describe and Understand the Diversity of the World?" *Social Sciences in China* 32, no. 4 (2011): 52–58.

Berg, Ulla Dalum and Robyn Magalit Rodriguez. "Transnational Citizenship Across the Americas." *Identities* 20, no. 6 (2013): 649–664.

Berg, M. L. and N. Sigona. "Ethnography, Diversity, and Urban Space." *Identities* 20, no. 4 (2013): 347–360.

Biles, John, A. Carroll, R. Pavlova, and M. Sokol. "Canada: Fostering an Integrated Society?" In *International Perspectives: Integration and Inclusion*, edited by James Frideres and John Biles, 79–110. Montreal/Kingston: McGill-Queen's University Press, 2012.

Biles, John and James Frideres. "Introduction." In *International Perspectives: Integration and Inclusion*, edited by James Frideres and John Biles, 1–16. Montreal/Kingston: McGill-Queen's University Press, 2012.

Blommaert, Jan. "Citizenship, Language, and Superdiversity: Towards Complexity." *Journal of Language, Identity, and Education* 12, no. 3 (2013): 1–4.

Bloemraad, Irene. "Theorizing and Analyzing Citizenship in Multicultural Societies." *The Sociological Quarterly* 56, no. 4 (2015): 591–606.

Bonikowska, Aneta, Feng Hou, and Garnet Picot. "Do Highly Educated Immigrants Perform Differently in the Canadian and U.S. Labour Markets?" Analytical Studies Branch Research Paper Series. Ottawa: Statistics Canada, 2011.

Brubaker, Rogers "The 'Diaspora' Diaspora." *Ethnic and Racial Studies* 28, 1 (2005):1–19.

Carr, Matthew. *Fortress Europe: Dispatches from a Gated Continent.* New York: New Press, 2012.

Carruthers, Ashley. "National Multiculturalism, Transnational Identities." *Journal of Intercultural Studies* 34, no. 2 (2013): 214–228.

Castles, Stephen. "Rethinking Australian Migration." *Australian Geographer* 47, no. 4 (2016): 391–398.

Castles, Stephen and Mark J. Miller. *The Age of Migration. International Population Movements in the Modern World.* 4/e New York: The Guilford Press, 2009.

Cavanagh, Matt, and Sarah Mulley. "Institute for Public Policy Research." *Fair and Democratic Migration Policy: A Principled Framework for the UK.* January 17, 2013. http://www.ippr.org/

Chazan, May, Lisa Helps, Anna Stanley, and Sonali Thakkar. "Introduction." In *Home and Native Land: Unsettling Multiculturalism in Canada.* edited by May Chazan et al., 1–14 Toronto: Between the Lines, 2011.

Chodos, Bob n.d. "Postmulticultural Ontario, Through the Eyes of a Quebecer." *Inroads Journal,* Issue 34 (2013).

Clarke, George Elliott. "Multiculturalism and Its (Usual) Discontents." *CanadaWatch,* Fall 2009: 24–25.

Collett, Elizabeth. "Europe: A New Continent of Immigration." In *Rethinking Immigration and Integration: A New Centre-Left Agenda.* edited by Olaf Cramme and Constance Motte, 10–18. London: Policy Network, 2010.

Cowen, T. "Cashing in on Cultural Free Trade: Don't Give Us Shelter: A U.S. Economist Sings the Praises of Canadian Artists." *National Post,* April 24, 1999.

Deloitte. "Welcome to Canada. Now What? Unlocking the Potential of Immigrants for Business Growth and Innovation." White paper summary of Deloitte's 2011 *Dialogue on Diversity.* November 2011. http://www.deloitte.com.

Donnelly, Michael J. *Canadian Exceptionalism. Are We Good or Are We Lucky? A Survey of Canadian Attitudes in Comparative Perspective.* Montreal: McGill Institute for the Study of Canada, 2017.

Drew, Kevin. "Switzerland Seen as Number One Country." *U.S. News and World Report,* 7 March 2017.

Duchastel, Jules. "Multiculturalism: What are Our Discontents About?" *CanadaWatch,* Fall 2009, 31–33.

Duchesne, Ricardo. "Will Kymlicka's Theory of Multiculturalism is a Dishonest Program to End 'Typically White Nations.'" *Council of European Canadians.* Posted August 10, 2016.

Economist. "What's the Point?" July 9, 2016.

Fleras, Augie. *The Politics of Multiculturalism: Multicultural Governances in Comparative Perspectives.* New York: Palgrave Macmillan, 2009.

Fleras, Augie. *Racisms in a Multicultural Canada.* Waterloo, ON: Wilfrid Laurier Press, 2014a.

Fleras, Augie. *Immigration Canada.* Vancouver: UBC Press, 2014b.

Fleras, Augie. "Beyond Multiculturalism: Managing Complex Diversities in Postmulticultural Canada." In *Revisiting Multiculturalism in Canada,* edited by L. Wong and S. Guo, 297–321. Rotterdam: Sense Publishers, 2015.

Fleras Augie. *Unequal Relations.* 8/e. Toronto: Pearson, 2016a.

Fleras, Augie. "Re-imagining Citizenship in Canada, New Zealand, and Australia: Transnational Dynamics, Postnational Complexities, Postcitizenship Possibilities." Plenary paper, Citizenship in a Transnational Context, University of Alberta, Edmonton, July 6–7, 2016b.

Fleras, Augie. *Inequality Matters.* Toronto: Oxford University Press, 2017a.

Fleras, Augie. "Rethinking Citizenship Through a Transnational Lens: Australia, Canada, and New Zealand." In *Citizenship in Transnational Perspective: Australia, Canada, and New Zealand,* edited by Jatinder Mann. 15–48. New York: Palgrave, 2017b.

Fleras, Augie. "Canadian Exceptionalism: From a Society of Immigrants to an Immigration Society." To be published in a future issue of *Canadian Ethnic Studies,* 2017c.

Foster, Lorne. "The Foreign Credentials Gap in Canada: The Case of Targeted Universalism." *Directions* (Canadian Race Relations Foundation) 6, no. 2 (2011): 23–36.

Frank, Kristyn. "Immigrant Employment Success in Canada: Examining the Rate of Obtaining a Job Match." *International Migration Review* 47, no. 1 (2013): 76–105.

Frank, K., F. Hou, and G. Schellenberg. "Life Satisfaction Among Recent Immigrants in Canada Compared with Source-Country Populations and the Canadian Born." Catalogue no 11FOO19M—No 363. Ottawa: Statistics Canada, 2014.

Fries, Christopher and Paul Gingrich. "A "Great" Large Family: Understanding of Multiculturalism Among Newcomers to Canada." *Refuge* 27, no. 1 (2009): 36–45.

Gaye, Nicola. "Superdiversity in Canada." *Policy Horizons.* Ottawa: Government of Canada, July, 2011.

Government of Canada. "Annual Report to Parliament on Immigration.". Retrieved from http://www.gic.gc.ac, 2016.

Griffith, Andrew. *Canada Faces Dramatic Drop in Citizenship, Prompting Concerns About Disengaged Immigrants.* Multicultural Meanderings. March 24, 2015.

Habacan, Alden E. "Beyond the Mosaic: Canada's Multiculturalism 2.0." Paper to the Annual Summer Conference. The Stranger Next Door: Making Diversity Work. Orillia ON: Couchiching Institute on Public Affairs, August 9–12, 2007.

Hampshire, James. *The Politics of Immigration: Contradictions of the Liberal State.* Boston: Polity Press, 2013.

Handa, Amita. *Of Silk Saris and Mini Skirts.* Toronto: Canadian Scholars Press, 2003.

Henry, Frances and Carol Tator (eds). *Racism in the Canadian University: Demanding Social Justice, Inclusion, and Equity.* Toronto: University of Toronto Press, 2009.

Hiebert, Dan. "Superdiversity in Canada: New Challenges of Integration." Presentation to the Cross Cultural Mental Health Conference. Vancouver, October 3–4, 2011.

Hiebert, Daniel. "What's So Special About Canada? Understanding the Resilience of Immigration and Multiculturalism." Migration Policy Institute. June 2016.

Hitchens, Christopher. "The Good Intentions Paving Company." *National Post,* June 25, 2010.

Hyman, Ilene, Agnes Meinhard, and John Shields. "The Role of Multiculturalism Policy in Addressing Social Inclusion Processes in Canada." Paper prepared for the Canadian Multicultural Education Foundation, 1 June 2011.

Javdani, Mohsen, David Jacks, and Krishna Pendakur. "What Have We Learned About Immigrants, Diversity, and Economy? 16 Years of Metropolis." Powerpoint Slides, 2012.

Jaworsky, John. "A Case Study of Canadian Federal Government's Multicultural Policies." Unpublished MA Thesis. Political Science. Ottawa: Carleton University, 1979.

Jedwab, Jack. "The Economic Integration of Immigrants in Canada and the Quebec Difference." In *Managing Diversity in Canada*. edited by D. Rodriguez-Garcia, 203–222. Kingston ON: School of Policy Studies, Queen's University, 2012.

Jedwab, Jack and Vic Satzewich "Introductory Essay." In *The Vertical Mosaic. An Analysis of Social Class and Power in Canada. 50th Anniversary Edition.* by John Porter, xvii-xxxvii. Toronto: University of Toronto Press, 2015.

Jin, Wen. *Pluralist Universalism: An Asian American Critique of U.S. and Chinese Multiculturalisms*. Athens, Ohio: Ohio State Press, 2012.

Karim, Karim. "Nation and Diaspora: Rethinking Multiculturalism in a Transnational Context." *International Journal of Media and Cultural Studies* 2, no. 3 (2007).

Kazemipur, A. *The Muslim Question in Canada: a Story of Segmented Integration*. Vancouver: UBC Press, 2014.

Kymlicka, Will. *Multicultural Odysseys: Navigating the New International Politics of Diversity*. Oxford: Oxford University Press, 2007.

Kymlicka, Will. "Prospects for a Multicultural Citizenship. Pluralism Forum—Reframing Europe's 'Multicultural Debates.'" Global Centre for Pluralism. April 2012.

Kymlicka, Will. "Trajectories of Multicultural Citizenship." In *Representation and Citizenship*, edited by R. Marback, 52–78. Detroit: Wayne State University Press, 2016.

Kymlicka, Will and Kathryn Walker. "Rooted Cosmpolitanism: Canada and the World." In *Rooted Cosmpolitanism: Canada and the World*, edited by W. Kymlicka and K. Walker, 1–27. Vancouver: UBC Press, 2012.

Labelle, Micheline and Daniel Salee. "Immigrant and Minority Representations of Citizenship in Quebec." In *Citizenship Today: Global Perspectives and Practices*, edited by T. A. Aleinikoff and D. B. Klusmeyer, 278–315. Washington: Brookings Institute Press, 2001.

Latham, Robert. "What are We? From a Multicultural to a Multiversal Canada." *International Journal* Winter (2007/08): 23–41.

Latham, Robert. "Canadian Society is not Just Multicultural; It is Multiversal." ResearchSnapShot. York University, Toronto, 2008.

Latham, Robert. "After Multiculturalism: Canada and Its Multiversal Future." *Canada Watch*, Fall (2009) 28–30.

Latham, Robert. "Post-Multiculturalism and Transnationality: Toward a Multiversal Citizenship." Paper presented to conference: Toward a Democratic Cosmopolis: Diasporas, Citizenship & Recognition. York University. March 25–26, 2014.

Lentin, Alana and Gavan Titley. *The Crisis in Multiculturalism. Racism in a Neoliberal Age*. London: Zed Books, 2011a.

Lentin, Alana and Gavan Titley. "Open Democracy." *The Crisis in Multiculturalism*. 2011b. Available online at http://www.opendemocracy.net.

Lewin, J., C. Meares, T. Cain, P. Spoonley, R. Peace, and E. Ho. "Namasté New Zealand: Indian Employers and Employees in Auckland." Research Report No. 5: Integration of Immigrants Programme. North Shore City, NZ: Massey University, 2011.

Ley, David. "Post-Multiculturalism?" Working Paper No. 05–17. Research on Immigration and Integration in the Metropolis. Vancouver: Vancouver Centre of Excellence, 2005.

Ley, David. "Multiculturalism: A Canadian Defence." *Research on Immigration and Integration in the Metropolis*, Working Paper Series No. 07–04, 2007: 1–20.

Li, Peter S. *Destination Canada: Immigration Debates and Issues*. Toronto: Oxford University Press, 2003.

Lister, Ruth. "Dialectics of Citizenship." *Hypatia* 12, no. 4 (1997): 6–26.

Lister, Ruth. "Inclusive Citizenship: Realizing the Potential." *Citizenship Studies*, 49–61. Published online May 30, 2007.

Malik, Kenan. "Canada's Multiculturalism is No Model for Europe." *The Guardian*, December 6, 2011.

Malik, Kenan. "In Defence of Diversity." *The New Humanist*. Winter, December 18, 2013. http://www.eurozine.com.

Mansur, Salim. *Delectable Lie: a Liberal Repudiation of Multiculturalism*. Mantua Books, 2011.

McNevin, Anne. *Contesting Citizenship: Irregular Migrants and New Frontiers of the Political*. New York: Columbia University Press, 2011.

Mistry, Rohinton. *A Fine Balance*. New York: Emblem Publications, 1995.

Motomura, Hiroshi. *Americans in Waiting: the Lost Story of Immigration and Citizenship in the United States*. New York: Oxford University Press, 2006.

Mudde, Cas. "The Relationship between Immigration and Nativism in Europe and North America." *Transatlantic Council on Migration*, 2012. http://www.migrationpolicy.org.

Murphy, Michael. *Multiculturalism: A Critical Introduction*. New York: Routledge, 2012.

Nagel, Caroline and Peter Hopkins. "Introduction: Spaces of Multiculturalism." *Space and Polity* 14, no. 1 (2010): 1–11.

Noonan, Norma C. and Vidya Nadkarni. "Introduction: A Century of Challenges." In *Challenge and Change*, edited by N. C. Noonan and V. Nadkarni, 1–11. New York: Palgrave Macmillan, 2016.

OECD. "Is Migration Good for the Economy?" *Migration Policy Debates*, May 2014.

O'Doherty, Hugo. "Canada the Second-best Country in the World to be an Immigrant, US Study Finds." *CIC News, Canada's Immigration Newsletter*. July 10, 2017.

Pakulski, J. "Confusions about Multiculturalism." *Journal of Sociology*, 50, no. 1 (2014): 23–36.

Pearson, David. "Citizenship, 'Culturalisms" and Civic Pluralism: Comparing New Zealand and Australia." In *Cultural Citizenship and the Challenges of Globalization*. edited by W. Ommundsen, M. Leach, and A Vandenberg, 147–164. Cresskill NJ: Hampton Press, 2010.

Perin, Roberto. "Ethnic Identity and Multiculturalism." *CanadaWatch*, Fall (2009): 20–21.

Peter, K. "Multi-cultural Politics, Money, and the Conduct of Canadian Ethnic Studies." *Canadian Ethnic Studies Association Bulletin*, 5 (1978): 2–3.

Picot, Garnett, and Arthur Sweetman. "Making It in Canada: Immigration Outcomes and Policies." IRPP Study No. 29. Montreal: Institute for Research on Public Policy, 2012.

Pinder, Sherrow O. *The Politics of Race and Ethnicity in the United States*. New York: Palgrave Macmillan, 2010.

Putnam, Robert. "*E Pluribus Unum*: Diversity and Community in the Twenty-First Century." *Scandinavian Political Studies* 30, no. 2 (2007): 137–174.

Raleigh, Elizabeth and Grace Kao. "Do Immigrant Minority Parents Have More Consistent College Aspirations for Their Children." *Social Science Quarterly* 91, no. 4 (2010): 1083–1102.

Reinhart, Anthony, and James Rusk. "Immigrants Suffer in Silence Within Walls of Suburbs." *Toronto Globe and Mail,* March 11, 2006.

Reitz, Jeffrey. "Assessing Multiculturalism as a Behavioural Theory." In *Multiculturalism and Social Cohesion,* edited by J. Reitz et al., 1–43. New York: Springer Science+Business Media, 2009.

Reitz, Jeffrey. "The Distinctiveness of Canadian Immigration Experience." *Patterns of Prejudice* 46, no. 5 (2012a): 518–40.

Reitz, Jeffrey. "Managing Immigration and Diversity in Canada and Quebec: Lessons for Spain?" In *Managing Immigration and Diversity in Canada,* edited by Dan Rodríguez-García, 61–86. Montreal/Kingston: McGill-Queen's University Press, 2012b.

Reitz, Jeffrey. "Who Succeeds in Integrating Muslim Immigrants: France, Quebec, or Canada? Research Profile by L. Ho and H. Natt." Global Migration Research Institute. University of Toronto, December 12, 2012c.

Reitz, Jeffrey. "Closing the Gaps between Skilled Immigration and Canadian Labour Markets: Emerging Policy Issues and Priorities." In *Wanted and Welcome? Policies for Highly Skilled Immigrants in Comparative Perspective,* edited by T. Triadafilopoulos, 147–62. New York: Springer Science and Business, 2013.

Roy, Jean-Louis. "Chers Voisins: Ce Qu'on ne Connait pas de l'Ontario." Montreal: Stanke, 2013.

Sakamoto, I., D. Jeyapal, R. Bhuyan, J. Ku, L. Fang, H. Zhang, and F. Genovese. "An Overview of Discourses of Skilled Immigrants and 'Canadian Experience': An English-Language Print Media Analysis." CERIS Working Paper No. 98. Toronto: Ontario Metropolis Centre, 2013.

Salee, Daniel. "Is Canada's Commitment to Multiculturalism Weakening?" *CanadaWatch,* Fall (2009): 34–35.

Sandercock, Leonie. "Planning in the Ethno-culturally Diverse City: A Comment." *Planning Theory and Practice* 4, no. 3 (2003): 319–323.

Sandercock, Leonie. "Mongrel Cities of the 21st Century: In Defense of Multiculturalism." UBC Laurier Lecture, 2006.

Saul, John Ralston. *A Fair Country. Telling Truths About Canada.* Toronto: Penguin, 2008.

Schmidtke, Oliver. "Citizenship and Multiculturalism in the 21st Century: the Changing Face of Social, Cultural, and Civic Inclusion." Working Paper Series for Metropolis British Columbia, 2014.

Simmons, Alan. *Immigration and Canada. Global and Transnational Perspectives.* Toronto: Canadian Scholars' Press, 2010.

Smith, Bryan and Pamela Rogers. "Towards a Theory of Decolonizing Citizenship." *Citizenship Education Research Journal* 5, no. 10 (2016): 59–72.

Spoonley, Paul and Erin Tolley E. (eds.). *Diverse Nations, Diverse Responses: Approaches to Social Cohesion in Immigrant Societies.* Queen's Policy Studies Series. Kingston: School of Policy Studies, Queen's University, 2012.

Vertovec, Steven. "Towards Post-Multiculturalism? Changing Communities, Conditions, and Contexts of Diversity." *International Social Science Journal* 61, no. 199 (2010): 83–95.

Vertovec, Steven. "'Diversity' and the Social Imaginary." *Archives Europeenes de Sociologies* LIII, no. 3 (2012): 287–312.

Vertovec, Steven. "Reading Super-Diversity." MPI-MMG. December 2013, Retrieved from http://www.mmg.mpg.de.

Vertovec. Steven and Wessendorf, Susanne. "Migration and Cultural, Religious, and Linguistic Diversity in Europe. An Overview of Issues and Trends." COMPAS. University of Oxford, 2004.

Walcott, Rinaldo. "Multiculturalism, the Canadian Academy, and the Impossible Dream of Black Canadian Studies." *CanadaWatch*, Fall (2009): 22–23.

Walton-Roberts, Margaret W. "Immigration, the University, and the Welcoming Second Tier City." *Journal of International Migration & Integration* (April 19, 2011). Published online/

Wessendorf, S. "Researching Social Relations in Super-Diverse Neighbourhoods: Mapping the Field." IRiS Working Paper, Series No 2. University of Birmingham, 2014.

Wong, L. L. "Transnationalism, Active Citizenship, and Belonging in Canada." *International Journal*, 63, no. 1 (2007/08): 79–100.

Wu, Z., C. M. Schimmele, and F. Hou. "Self-Perceived Integration of Immigrants and Their Children." *Canadian Journal of Sociology* 37, no. 4 (2012): 381–392.

PART 3
A POSTCITIZENSHIP WORLD: EMERGING REALITIES, SHIFTING DISCOURSES, NEW PRACTICES

· 6 ·

A TRANSNATIONAL CITIZENSHIP, ACROSS BORDERS; POSTNATIONAL CITIZENSHIP, BEYOND BORDERS

Introduction: Identity and Belonging in a Transnational World of Transmigration

"People cross borders. It's been that way ever since borders crossed people."
(Antoine Cassar)

The 21st century will be defined by the movement of peoples from one country to another, from one continent to another (Castles, de Haas, and Miller, 2013). With up to 245 million people (in 2016) on the move outside of their homeland—a population equivalent to that of Brazil as the world's fifth most populous country—few countries have been untouched by international migration (Papademetriou, 2003; Simmons, 2010). People from around the world are in a constant quest to improve their lives, to flee from confining environments, and to escape from natural and social disasters. People are being "pushed" from their homelands because of political oppression, ethnic conflicts, demographic pressure, and economic stagnation (Fleras, 2014). They also are "pulled" into other countries to take advantage of opportunity and freedom or, alternatively, to seek out adventure and excitement. In some cases, people are seeking asylum by fleeing persecution, human rights abuses, and armed conflicts; in other cases, they are escaping hardship and the lived-uncertainties in those developing countries with weak economies and unstable political systems (also Spoonley and Bedford, 2012). The immediate future promises yet more displacement: Climate change and natural disasters will render human existence increasingly unsustainable especially in low-lying coastal regions or in locales undergoing desertification. As well, the punishing gaps between the affluent and the destitute will induce many to uproot and seek their fortunes elsewhere, despite the attendant risk of danger and disappointment. The conclusion is inescapable as Pecoud and de Guchteneire (2005) point out: "In this globalized era of human uprootedness and migration, the movement of people is not an anomaly, but a normal process that may prove impossible to curb or control."

Theorizing the worldwide movements of migrants has attracted widespread academic attention in search of models to account for global patterns, processes, and politics (Castles et al., 2013; Simmons, 2010). Two models of international immigration and immigrant integration prevail: *nationalist* vs *transnationalist* (Fleras, 2014). A nationalist model conceptualizes immigration as a fixed field of location between "a" (the sending country) and "b" (the host or receiving country). With its emphasis on finalities and binary oppositions ("here" vs "there"), a nationalist model framed immigrants as individuals who permanently uprooted themselves from their home country. Over time, they discarded any lingering attachment to their homelands for affiliation with their new "hostland" to which they pledged an unswerving allegiance. Governments and host communities were clear in their expectations of immigrant behavior, commitments and obligations—namely, undivided identification with and political loyalty to a single national community. Society building was thus predicated on a process of selecting preferred classes of individuals for admission and inclusion, while excluding the unpreferred through restricted modes of entry or incorporation. Multiple allegiances and divided attachments were discouraged or disallowed as unnecessary accoutrements that complicated the governing process. Conferral of a national citizenship symbolized the definitive marker of proof that newcomers had transferred their loyalty from "there" to "here" (Spoonley, 2010).

But many now criticize the national model of immigration and immigrant integration as simplistic and inaccurate (Fleras, 2014; Satzewich and Wong, 2006). Framing immigration as a finality between two fixed fields of location ("a thing") has given way to a discursive framework that focuses on global flows and trans-linkages ("a *process*"), around transnational networks of numerous actors, across diverse domains, and at different levels of incorporation (Simmons, 2010). State-centric notions of migrant identity, attachment, and belonging have been unsettled by the combination of low cost travel, digital communication technologies, and the aggressive recruitment of skilled and highly mobile professionals (Spoonley, 2010; Spoonley and Bedford, 2012). A national citizenship model finds it increasingly difficult to address transnational discourses and practices that inform how we think, talk, and do citizenship (also Fox, 2005). A transnational model of citizenship is preferred, one that acknowledges the creation of new transnational social spaces of identity and belonging along geographically discontinuous lines of cross-border transactions (Faist, 2007; Wong, 2007/08). A transnational lens underscores the existence of multiple memberships that span political boundaries within and between sovereign states (Bloemraad et al., 2008). Framing citizenship within the context of transnational movements and global actors not only calls into question fixed and spatialized notions of citizenship, but also offers opportunities for rethinking the multi-dimensions of identity and belonging beyond the pale of the national (Kallio and Mitchell, 2016).

The transnationalization of migration is proving a formidable citizenship challenge (Castles, de Haas, and Miller, 2013; Fleras, 2014; Garcea et al., 2008; Kraus, 2011). Hardly surprising, given the number and range of countries impacted by the magnitude and scope of migrant movements, together with the complexities of global mobility patterns (Wessendorf, 2014). The seemingly ceaseless movement of people also intensifies global anxieties over a "coming anarchy" in unsettling long established national markers of identity and belonging, unity and security. The dynamics of mobility are known to foster a raft of challenging outcomes: (a) blur a defence of territorial boundaries, (b) encourage cross-border movements of migrants in search of safety or success, (c) undermine national regimes of multicultural governance, (d) transform public space into a contested site, (e) coax identities away from a strict national focus, and (f) complicate the search for citizenship models that balance a respect for diversities with a commitment to community and consensus. Not unexpectedly, national jurisdictions in the post 9/11 era want to discipline citizenship by tightening up conditions for naturalization; introducing tougher criteria as precondition for integration and citizenship (Winter, 2014); imposing more restrictive measures to avert unwanted immigration flows; ramping up border enforcement and multi/bi/lateral agreements over deterrence and deportation; and promoting the "culturalization" of nation-states as communities of value and values rather than a disparate collection and random coexistence of diverse migrants (Anderson, 2014).

Ongoing debates over migration and citizenship in a transmigratory world reinforce the futility of applying binary analysis as explanatory framework (Ang, 2011). As critics argue, it doesn't make sense to impose a dichotomy between "a" and "b" in a globalizing world where references to here and there by way of the in between are increasingly blurred, overlapping, and contested. Consensus is mounting that transmigratory connections are not necessarily contradictory but may concur simultaneously in a mutually reinforcing fashion. Compounding the misunderstanding is yet another misconception. Too often identity and belonging were mistakenly addressed in zero sum terms in which attachment to one jurisdiction (or citizenship) seemingly detracted from the other (but see Jedwab, 2007/08). But belongings and identities within a framework of transmigration and transnational social networks do not necessarily undermine any senses of allegiance and affiliation. Migrants may use their transmigration connections to carve out an identity and belonging consistent with a national (universal) citizenship, while creating a transnational sense of affiliation to offset the strains of uprooting, transitioning, and settling in (Akesson, 2010).

Insofar as individuals possess multiple identities and belongings—from the local and national to the diasporic or cosmopolitan (Parekh, 2007; Wong, 2007/08)—immigrant identity and belonging are no longer what many assumed them to be, namely, fixed, singular, determinative, and irreversible. Rather identities are better envisaged as fluid, negotiated, and multidimensional, especially when the identification process is delinked from geographical location and rekindled around the hybridities of a transnational context. A new type of immigrant experience is emerging, one that neither severs ties with the home country nor passively assimilates into the host country. Transmigrants construct transnational communities that offer solidarity, support, information, and identity, across multiple jurisdictions as they settle and integrate, without necessarily discarding an attachment to a specific locale or denying a mix of multiple identities. Such a commitment and involvement is not without criticism and second-guessing. Questions include: Will transnationals integrate into mainstream society or into an immigrant enclave? Will transnational loyalties impede or improve integration? Will transnationals simply become citizens of conviction or citizens of convenience, given the ease with which citizenship may be acquired, maintained and transmitted (Metropolis, 2007)?

Views of how we think, talk, and do citizenship are shifting in response to these transnational discourses and transmigrant practices (Mann, 2017). References to a nationally bounded citizenship that tethered individuals to one nation state are making way for new citizenship models that acknowledge transmigrant claims in both the host and home county as part of a broader human rights discourse. Transformations in the politics and ideologies of the global system have redefined citizenship's normative and institutional core beyond the parameters of the national with respect to membership, identity, and entitlements (Triadafilopoulos, 2012). Two ideal typical dynamics are at play: the concept of transnational citizenship encompasses the idea of crossing borders to establish dual (or multiple) citizenships; a postnational citizenship as concept envisages a citizenship that transcends (or goes beyond) borders in fostering a more cosmopolitan citizenship ideal. To be sure, it's not a case of either-or in debating the postnational or the transnational, but rather an analytical separation of an interlinked dynamic. Or as aptly put by Cristina Rodriguez (2008: 1117), "This emerging transnational trope is organized around the idea that we have entered a postnational era…"

This chapter is predicated on the principle that applying a both a transnational and postnational citizenship lens is paying dividends in rethinking citizenship with respect to who belongs, how they belong, and what belonging entitles (Fleras, 2017). The chapter begins by looking at the concept of transmigration and transnationalism, followed by an examination of a transnational citizenship as status, discourse, and activity, with special attention to the realities and politics of a dual citizenship modality. This chapter also addresses the nature and worth of postnational citizenship as a discursive practice within the context of an evolving postnational era. The chapter demonstrates how reframing citizenship through a postnational lens and within a transnational framework reinforces the possibility of a more inclusive ("differentiated") citizenship without rejecting the benefits of a national ("universal") citizenship. The next chapter puts the principle of postnational citizenship into practice by addressing the politics of Indigenous citizenship. This chapter concludes by exploring the concept of cosmopolitanism as a global citizenship idea, with its rootedness in the ideals of universal personhood and the internationalization of human rights as basis for identity and belonging.

Reframing Citizenship Through a Transnational Lens

The forces of globalization and transnationalism[1] have transformed how we think, talk, and do citizenship. Globalization entails the global movement of people that cross and transcend borders in forging new social fields by linking countries of origin to those of settlement (Glick Schiller et al., 1992; Sandercock, 2006). The dynamics of transmobility associated with globalization not only challenge conventional understandings of citizenship as a territorially-based polity of belonging and identity. They also exert pressure on unpacking the meaning of citizenship by refracting it through a transnational lens (Bloemraad, 2015). Not surprisingly, many are critical of T.H. Marshall's formulation of citizenship as a unified bundle of civil, political, and social rights for nation state members, on grounds that memberships rights may be unbundled from territorial boundaries (Benhabib, 2003, 2007; Glover, 2011; Soysal, 2004). A transnational citizenship complements a person's singular national loyalty to one sovereign state with an attachment to another political entity through the social spaces that cross territorial boundaries (Benhabib, 2003, 2007). Reference to transnational citizenship as concept, reality, and interpretive lens reinforces the centrality of multiple allegiances, splintered identities, and overlapping networks that traverse nation state borders, thereby generating new transnational spaces that deterritorialize yet, paradoxically, also re-spatialize (Castles et al., 2013; Fleras, 2014; Rodriguez, 2008).

What counts as transnational citizenship? If citizenship is a relational concept between citizens and the state, to what do we owe a transnational citizenship? Defining the concept of transnational citizenship is proving problematic (Fox, 2005). Vastly different forms of identity and belonging as well as status and rights may be subsumed under a transnational umbrella (Fleras, 2016). A transnational citizenship may encompasses the concurrent possession of two or more citizenships, a single citizenship with emotional ties that cross another polity, or a new citizenship space that transcends political boundaries (for example, flexible citizenships or multiple passports that allow subjects to respond quickly and opportunistically to changing economic and political circumstances [Ong, 1999]). References to transnational citizenship in the singular conceals the possibility of more multifaceted dimensions, including diasporic and dual citizenship, both of which foster a rethinking of citizenship and its relationship to national communities (Welsh, 2011). A global or cosmopolitan citizenship may also be included in a transnational category, although this chapter prefers to categorize it under the postnational.

The term transnational is commonly used to describe how people's lived-realities cross and/or transcend a single geographical space and national borders. In its narrowest terms, it can be defined as the ability of migrants to forge and maintain ties that span national borders by creating new social spaces that are multilocal and multidimensional (Sandercock, 2006). Those patterns of belonging and identity that encompass more than one country provides a conceptual framework for rethinking the nature and dynamics of citizenship in a highly mobile world (Conference Notes, 2012). In its broadest sense, the prefix "trans" in transnational is employed to incorporate multiple dimension: *across* national borders (dual citizenship); *beyond* national borders (cosmopolitanism and universal human rights); *transcending* national borders (diaspora + transmigrants + cosmopolitanism); *transecting* national space (multiversal citizenship); as *oppositional* (Indigenous citizenship); and *transforming* via disruptive change (Fleras, 2016). A "trans" perspective that transverses borders (internal and external) and crosses frontiers offers a new way of seeing, thinking, and talking about citizenship and citizenship regimes. It should be noted that risks prevail in any framing. Used narrowly, only dual citizenship would qualify as transnational citizenship; used broadly, a conceptual stretching may well risk emptying the concept of any meaning (Fox, 2005).

A distinction between transnationalism and transnational citizenship is useful. Transnationalism refers to cyclical and nonlinear movement of transmigrants who establish new linkages and social spaces *across* the borders of existing states and national affiliations, with the result that citizens live within the context of two or more polities, jurisdictions, and societies (Leggewie, 2013; Rodriguez, 2008). The concept of transnational as transmigration acknowledges that people have multiple notions of identity, belonging, commitment, loyalty because of diverse and multilayered ties that link individuals or institutions across nation-state borders (Metropolis, 2007). The traversing of pre-established national borders gives rise to modern meaning of citizenship in a globalized world (Fox, 2005), including the idea of dual or multiple citizenships thus securing citizenship rights in two or more nation-states. In other words, transnationalism is objectively real since it's reflected in empirical and measurable reality. By contrast the concept of a transnational citizenship is not real in the naturally occurring sense of possessing an objective legal standing (dual citizenship notwithstanding [Fox, 2005]). Except as a lens, ideal, or model, there is no such thing as a transnational citizenship that supersedes the authority and borders of existing nation-states. But what a reference to a transnational citizenship does offer is a new way of reinterpreting the meaning of citizenship in a hyperdiverse world of coming and going. Applying a transnational lens to citizenship draws attention to how people's sense of membership, identity and lived-realities are neither exclusively sourced in the authority of the state nor entirely delimited by it. Rather they span borders without necessarily repudiating the centrality of the nation-state as the primary container and legal repository of citizenship rights (Soysal, 2011).

Dimensions of a Transnational Citizenship

Increasing recognition of dual citizenship and extension of state benefits and policies to diasporic communities have been interpreted in varying ways. For some, reference to a diasporic citizenship is proof that nation-states are abandoning a commitment to exclusive nationality and habitual residence as a precondition for citizenship rights (Pedroza and Palop-Garcia, 2017). For others, there are attendant dangers associated with societal unity and national identity in forsaking a singular and place-based citizenship. Still others acknowledge the possibility that both interpretations are inevitable in framing the politics of citizenship in world both transnational and postnational.

Diasporic Citizenship

We live in a diasporic world of transmigration. Far broader in scope than in the past of persons who explicitly yearned to return, modern references to diaspora expand to include individuals who no longer reside in their country of birth but are dispersed in space yet remain bound together to language, culture, identity, and ties to the homeland (Berns-McGowan, 2007–2008; Brubaker, 2005). The essential features of such a "diasporic diaspora" (refers to how the meaning of diaspora is dispersed across semantic, conceptual, and disciplinary space [Brubaker, 2005: 2]) are as follows: Dispersion and cross border linkages in two or more locales, ongoing orientation toward communities of origin and settlement, and boundary-maintenance of transnational migrant communities and translocal collective identities (Fox, 2005; Gamlen, 2007). The combination of accessible communication technologies and relatively inexpensive travel simplifies yet intensifies the diasporic process. Diasporas organized round the internet and social media ("digital diaspora") benefit from access to information and problem solving, a capacity to mobilize communities around shared goals, and the amplification of voices once silenced.

Precise figures for tallying up the number of diasporic individuals around the world don't exist. It is estimated that one million Australians (or 5% of the population) are working and living abroad (Banfield, 2017), most of whom appear to be relatively young, skilled and educated, and willing to do whatever necessary to advance their careers. A similar situation exists in New Zealand where the popularity of working overseas is captured by the popular phrase "OE" (overseas experience). Canada, too, is no stranger to transnational migrants, including up to 9 percent of its population who reside overseas. Public reaction to diasporic Canadians is varied (Nyers, 2010). To one side, Canadians tend to think of citizenship in non-geographic terms but "wherever Canadians are" (Welsh, 2011); to the other side are those who believe citizenship should be earned (a "privilege") through physical settlement and active contribution to Canadian society (Griffiths, 2009). Yet others express concern over the consequences of disengaging a singular citizenship from a fixed state. The danger lies in expanding yet diluting the concept to the point where a Canadian citizenship loses any semblance of meaning except as a largely unenforceable claim to human rights or hazy reference to a global community. Kallio and Mitchell (2016: 262) write to this effect when they explain: "[B]y giving up the *geographies* of citizenship, we risk losing the *politics* of citizenship, as the political exists *in abstracto* only in political philosophical principles"

Dual Citizenship: Split Loyalties or Bridge-Building?

A dual citizenship at its most basic level involves the concurrent holding of at least two citizenships (Renshon, 2005). Dual citizens consists of those individuals whose lives span the border of two or more nation-states, not only participating in and contributing to both polities, but also claiming rights, membership, and privileges (Glick Schiller, 2005). Dual citizenship may be differently acquired, including inheritance from a parent, birth in a territory that recognizes birthright, ancestral claims, process of naturalization, and marital arrangements (Goodman, 2014). Several dual citizen pathways exist in Canada and the United States, the most common include:birth in Canada or the United States to a foreign national; born abroad to a Canadian or American parent; or birth in a country that recognizes the duality of citizenship arrangements. In the United States, dual citizens face few restrictions or consequences of any kind even if they fight in a foreign country (Renshon, 2005). Nevertheless, the Constitution affords one advantage to American born citizens: the right to run for office of the President of the United States. The American Constitution limits the presidency to a "natural born citizen"—a citizen from birth (including persons born abroad to a US citizen parent who do not require a naturalization process [Katyal and Clement, 2015]).

References to dual citizenship should not be confused with the concept of postnational citizenship. A dual citizenship falls under the category of transnational citizenship inasmuch as it entail the crossing (not a transcending) of borders without repudiating the reality, necessity, and importance of the nation-state and national citizenship. For scholars of transnationalism as re-territorialized citizenship, dual citizenship acknowledges how immigrants cross borders and create new social spaces around existing jurisdictions (Bloemraad, 2004). And whereas the concept is usually used in the international sense, dual citizenship can exist internally within the nation-state; for example Native Indigenous Americans have enjoyed de jure dual citizenship since 1924, while Indigenous peoples in Canada enjoy a kind of de facto dual citizenship as members of their tribes as well as membership in the Canadian community. Or consider how the Nisga'a First Nations in Canada possess a quasi-dual citizenship based on an arrangement with the federal government that came into effect in 2000 (see Chapter 7 for details). By contrast, postnational notions of citizenship tend to question the idea of citizenship as formal membership in one or more states. Rather citizenship rights are increasingly thought to be vested in the principle of universal personhood and internationalization of human rights—an investiture that transcend borders rather than simply crosses them. Or alternatively, the concept of a postnational citizenship may also be applied to substate national minorities and Indigenous peoples who transcend the nation-state through politicized claims as the "citizens within".

What does acceptance of dual citizenship in over 100 countries, including Canada since 1978, say about the meaning of citizenship (Faist, 2007; Faist and Gerdes, 2008; Preston et al., 2007; Sejersen, 2008)? The concept of dual or multiple citizenships was once condemned as unthinkable or an "abomination" for eroding state-centric identities, diminishing the intensity of the state-citizen affiliation, and unravelling the bonds among individuals (Rodriguez, 2010; Spiro, 2006). The concept is now widely tolerated and accepted, in part because the reasons for rejecting it have become less compelling (Kivisto, 2007), especially with international norms increasingly tolerant of the principle of plural (dual) citizenship (Spiro, 2008). Acceptance of dual citizenship acknowledges a fundamental reality. The interplay of economic globalization, rapid developments in communication technology, and vastly increased personal mobility is transforming peoples' ideas about national identity, national governance, and national citizenship (Macklin and Crepeau, 2010; Millbank, 2000). A dual citizenship is no longer dismissed as a problem that complicates issues over integration, loyalty, foreign policy, and diplomatic protection. Instead it's increasingly framed as a possibility to be actively encouraged or, at minimum, to be pragmatically tolerated. To be sure, reaction to dual citizenship—acceptance, tolerance, rejection—may prove selective; for example, Europeans tend to accept dual citizenships for Europeans abroad, but are less accepting of dual citizenship for foreign nationals in a European country.[2]

Despite inconsistencies, dual citizenship regimes will likely continue to flourish in domains where the principles of jus soli and sanguinis principles coexist, a greater commitment to equality and inclusion prevails, and patterns of international mobility and cosmopolitanism continue apace (Joppke, 2008).

For critics, dual citizenships remain an anathema. Dual citizens perceived as citizens of convenience are thought to lack a meaningful ("emotional") commitment to one or both countries, claim services but supposedly do not pay taxes,[3] and express divided loyalties over military service (Renshon, 2005). Dual citizenship disturbs the sense of boundedness that has long defined citizenship as a spatially rooted concept—from a city-state to the nation-state (Preston et al., 2007)—in arbitrating the relationship between citizen and alien, insider and outsider, member and non member (Kivisto, 2007). A dual citizenship is also thought to undermine the exclusive bond between individuals and membership in sovereign state, with outcomes ranging from split loyalties to conflicting diplomatic protection (Bloemraad, 2004; Macklin, 2007). Or as Jack Granastein (2006) writes in criticizing what he sees as Canada's casual approach to naturalizing newcomers and dispensing dual citizenship, "Does citizenship mean anything or is Canada just a hotel where people of the world check into when it suits them." Take for example, how the costly evacuation of 15,000 so-called Canadians of convenience from a war ravaged Lebanon stirred public outrage over dual citizenship (Nyers, 2010), especially when it was alleged that many of those rescued had subsequently returned to Lebanon once hostilities ceased (Joppke, 2008; Welsh, 2011). In short, major objections to dual citizenship dismiss it for promoting shallowness and disloyalty, while fostering unfairness and unwieldiness (Joppke, 2008) while others believe it leads to conflict of interest or awkward attachments. Still others pounce on it for degrading the symbolic value of citizenship to the level of a commodity, either for economic (tax advantages or employment opportunities) reasons or for travel convenience (see Millbank, 2000).

Others such as Macklin and Crepeau (2010; also Welsh, 2011; Winter, 2016) challenge the validity of these criticism. Contrary to popular perception of societal collapse or individual anomie, dual citizenship may facilitate loyalty, identity, and belonging by allowing individuals to maintain other affiliations while freeing them from the discomfort of making painful choices (Goodman, 2014; Rodriguez, 2010). For example, Jack Jedwab (2007/08) has argued on the basis of survey data that dual citizens may possess a stronger sense of belonging to and identification with Canada than those with a single Canadian citizenship. As well, dual citizens may be enlisted as key players in facilitating Canada's goal to foster international commerce, expand investment opportunities, and explore trade linkages (Nyers, 2010). Admittedly, the possibility of diluting national unity and identity because of conflicting citizenships should not be dismissed out of hand, although there is little evidence in support of this scenario, given the difficulties in both operationalizing and measuring emotional attachments (Banulescu-Bogdan, 2012; Macklin and Crepeau, 2010). Nevertheless, citizenship in Canada and elsewhere remains subject to a range of securitizations in law, policy, and practice after "9/11", with dual citizenship a prime target of attention, in effect reinforcing the fragility of citizenship rights for dual citizens (Nyers, 2010).

Postnational Citizenship: Think Globally, Talk Nationally, Act Locally

The growing influence of transnationalism and the ubiquity of human rights norms is prompting a rethinking of how we think, talk, and do citizenship. New citizenship discourses and practices are disrupting the conventions of identity and belonging associated with a nationally-bounded definition of citizenship (Grundy and Smith, 2006). Once thought to be the exclusive preserve of a national community, citizenship rights are increasingly sourced and legitimated within a global framework of human rights rather than anchored in the nation-state. And although, nation-states and their boundaries remain in control, universalistic principles of personhood transcend these borders, giving rise to new and more complex patterns of belonging and identity (Soysal, 2011). Reference to a universal personhood points to the emergence of a postnational citizenship model wherein rights are attached to individuals as humans rather than nation-state members, to humanity rather than nationality, to world citizens rather than national citizens, to personhood rather than nationhood. The locus of citizenship as discourse or activity has evolved as well, from city, to empire, to fiefdom, to nation-state and more recently to the world stage. Nation-states are not always the leading players on the international stage, especially as political authority is dispersed among local, national, and transnational levels, while a national citizenship no longer serves as an exclusive container that bonds people to each other or binds them to the nation-state. No more so, it would appear, then when a neoliberal globalization privileges the primacy of market fundamentalism over the principle of personhood in articulatingmembership and entitlements (Deckhard,

2016). In short, the implications are vast for living in a postnational world of globalized economy, universal human rights norms, trade interdependencies, permeability of borders, and vast communication networks. It becomes more difficult than ever for the nation-state to protect its citizens, solve their problems, define collective identities or secure territorial integrity. In turn, the notion of a postnational citizenship discourse informed by the principles of globalization and cosmopolitanism allows immigrants and permanent residents to enjoy a wider range of citizenship entitlements on grounds of residency and rights rather than on the basis of legal status (Seymour, 2012; Soysal, 1994; Urzi and Williams, 2016).

This challenge signals the onset of postnational discourses and citizenship practices. Pressure is exerted to dislodge the exclusive authority of the nation-state in defining the parameters of who belongs, how they belong, and what belonging brings to the table (Banerjee, 2014). According to this line of thinking, any compelling reason for identifying with a single national citizenship is undone by the decline in absolute state authority over identity and belonging, coupled with the rise of supra-state attachments (Spiro, 2007). Evolving discourses and emergent practices about identity and belonging are transforming—and being transformed by—how we think, talk, and do citizenship. This discursive shift does not mean that nation states are dispensing with conventional channels for accessing citizenship status and enforcing citizenship rights (Foran, 2017). To the contrary, borders have become more militarized in attempting to deter unwanted newcomers from admission to national citizenship (Smith, 2004; Williams, 2016). Moreover, reference to postnational neither portends the end of nation-state nor condones its banishment from domestic affairs; more accurately, it calls attention to the end of citizenship as we know it. Instead of a national citizenship model, what is proposed is a postnational citizenship model for interpreting new citizenship realities and dynamics. A new discursive framework is proposed for becoming, being, and doing citizenship in a postnational world that demands space for multiple identities and splintered belongings yet recoils at the prospect of discarding the legal authority of national citizenship.

Reformulating the concept of citizenship within a postnational world challenges the controlling and homogenizing logic of national citizenship (Maas, 2013). Reference to postnational citizenship contests the once uncontested status of citizenship as universal and unitary by advocating a framework consistent with multilayered patterns of belonging, identity, and entitlements. Such a nested arrangement conjures up images of Russian dolls where smaller dolls fit into larger dolls in an expanding/contracting order of compartments. Take the case of European Union as exemplifying a postnational (or supranational) site of nested citizenships (Kivisto and Faist, 2008). Every national (or citizen) of a member state is a European citizen, although the EU is not a state per se, while EU citizenship is unattainable without citizenship in a member state (Guild, 2014). The end result is a multilayered citizenship involving different levels of meaning, from the national to the postnationality of supra-European state, each of which is constructed and constrained by the proximity of adjoining layers (Maas, 2013,; Yuval-Davis, 1999). The implication of framing citizenship through a nested lens is critical. If people's identities are nested or multi-layered, a proper a citizenship frame is required, one unfettered from the monopoly of the nation state but located in expanding circle of attachments that incorporate a local/national/global nexus (Kivisto, 2007).

Cosmopolitanism as Postnational Citizenship

Should citizenship as belonging, entitlements, and identity be defined on territorial grounds and embedded in a politically demarcated polity? Or should citizenship be framed around a commitment to an ideal involving an attachment to humanity and the principle of universal personhood—especially when individuals increasingly envision themselves as global citizens of the world rather than as national citizens of a society? What is the relationship between the concept of cosmopolitanism and that of a global citizen/citizenship? Does reference to the concept "global citizen" possess any formal legitimacy or heuristic worth? Or is it more accurate to approach the concept as code for re-imagining citizenship against a postnational backdrop and within a global context (see also Gerzon, 2009)? Answers to these question are more important than ever. A growing number of people around the world increasingly identify as citizens of the world rather than as citizens of their own country (Soffel, 2016). According to a BBC World Service Poll conducted by Globescan involving 20,000 respondents in 18 countries, 51 percent of the respondents prefer to self-identify as global citizens, including over 70 percent of those from Nigeria, China and Peru who concurred with the statement "I see myself more as a global citizen than a citizen of my country". Canadians at 54 percent and American at 43 percent were bunched in the middle of the pack, with Russia last at 24 percent. Clearly, then, a new worldview about identity and belonging is transforming our concepts of humanity and citizenship (Bourne, 2009)—thanks in part to the interplay of online and social media, globalization, environmental activism, and awareness of humanitarian disasters (Israel, 2012; Khanna, 2017). Moreover Canada provides an especially fecund domain for exploring the concept of cosmopolitanism and global citizenship. Public debate and academic discourse have long endorsed the idea that Canadianess is reflective of "being a good citizen of the world" (Kymlicka and Walker, 2012: 1; Tan, 2015). More recently, endorsing the doctrine of "Responsibility to Protect" (R2P) reinforces Canada's stature as a "global good Samaritan" (Brysk, 2009). Reference to Canada as a *notion* ("idea and ideal") rather than a *nation* further cements its status as a postnational society in the throes of rethinking its citizenship agenda.

Insight Post

Rebranding Canada: Redoing the Citizenship Project—From Nationhood to Notionhood

Canada claims to be a postnational society. It justifies this claim by proposing to transcend the tired narratives of identity based on blood or history as basis for society-building (Kingwell, 2017). Prime Minister Justin Trudeau referred to Canada as the world's first postnational state when he claimed "There is no core identity, no mainstream in Canada. There are shared values,—openness, respect, compassion, willingness to work hard, to be there for each other, to search for equality and justice" (Lawson, 2015) (Prime Minister Jean Chretien made similar remarks in the mid-1990s). Others too point to Canada as postnational and postWestphalian on the grounds that it downplays its history, fosters ethnic and regional loyalties, espouses a loosely defined national identity, encourages highly personalized forms of community and belonging, and imposes relatively few demands on its citizens (Griffiths, 2009).

This assessment is criticized by some as reckless or naive, especially among those who regard the nation-state model as sacrosanct despite the reality of dissolving borders, widespread exodus and diasporic citizens, and diminished sovereignty (Griffiths, 2009; Todd, 2016). For others, this assessment heralds the onset of a postnational model of *notionhood*, one that thinks outside the nation-state box. As Charles Foran (2017) points out, reference to postnational is not about shredding passports, disbanding state governance, or ditching the national anthem. More accurately, it's about employing a different set of lens to rethink the challenges of living together with/in/through diversity. Reference to Canada as a notion rather than nation speaks of a country that is largely unshackled by notions of completeness and history, an adherence to blood and descent for recognition or reward, a preoccupation with cohesion and homogeneity, and a nativist fervour in defence of or (or in search of) the promised land. Reference to notionhood also points to a rethinking of Canada as a postnational experiment in populating a vast yet unified territorial space with the diversities of world, in large part because it can afford to differently build a society in light of its geographical isolation and physical space (Foran, 2017).

In securing its postnational bona fides, Canada does it differently. It supports a relatively decentralized system of governance based on federal, provincial, and Indigenous levels of government; an adherence to the principles of a civic nation as basis for belonging and identity; a commitment to a relatively easy naturalization of newcomers; and endorsement of multicultural principles as a governance framework for living together differently yet cooperatively. But clarification is required: Canada may be postnational in discourse and practice, but not in the Trudeauian claim that Canada has no core identity or that it lacks a mainstream (Todd, 2016; Fernandes, 2016). Rather Canada's postnationality exists in the sense that it *claims* to have dispensed—at times by intent at other times by expediency —those conventional tropes for society/nation-building such as a strong central government, an immovable national identity, an ethnicity-based nation-state coupled with a jus sanguinis concept of citizenship, and a commitment to homogeneity as recipe for unity and identity.

Admittedly, reference to Canada as a postnational society is less an accurate appraisal of reality but more of an ideal or an aspiration. It reflects a rebranding of Canada for the 21st century beyond those nationalisms that espouse a narrow-minded xenophobia and intolerance of difference. Alluding to Canada as postnational is an admission that Canada cannot afford to abide by conventional models of society-building, namely a strong central core, a homogenizing logic of governance, and a uniform population that subscribes to a single identity and singular way of belonging to Canada. A postnational ("postWestphalian") view of Canada that endorses doing citizenship differently is timely if it wants to stay in the game of being globally competitive yet nationally viable.

The concept of global citizen/citizenship traces its origins to the antiquity of ancient Greek philosophers who promulgated the idea of people as "citizens of the world" (ie cosmopolitans) (Karas, 2015). But consensus over the concept remains elusive despite the passage of time, resulting in a term fraught with uncertainty and imprecision (Kymlicka and Walker, 2012). This assessment is hardly surprising. Populations have historically organized themselves into groups or nations based on shared identity and singular membership. And they continue to do so despite the combination of modern communication and cosmopolitan idealogies that foster global outlooks of identity, community, and belonging (Israel, 2012). Complicating any clarification is an awareness that any reference to the cosmopolitanism of global citizen/citizenship is neither simple nor straightforward. Rather, it reflects a wide-ranging label for a host of disparate actions and outlooks, including those who (a) want to help the less fortunate of the world, (b) desire to easily travel and work outside of their home country (c) believe everyone should have the right to live and work wherever they choose based on an unfettered right to migrate or (d) are critical of national citizenships and nationalism as the source of much controversy and conflict. For some, a global citizen/citizenship connotes persons of education and insight, generally aware of contemporary issues such as social injustice, engaged in their communities and politics, and concerned with responsibility and caring for others beyond the borders of one's country (Byers, 2005). For others, global citizens embody a coalition of activist groups who put pressure on governments and corporations to enhance their public accountability and corporate responsibility, improve trade and labour practices, and display a commitment to environmental stewardship (Bennett, forthcoming). For still others, it calls attention to a set of institutional arrangements within the framework of a supra-state governance that value the inclusion of all humans regardless of where they live or who they are (Karas, 2015).

Reference to global citizen/citizenship represents a mode of identity and belonging based on the principle of universal personhood and the internationalization of human rights. In contrast to national patterns of identity formation, global citizens constitute individuals with a shared identity of an emerging world community and whose actions contribute to advancing the values and practices of this community (Israel, 2012). Cosmopolitans first and foremost see themselves as citizens of a world community rather than citizens of a specific country. Citizenship is applied to persons beyond the jurisdiction of the nation-state in a worldwide system that embraces a multi-centric (not state-centric) platform as basis for global governance. Weaker forms of cosmopolitanism put the emphasis on fostering moral concerns for all human beings, whereas stronger versions demand inclusion through equitable ("substantive") treatment (Miller, 2007).

Of course, the concept of global citizen in a cosmopolitan world does not constitute a legal status. What prevails, instead, is a discursive shift in rethinking the purpose of a national citizenship within a broader global context. It represents an exhortation (or an aspiration) to think, talk, and act *as if* the world was an imagined global community (Stromquist, 2009) A path is proposed for relating to humanity at large by applying an international perspective when addressing challenges such as respect for diversity, demands for social justice, and commitment to planetary survival (Sakhi, 2016; Shachar, 2009). Nor is the concept the same as or equivalent to national citizenship transposed to the global level (Byers, 2005). Citizenship rights do not exist at the international level—as proof consider the millions of stateless (without citizenship) persons in the world who languish in refugee camps or shantytowns without any legal rights or citizenship protections. Gross human rights abuses from Syria to Myanmar should further disabuse anyone of the futility in believing that repeating the mantra of a universal personhood will usher in a more humane world. Advocated instead under a cosmopolitan ideal is a new configuration of commitments, entitlements, and responsibilities beyond national-territorial boundaries—not in the sense of displacing national citizenship, but in extending its positives into a global sphere so that monopolies of power become accountable to those most affected by them (Lee, 2014; Linklater, 1998).

The link between global citizen/citizenship and cosmopolitanism is unmistakable. The idea of global citizenship may well provide a proxy or code to represent a cosmopolitan outlook that expresses loyalty and commitment to humanity at large rather than membership in a particular community (Bosniak, 2000; Israel, 2012). First principles are invoked to justify the cosmopolitans claim that we are first and foremost human beings, that our first allegiance is to the family of humankind rather than to nation or state, and that borders unjustly favour one group of individuals over the singular reality of humanity (Milikh, 2016). For example, critics of Australia's offshore refugee program argue that this country's obligation toward the broader community should take precedence over any threat to its sovereignty that boat-born asylum seekers might pose (Castles, 2016; Laughland-Booy et al., 2015). A global citizenship within a cosmopolitan context reflects a mindset that embraces the entirety of humanity by virtue of attending to common values and moral ideals of global responsibility and connectedness (Sfier, 2015). This global-friendly commitment is thought to transcend the biases, elitism, or dogmatism of particular cultural or religious groups; embrace a collective responsibility to protect and preserve the natural and human world; and endorse a deep investment in the world as a whole rather than identities defined in opposition to the national or ethnic other (Byers, 2005; Smith, 2007).

The implications of a cosmopolitan citizenship-global citizen nexus are far-reaching: As far as globalists and cosmopolitans are concerned, it's time to move beyond the stifling parameters of a national citizenship. For far too long, they argue, conceptions of citizenship revolved around the nation-state paradigm—a paradigm that generally rejects those multiple memberships and cross-border identities reflective of contemporary realities, while impeding the emergence of nested or multilayered polities that situate individuals as citizens of substate polities, the nations within, and suprastate communities (Baubock, 2007). The notion of a cosmopolitan citizenship (or more accurately, reframing citizenship from a cosmopolitan perspective) transcends this limitation by proposing an imagined citizenship ideal over a territorialized mode of belonging and spatialized identities (Nyamnjoh, 2007). Besides, cosmopolitans contend, narrow-minded identities and exclusive allegiances have reached the limits of their usefulness—an outdated vision of the world increasingly unliveable because of nationalist excesses (Gerzon, 2009; Israel, 2012). Or to paraphrase Einstein, we cannot solve problems by using the same thinking that created them. Our awareness must aspire to a new level by balancing the logic of national citizenship with the principle of universal personhood (Soysal, 1994).

Not everyone concurs with this aspirational ideal. Critics disagree with the concept of postnational, global, and cosmopolitan citizenship as a commitment that elevates the concept of status, identity, and belonging beyond the confines of a territorially-bounded nation-state. For them, citizenship only makes sense only in a context that emphasizes rights and enforces duties which individuals possess as members of bounded sovereign polities (Linklater, 1998; Miller, 2011). Outside of a state-centric context, the citizenship concept loses its meaning, rationale, and legitimacy, especially when divorced from territoriality, sovereignty, and nationality. Others disagree with this criticism. Reference to cosmopolitanism and global citizenship acknowledges the obvious. We no longer live in national citizenship world of discrete and sovereign nation-states that comprise the global order. Rather, reality and practices are pointing to increasingly trans-territorial and denationalized patterns of political, cultural, and social life including a commitment to a vision of citizenship that condones the universalistic principles of compassion, inclusion, responsibility, and openness to all. For in the final analysis, we are global citizens by definition of birthright and that alone behoves us to put the aspirational into practice through ideological platforms and institutional arrangements that recognize and promote our common humanity (Lee, 2016).

To be sure, an endorsement of both cosmopolitanism and global citizenship does not repudiate the centrality and guarantees of a national citizenship. A world convulsed by global flows and worldwide anxieties reinforces the centrality of nation-states and national citizenship in anchoring the protection of social and political rights (Skey, 2013). A "rooted cosmopolitanism" is proposed —*rooted*, as in particularist commitments, claims, and attachments; *cosmopolitanism* as in global commitments and universal aspirations. The idealized result is a shared social space that combines the equal moral worth of all individuals ("cosmopolitanism") with a sensitivity to the importance of local obligations, traditions, and relationships ("rootedness") (Appiah, 1997; Moore, 2010; Walker, 2011). Kwame Anthony Appiah (1997: 22) writes of a world where the national combines with a cosmopolitanism to transcend local borders:

> The cosmopolitan patriot can entertain the possibility of a world in which everyone is a rooted cosmopolitan, attached to a home of his or her choice, with its own cultural peculiarities, but taking pleasure from the presence of other, different, places that are home to other, different, people.

In other words, a commitment to global citizen/citizenship as rooted cosmopolitans neither precludes an identification with a national culture or attachment to co-nationals nor excludes a sense of belonging to a particular political community (Tan, 2015). A state of creative tension prevails instead that mediates the mutually reciprocating ideals of cosmopolitanism as justice and inclusion with that of nationality as identity and belonging.

To summarize, reference to global citizen/citizenship represents a new way for thinking, talking, and doing citizenship in the postnational age of globalization. Two aspects of globalization impact citizenship: First, the movement of people across more permeable borders raises the question of membership and rights; second, the proliferation of supra-state institutions and ideologies tend to diffuse those identities and belongings once monopolized by a national citizenship (Gans, 2005). To counterbalance these dynamics, a rooted global (cosmopolitan) citizenship reinforces how nation-states continue to matter as sources of identity, repositories of belonging, and channels for collective action (Kymlicka and Walker, 2012). It also accept the reality that national citizenships provide a bulwark against the excesses of inward looking ethnicities and insurgent nationalisms (Calhoun, 2007). The reconceptualization of citizenship within the cosmopolitanism of a postnational context provides a reminder of the challenges in store in balancing the global with the national. As Kymlicka and Walker (2012: 3) point out, any cosmopolitanism must be postcolonial in process and outlook insofar as cultural homogenization or political unification are rejectedin favour of cultural diversity and patterns of local autonomy. The objective of a rooted cosmopolitan citizenship instills a sense of national identity and belonging within each constituent group in society as well as promoting a kind of overarching identity and belonging that binds members into a national/global matrix (Kymlicka, 2001). Such a responsibility also adds another layer of responsibility to a worldwide network of community members who share a similar mindset in normatively valuing specific traditions yet simultaneously endorsing global values (Israel, 2012; Lenard and Moore, 2012).

Notes

1. Issues related to meaning of citizenship and what it means to be a citizen have assumed a renewed salience because of globalization and transnationalism (Preston et al., 2007). The terms 'globalization' and 'transnationalism' are not synonymous; rather, they differ (at least in theory if not necessarily in practice) in underlying assumptions about the role of the state with respect to the meaning of citizenship as identity and belonging. Globalization discourses focus on social processes that are largely decentred from and transcend specific national territories—i.e. the growing insignificance of borders and sovereign spaces to create interdependent market economies. By contrast, transnationalism draws attention to relations and processes that remain anchored in nation states (keep in mind the continuing significance of borders, sovereignties, national identities) even as transnational dynamics cross national borders or define political spaces to create new and lived-in fields of activity. Thus, the nation-state and transnational practices are constitutive of each other rather than mutually exclusive (Smith, 2003).

2. European nationals possess a unique dual citizenship arrangement. According to the 1992 Maastricht Treaty, every individual holding the nationality (citizenship) of a member state will be deemed to be a citizen of the European Union. Citizenship in the Union is a non legal status but focuses on the right to live and work anywhere in Europe, while remaining dependent on the nationality of a member state (Maas, 2013).

3. Canadians working abroad must pay federal and provincial tax on all or a portion of the income they earn if they continue to maintain a factual residency in Canada. Some argue the Canadian diaspora pay $6 billion in taxes each year yet rarely use the government services whose costs they help to defray (MacKinnon, 2015).

References

Akesson, Lisa. "Multicultural Ideology and Transnational Family Ties among Descendents of Cape Verdeans in Sweden." *Journal of Ethnic and Migration Studies* 37, no. 2 (2010): 217–235.

Anderson, Bridget . "Exclusion, Failure, and the Politics of Citizenship." Ryerson Centre for Immigration and Settlement. Working Paper No 2014/1. January, 2014.

Ang, Ien. "Navigating Complexity: From Cultural Critique to Cultural Intelligence." *Continuum: Journal of Media & Cultural Studies* 25, no. 6 (2011): 779–794.

Appiah, Kwame Anthony. "Cosmopolitan Patriots." *Critical Inquiry* 23, no. 3 (1997): 617–639.

Banerjee, Kiran. "Toward Post-National Membership? Tensions and Transformations in German and EU Citizenship." *Journal of International Law and International Relations* 10, (2014): 4–30.

Banfield, Samantha. "Australians Abroad: Preliminary Findings on the Australian Diaspora." Advance. Connecting Australians Globally. Retrieved from https:///www.advance.org. 2017

Banulescu-Bogdan, Natalia. "Shaping Citizenship Policies to Strengthen Immigrant Integration." MPI, August 2, 2012.

Baubock, Rainer. "Why European Citizenship? Normative Approaches to Supranational Union." *Theoretical Inquiries in Law* 8 (2007): 453.

Benhabib, Seyla. "Globalization Changing Nature of Citizenship Says Scholar. By Gila Reinstein." *Yale Bulletin & Calendar* Vol 31, 17. February 7, 2003.

Benhabib, Seyla. "Twilight of Sovereignty or the Emergence of Cosmopolitan Norms: Rethinking Citizenship in Volatile Times". *Citizenship Studies* 11, no. 1 (2007): 19–36.

Bennett, W. Lance. "Branded Political Communication: Lifestyle Politics, Logo Campaigns, and the Rise of Global Citizenship." In *The Politics Behind Products*. edited by M Micheletti, A. Follesdal and D. Stolle. New Brunswick NJ: Transaction Books, forthcoming.

Berns-McGown, Rima. "Redefining 'Diaspora': The Challenge of Connection and Inclusion." *International Journal* 63, no. 1 (2007–08): 3–21.

Bloemraad, Irene. "Who Claims Dual Citizenship? The Limits of Postnationalism, The Possibilities of Transnationalism, and the Persistence of Traditional Citizenship." *IMR* 38, no. 2 (2004): 389–426.

Bloemraad, Irene. "Theorizing and Analyzing Citizenship in Multicultural Societies." *The Sociological Quarterly* 56, no. 4 (2015): 591–606.

Bloemraad, Irene Anna Korteweg, and Gokce Yurdakul. "Citizenship and Migration: Multiculturalism, Assimilation, and Challenges to the Nation-State." *Annual Review of Sociology* 34 (2008): 153–179.

Bosniak, Linda. "Citizenship Denationalized (the State of Citizenship Symposium)." *Indiana Journal of Global Legal Studies* 7, no. 2 (2000): 447–512.

Bourne, Edmund J. *Global Shift: How a New Worldview is Transforming Humanity*. New Harbinger and Noetic Books, Oakland, CA., 2009.

Brubaker, Rogers. "The 'Diaspora' Diaspora." *Ethnic and Racial Studies* 28, no. 1 (2005): 1–19.

Brysk, Allison. *Global Good Samaritans: Human Rights as Foreign Policy*. New York: Oxford University Press, 2009.

Byers, Michael. "Are You a 'Global Citizen?" *The Tyee* October 5, 2005.

Calhoun, Craig. *Nations Matter: Culture, History, and the Cosmopolitan Dream*. New York: Routledge, 2007.

Castles, Stephen. "Rethinking Australian Migration." *Australian Geographer* 47, no. 4 (2016): 391–398.

Castles, Stephen, Hein de Haas and Marvin Miller. *The Age of Migration*. 5th edition. New York: Palgrave, 2013.

Conference Notes. "Rethinking the Transnational Perspective: Shortcomings and New Approaches." International Workshop, University of Fribourg, September 13–14, 2012.

Deckhard, Natalie Delia. "After Postnational Citizenship: Constructing the Boundaries of Inclusion in Neoliberal Societies." *Sociology Compass* 10, no. 4 (2016): 294–305.

Faist, Thomas. "Introduction: The Shifting Boundaries of the Political." In *Dual Citizenship in Global Perspective: From Unitary to Multiple Citizenship*, edited by T. Faist and P. Kivisto, 1–26. New York: Palgrave Macmillan, 2007.

Faist, Thomas and Jurgen Gerdes. "Dual Citizenship in an Age of Mobility." Transatlantic Council on Migration, a Project of the Migration Policy Institute, 2008.

Fernandes, Michael. "Is Canada a Post-National State?" *The Canadian Journal* July 28, 2016.

Fleras, Augie. *Immigration Canada*. Vancouver: UBC Press, 2014.

Fleras, Augie. "Beyond Multiculturalism: Managing Complex Diversities in Postmulticultural Canada." In *Revisiting Multiculturalism in Canada*, edited by L. Wong and S. Guo, 297–321. Rotterdam: Sense Publishers, 2015.

Fleras, Augie. "Re-imagining Citizenship in Canada, New Zealand, and Australia: Transnational Dynamics, Postnational Complexities, Postcitizenship Possibilities." Plenary Paper, Citizenship in a Transnational Context, University of Alberta, Edmonton, July 6–7, 2016.

Fleras, Augie. "Rethinking Citizenship Through a Transnational Lens: Australia, Canada, and New Zealand." In *Citizenship in Transnational Perspective: Australia, Canada, and New Zealand*, edited by Jatinder Mann, 15–48 New York: Palgrave, 2017.

Foran, Charles. "The Canada Experiment: Is This the World's First 'Postnational' Country?" *The Guardian* January 4, 2017.

Fox, Jonathan. "Unpacking 'Transnational Citizenship.'" *Annual Review of Political Science* 8 (2005): 171–201.

Gamlen, Alan. "Making Hay While the Sun Shines: Envisioning New Zealand's State-Diaspora Relations." *Policy Quarterly* 3, 4 (2007): 12–23.

Gans, Judith. "Citizenship in the Context of Globalization." Immigration Policy Working Papers, June. University of Arizona, 2005.

Garcea, J., A. Kirova, and L. Wong, "Introduction: Multiculturalism Discourses in Canada." *Canadian Ethnic Studies*, 40, 1 (2008): 1–10.

Gerzon, Mark. "Global Citizens, Part 1." *Kosmos* May 12, 2009.

Glick Schiller Nina. "Transborder Citizenship: An Outcome of Legal Pluralism within Transnational Social Fields." In *Mobile People, Mobile Law. Expanding Legal Relations in a Contracting World*, edited by F. Bender et al. 27–49. London: Ashgate, 2005.

Glick Schiller, Nina, Linda Basch, and Cristina Blanc-Szanton. "Transnationalism: A New Analytic Framework for Understanding Migration." *Annals of the NY Academy of Sciences* 645 (1992):1–24.

Glover, Robert W. "Radically Rethinking Citizenship: Disaggregation, Agonistic Pluralism, and the Politics of Immigration in the United States." *Political Studies* 59, no. 2 (2011): 209–229.

Goodman, Sara Wallace. *Dual/Multiple Citizenship*. Retrieved from http://www.springerreference.com. May 27, 2014.

Granastein, Jack. "Conflicted Over Citizenship." *Globe and Mail*, July 31, 2006.

Griffith, Andrew. "What Should Expatriate Voting Rights Be?" *Policy Options*, June 7, 2016.

Griffiths, Rudyard. *Who We Are: A Citizen's Manifesto*. Vancouver: Douglas & McIntyre, 2009.

Grundy, John and Miriam Smith. "The Politics of Multiscalar Citizenship: the Case of Lesbian and Gay Organizing in Canada." *Citizenship Studies*. Published online August 19, 2006: 389–404.

Guild, Elspeth. "Migration, Security, and European Citizenship." In *Routledge Handbook of Global Citizenship Studies*, edited by E. Isin and P. Nyers. 284–292. New York: Routledge, 2014.

Isin, Engin F. and Peter Nyers. "Introduction: Globalizing Citizenship Studies." In *Routledge Handbook of Global Citizenship Studies*, edited by E. Isin and P. Nyers. 1–11. New York: Routledge, 2014.

Israel, Ronald C. "What Does it Mean to be a Global Citizen?" *Kosmos*. Spring/Summer 2012.

Jedwab, Jack. "Dually Divided? The Risks of Linking Debates over Citizenship to Attachment to Canada." *International Journal* 63, no. 1 (2007–08): 65–78.

Joppke, Christian. "Dual Citizenship and Transnationalism in Europe." *Canadian Diversity* 6, no. 4 (2008): 17–20.

Kallio, Kirsi Pauliina and Katharyne Mitchell. "Re-Spatializing Transnational Citizenship." *Global Networks* 16, no. 3 (2016): 259–267.

Karas, Martin. "Europa." *Global Citizenship as Identity: Viable Alternative to Development or Reproduction of Western Hegemony? European Year of Development*. 2015. Retrieved from https://europa.eu

Katyal, Neal and Paul Clement. "On the Meaning of 'Natural Born Citizen.'" *Harvard Law Review* 128, 2110–2165, (2015)

Khanna Parag. *Connectography: Mapping the Future of Global Civilization*. New York: Random House, 2017.

Kingwell, Mark. "No Exceptionalism Please, We're Canadian." *Globe and Mail*, January 14, 2017.

Kivisto, Peter and Thomas Faist. *Citizenship: Discourse, Theory, and Transnational Prospects*. Oxford: Blackwell, 2008.

Kivisto, Peter. "Conclusion: The Boundaries of Citizenship in a Transnational Age." In *Dual Citizenship in Global Perspective: From Unitary to Multiple Citizenship*, edited by T. Faist and P. Kivisto, 272–284. New York: Palgrave Macmillan, 2007.

Kraus, Peter. "The Politics of Complex Diversity: A European Perspective." *Ethnicities* 12, 1 (2011):3–25.

Kymlicka, Will. *Politics in the Vernacular. Nationalism, Multiculturalism, and Citizenship*. Toronto: Oxford University Press, 2001.

Kymlicka, Will and Kathryn Walker. "Rooted Cosmpolitanism: Canada and the World." In *Rooted Cosmpolitanism: Canada and the World*, edited by W. Kymlicka and K. Walker, 1–27. Vancouver: UBC Press, 2012.

Laughland-Booy J., Z. Skrbis, and B. Tranter. "Crossing Boundaries: Understanding the Pro-Asylum Narratives of Young Australians." *Ethnicities* (2015): 1–18.

Lawson, Guy. "Trudeau's Canada, Again." *NY Times Sunday Magazine*, December 13, 2015: 1–13.

Lee, Charles T. "Decolonizing Global Citizenship." In *Routledge Handbook of Global Citizenship Studies*, edited by E. Isin and P. Nyers. 75–85. New York: Routledge, 2014.

Lee, Charles. *Ingenious Citizenship: Recrafting Democracy for Social Change*. Durham, NC: Duke University Press, 2016.

Leggewie, Claus. "Eurozine." *Transnational Citizenship. Ideals and European Realities*. Retrieved from http://www.eurozine.com, February 19, 2013.

Lenard, Patti Tamara and Margaret Moore. "A Defence of Moderate Cosmopolitanism and/or Moderal Liberal Nationalism." In *Rooted Cosmpolitanism: Canada and the World*, edited by W. Kymlicka and K. Walker, 47–68. Vancouver: UBC Press, 2012.

Linklater, Andrew. "Cosmopolitan Citizenship." *Citizenship Studies* 2, no. 1 (1998): 23–41.

Maas, Willem. *Multilevel Citizenship*. Philadelphia: University of Pennsylvania Press, 2013.

MacKinnon, Mark. "I Am Canadian—But Not as Much as I Used to Be." *Globe and Mail*, July 24, 2015.

Macklin, Audrey and Francois Crepeau. "Multiple Citizenship, Identity, and Entitlement in Canada." *IRPP*, June 22, 2010.

Macklin, Audrey. "The Securitization of Dual Citizenship." In *Dual Citizenship in Global Perspective: From Unitary to Multiple Citizenship*, edited by T. Faist and P. Kivisto, 42–68. New York: Palgrave Macmillan, 2007.

Mann, Jatinder (ed.). *Citizenship in a Transnational Perspective*. New York: Palgrave, 2017.

Metropolis. "Transnationalism and the Meaning of Citizenship in the 21st Century." Metropolis Conversation Series, 2007.

Millbank, Adrienne. "Dual Citizenship in Australia." *Current Issues Brief* 5 (2000–2001), November 28, 2000.

Milikh, Arthur. "Immigration, Citizenship, and Cosmopolitanism." *Public Discourse*, January 6, 2016.

Miller, David. "National Responsibility and Global Justice." Oxford Scholarship, 2007.

Miller, David. "The Idea of Global Citizenship." *Nuffield's Working Paper Series in Politics*, February 16, 2011.

Moore, Margaret. "Rooted Cosmopolitanism: A Defence of Moderate Cosmopolitanism and/or Moderate Liberal Nationalism." Paper presented to the Annual Meeting of the American Political Science Association, Washington, DC, September 2–5, 2010.

Nyers, Peter. "Dueling Designs: The Politics of Rescuing Dual Citizens." *Citizenship Studies* 14, no. 1 (2010): 47–60.

Nyamnjoh, Francis B. "From Bounded to Flexible Citizenship: Lessons from Africa." *Citizenship Studies*, Published online May 30, 2007.

Ong, A. *Flexible Citizenship.* Durham, NC: Duke University Press, 1999.

Papademetriou, Demetrios G. "Managing Rapid and Deep Change in the Newest Age of Migration." *The Political Quarterly*, Special Issue (2003): 39–58.

Parekh, Bhikhu. *A New Politics of Identity: Political Principles for an Interdependent World.* New York: Palgrave Macmillan, 2007.

Pecoud, Antoine and Paul de Guchteneire. "Global Migration Perspectives." No 27. Switzerland: Global Commission on International Migration, 2005.

Pedroza, Luicy and Pau Palop-Garcia. "The Grey Area Between Nationality and Citizenship: An Analysis of External Citizenship Policies in Latin America and the Caribbean." *Citizenship Studies.* Published online, April 19, 2017: 1–19.

Preston, Valerie, Myer Siemiatycki, and Audrey Kobayashi. "Dual Citizenship Among Hong Kong Canadians: Convenience or Commitment?" In *Dual Citizenship in Global Perspective: From Unitary to Multiple Citizenship*, edited by T. Faist and P. Kivisto, 203–221. New York: Palgrave Macmillan, 2007.

Renshon, Stanley. "Reforming Dual Citizenship in the United States." *Center for Immigration Studies.* October 2005.

Rodriguez, Cristina M. "Review: the Citizenship Paradox in a Transnational Age." *Michigan Law Review* 106, no. 6 (2008): 1111–1118.

Rodriguez, Cristina M. "Review: Beyond Citizenship: American Citizenship after Globalization." Peter Kivisto. New York University School of Law. Working Paper no 10–35, July 2010.

Sakhi, A. J. "Are You a Global Citizen?" *Huffington Post*, July 24, 2016.

Sandercock, Leonie. *Mongrel Cities of the 21st Century: In Defense of Multiculturalism.* Vancouver, UBC Laurier Lecture, 2006.

Satzewich, Vic, and Lloyd Wong (eds.). *Transnational Identities and Practices in Canada.* Vancouver: University of British Columbia Press, 2006.

Sejersen, T. B. "'I Vow to Thee My Countries'—The Expansion of Dual Citizenship in the 21st Century." *International Migration Review* 42, no. 3 (2008): 523–549.

Seymour, Michel. "Research Gate." *On Postnational Identity.* 2012. Retrieved from http://www.researchgate.net.

Sfier, Ghada. "A Cosmopolitan Outlook on Canadian Citizenship: A Case Study in Montreal." *In Education* 21, no. 1 (2015).

Shachar, Ayelet. *The Birthright Lottery: Citizenship and Global Inequality.* Boston: Harvard University Press, 2009.

Simmons, Alan. *Immigration and Canada. Global and Transnational Perspectives.* Toronto: Canadian Scholars' Press, 2010.

Skey, Michael. "Why Do Nations Matter? The Struggle for Belonging and Identity in an Uncertain World." *The British Journal of Sociology* 64, no. 1 (2013): 81–98.

Smith, Peter J. "The Impact of Globalization on Citizenship: Decline or Renaissance?" In *From Subjects to Citizens: A Hundred Years of Citizenship in Australian and Canada*, edited by P. Boyer et al., 301–309. Ottawa: University of Ottawa Press, 2004.

Smith, William. "Cosmopolitan Citizenship. Virtue, Irony, and Worldliness." *European Journal of Social Theory* 10, no. 1 (2007): 37–52.

Smith, Michael Peter. "Transnationalism and Citizenship." In *Approaching Nationalisms*, edited by Brenda Yeoh, 15–38. Boston: Kluwer, 2003.

Soffel, Jenny. "Are You a Global Citizen? New Poll Suggest Global Trumps National Identity." *World Economic Forum*, April 28, 2016.

Soysal, Yasemin Nuhoglu. *Limits of Citizenship*. Chicago: University of Chicago Press, 1994.

Soysal, Yasemin Nuhoglu. "Postnational Citizenship: Reconfiguring the Familiar Terrain." In *The Blackwell Companion to Political Sociology*, edited by Kate Nash and Alan Scott. Hoboken NJ: Blackwell, 2004.

Soysal, Yasemin Nuhoglu."Postnational Citizenship: Rights and Obligations of Individuality." Heinrich Boll Stiftung. Migrations Politisches Portal. May 18, 2011. Retrieved from https://heimatkunde.boell.de

Spiro, Peter J. "Dual Citizenship—A Postnational View." In *Dual Citizenship: Democracy, Rights, and Identities Beyond Borders*, edited by T. Faist. 1–18. New York: Palgrave Macmillan, 2006.

Spiro, Peter J. *Beyond Citizenship. American Identity After Globalizations*. New York: Oxford University Press, 2008.

Spoonley, Paul. *Rethinking Immigration*. Wellington: Asia-New Zealand Foundation, 2010.

Spoonley, Paul and Richard Bedford. *Welcome to our World? Immigration and the Reshaping of New Zealand*. Auckland: Dunmore Publishing, 2012.

Stromquist, Nelly P. "Theorizing Global Citizenship: Discourses, Challenges, and Implications for Education." *Inter-American Journal of Education for Democracy* 2, no. 1 (2009).

Stasiulis, Daiva. "Respatializing Social Citizenship and Security Among Dual Citizens in the Lebanese Diaspora." Paper presented to the Citizenship in Transnational Perspective Conference. Edmonton, University of Alberta, July 6–7, 2016.

Stasiulis, Daiva. "The Extraordinary Statelessness of Deepan Budlakoti: The Erosion of Canadian Citizenship Through Citizenship Deprivation." *Studies in Social Justice* 11, no. 1 (2017): 1–26.

Tan, Kathy-Ann. *Reconfiguring Citizenship and National Identity in the North American Literary Imagination*. Detroit: Wayne State University Press, 2015.

Todd, Douglas. "Trudeau Channelling John Ralston Saul on "Postnational" Canada." *Vancouver Sun*, March 17, 2016.

Triadafilopoulos, Triadafilos. *Becoming Multicultural. Immigration and the Politics of Membership in Canada and Germany*. Vancouver: UBC Press, 2012.

Urzi, Domenica and Colin Williams. "Beyond Post-national Citizenship: An Evaluation of the Experiences of Tunisian and Romanian Migrants Working in the Agricultural Sector of Sicily." *Citizenship Studies*. Published online, November 10, 2016, 136–150.

Walker, Kathryn. 2011. "Is Rooted Cosmopolitanism Bad for Women?" Retrieved from https://www.cpsa-acsp.ca.

Weinfeld, Morton. "Canadian Jews, Dual/Divided Loyalties, and the Tebbet "Cricket" Test." In *Revisiting Multiculturalism in Canada: Theories, Policies and Debates*, edited by Shibao Guo and Lloyd Wong, 141–158. Rotterdam: Sense Publishers, 2015.

Welsh, Jennifer. "Our Overlooked Diaspora." *Literary Review of Canada* (March 2011): 1–15.

Wessendorf, S. *Researching social relations in super-diverse neighbourhoods: Mapping the field.* IRiS Working Paper Series No 2. University of Birmingham, 2014

Williams, Rowan. "What Does a Good 21st Century Immigration Policy Look Like?" *New Statesman*, December 28, 2016.

Winter, Elke. "Becoming Canadian: Making Sense of Recent Changes to Citizenship Rules." IRPP Study No 44. January, 2014.

Winter, Elke. "Report on Citizenship Law: Canada." European University Institute, Florence, Robert Schuman Centre (2015).

Winter, Elke "Balancing Citizenship Rights in an Era of Globalization." Lightening Policy Brief Series. Carleton University Centre for European Studies/Canada-Europe Transatlantic Dialogue, March (2016).

Wong, L. L. "Transnationalism, Active Citizenship, and Belonging in Canada." *International Journal*, 63, no. 1 (2007/08): 79–100.

Yuval-Davis, Nira. "The 'Multi-layered' Citizen. Citizenship in the Age of 'Glocalization.'" *International Feminist Journal of Politics* 1, no. 1 (1999): 119–136.

· 7 ·

INDIGENIZING CITIZENSHIP, CITIZENIZING INDIGENEITY: CITIZENSHIP IN THE POSTCOLONIES

Introduction: The Citizens Within

The previous chapters have made it abundantly clear. The framework for becoming, being, and doing citizenship is undergoing a discursive shift in a world of posts, trans, and isms (Fleras, 2017b). The politics of accommodating new diversity dynamics and patterns—simultaneously fluid and non-linear as well as contested and politicized—put pressure on re-conceptualizing the accommodation of increasingly complex citizenship arrangements (Mann, 2017). Less credibility is attached to the once snug fit between citizenship and nationality that locked citizens into a specific nation-state and around a common set of values and entitlements. More credence is assigned to reformulating citizenship in a more nuanced way while questioning its embeddedness in territorially bounded nation-states increasingly at odds with a post-sovereign global order (Lightfoot, 2013). The attendant conflict of interest between nation-states and the nations-within generates an inherent ambiguity and instability which, in turn, expose the citizenship realm to controversy and change (Barreto and Lozano, 2017; Isin and Nyers, 2014).

Indigenous peoples represent another layer of complexity that complicates the dominant narrative of a national citizenship model. The challenge is animated in part by their constitutional status as the descendants of the original occupants who predated the creation of modern nation states, in part because of the transnational character of their territories, including the Haudenosaunee (Iroquois) Confederacy whose traditional lands span the Canadian-American border. Nation-state responses to these challenges such as unilaterally imposing yet more universal citizenship rights have proven largely unsatisfactory since such impositions tend to compromise inherent Indigenous rights to self-determining autonomy over identity and belonging. Even nation-states nominally committed to the principle of Indigenous rights are vexed by the prospect of forging a mutually satisfying framework that synthesizes state interests with Indigenous rights, while ensuring full and simultaneous exercise of Indigenous citizenship in both tribal nations and settler states (Cattelino, 2010). In an effort to unblock this governance gridlock, Indigenous activists and leaders are looking into multilevel (or dual or differentiated) citizenship models that, for all their imperfections, secure a working model for reconciling competing citizenship regimes. An Indigenous citizenship model also imparts a more inclusive yet customized framework for citizenship-making that addresses the complicated historical realities and trans-border complexities of Indigenous peoples politics (Lightfoot, 2013).

The politics of a postcolonial citizenship remains a contested site that pits Indigenous citizenship narratives against settler society prototypes (Cairns, 2001; Spoonley, 2015, 2016; Tawhai, 2016). Indigenous peoples have long experienced a complex and contradictory relationship to a national citizenship (Lightfoot, 2013). Too often they were denied citizenship on grounds of being too primitive or too doomed; or, conversely, they endured often aggressive pressure to citizenize through absorption into a settler citizenship (Maas, 2013). Citizenship symbolized a device of coercive exclusion and forcible inclusion insofar as Eurocentric assumptions and founding principles informed the concept of who belonged, how, and why. The imposition of a national citizenship regime tended to obscure the violence and suppression that accompanied the seemingly benign settler impositions of "peace, order, and good government" (Menon, 2009). Predictably settler-centric models of citizenship rarely resonate with the lived-realities of Indigenous peoples—especially when they are deprived of the right to *refuse* (emphasis, Humpage, 2008: 254) incorporation into what many perceive as assimilation by another name (also Simpson, 2007, 2014). Nor do state promises of justice through a universal citizenship carry much clout; after all, the Eurocentrism implicated in such a citizenship model neither reflects Indigenous realities nor advances their interests. It is both telling and alarming that governments in settler societies continue to endorse the principle of universality (namely, the incorporation of Indigenous peoples into society as equal citizens), despite Indigenous peoples demands for doing it differently. Such universalistic claims expose the homogenizing and controlling agendas of a national citizenship that often clash with Indigenous models of self-determining autonomy over identity and belonging (Humpage, 2015; Maaka and Fleras, 2005).

Clearly, then, the concept of a national citizenship poses a poor fit for Indigenous peoples (Chabot, 2007; Green, 2016). The domain of citizenship in settler societies countries is fraught with ambiguities and difficulties, inasmuch as they are constructed on assumptions that pre-empt the claims of Indigenous peoples for full recognition as the nations within (Dodson, 1993; Fleras and Elliott, 1991). A national citizenship represents a largely legalistic, territorially bounded, and Euro/state-centric concept whose universal and linear logic (i.e., undivided sense of loyalty and identity) and a politically infused values (such as liberal universalism) privilege vested interests at the expense of Indigenous peoples realities (Alfred, 2009). Reference to the idea of rights-bearing individuals under a liberal citizenship poses a problem in those Indigenous contexts that prefer to embed the collective concept of self hood within the reassuring confines of family, kin, community (Richardson, 2015). To further complicate matters, there is no neutral language that can be used to analyze Indigenous people's citizenship, apart from a Western context, given how a Euro-systemic bias informs the social constructedness of the citizenship concept. Nevertheless, Canada's Indigenous peoples often refer to themselves as citizens of nations rather than band members (Chabot, 2007), in effect appropriating the language of neocolonialism to frame their concerns and advance their interests (Dickson-Gilmore, 1999).

Such a governance dilemma raises a series of interesting questions. Is it possible to truly understand Indigenous citizenship models when filtered through the prism of Eurocentric lens? For example, the emergence of a cosmopolitan Indigenism incompasses a worldwide framework of belonging and identity through the creation of a global Indigenous identity that transcends national spaces (Levi and Durham, 2015). Yet such an Indigenous cosmopolitanism also embodies a contradiction. An Indigenous citizenship is, by definition, rooted and bounded, whereas cosmopolitanism reflects a global commitment to unbounded humanity above all other attachments. In other words, what happens when Indigenous notions of belonging and identity are no longer fastened to a fixed territorial setting (Forte, 2010) but exposed to the freer-floating realities of a universal personhood and transmigrant movements?

Such provocations make it doubly important to explore the mutually related concept of Indigenizing citizenship and citizenizing Indigeneity, that is, of seeing Indigeneity through the lens of citizenship and, at the same time, analyzing the concept of citizenship from an Indigenous perspective.

Indigenous peoples have taken measures to advance an Indigeneity-inclusive citizenship model. In doing so, they hope to disrupt the prevailing narrative of nation-state as a specific geographical space of one nation with a singular and uniform citizenship (Fleischmann and Styvendale, 2011). The challenge lies in establishing a multidimensional citizenship model that balances the individual rights of a national citizenship with collective rights of an Indigenous model within a context of shared commonalities yet distinct identities (Green, 2014; Lightfoot, 2013; MacDonald and Wood, 2016; Yashar, 2005). The rationale is justified on the basis of a key sociological distinction. To one side are voluntary minorities and migrants who want to "get in" to the existing system; to the other side are involuntary peoples who want to "get out" of a forcibly imposed political arrangement that doesn't work for them (Fleras, 2016): Whereas the conferral of dual citizenship among transmigrant or multicultural groups reinforces their inclusion as equals into Canadian society (Kymlicka and Norman, 2000), Indigenous citizenship models embrace the politics of refusal (Simpson, 2014)—a strategic exclusion from a national citizenship mode that contains and controls (also Merry, 2013). Of particular relevance in advancing an Indigenous citizenship model is a commitment to governance arrangement anchored in the nation-to-nation principle of intra-state sovereignty, a relationship built on a resource-based and a power-sharing partnership, and a commitment to constructive engagement that embraces yet simultaneously resists state-centric authority (Humpage, 2008; Maaka and Fleras, 2005). And yet, despite the injuries and exclusions of a national citizenship, both in the past and at present, Indigenous nations are unwilling to discard those individual rights and entitlements that flow from this legal status. They prefer, instead, to differentiate themselves as the "citizens within" who combine belonging to Indigenous communities with membership in the nation state. Or phrased differently, Indigenous peoples possess the right to maintain their rights to Indigenous citizenship models while reclaiming their right as national citizens to participate freely in the political affairs of the state (Maas, 2013). In doing so, the concept of an Indigenous citizenship in a postnational context represents a postcolonial shift not only in how we think, talk, and engage citizenship, but also in the notion of becoming, being, and doing citizenship.

The CANZUS countries have responded to these challenges in different ways. Responses have revolved around measures that, at times, reinforce the exclusion of Indigenous peoples from full and equal citizenship rights ("citizen-minus"); at other times through initiatives that promote inclusion ("fitting into") by way of a *citizens-plus* ("add-on") status (Cairns, 2001); at still other times through inclusivity measures that attend to Indigenous citizenship models in redefining ("refitting") the rules for belonging and identity along an *Indigeneity-plus* matrix. The citizenship situation of Native Americans is somewhat more complicated and deserving of attention because of their Indigeneity-minus status as "domestic dependent nations" (Fleras and Elliott, 1991). This chapter advances the concept of a postnational citizenship by demonstrating how Indigenous citizenship models challenge the (neo)colonialism that informs Indigenous peoples-state relations, reject the legitimacy of a settler citizenship agendas, traverse the internal boundaries of a national citizenship model, and bolster a pan-Indigenous sense of identity that advances a global embrace in tandem with a tribal orientation. The chapter examines the relational status of Indigenous peoples in the CANZUS countries with respect to the citizenizing of Indigeneity as a political project. Their constitutional status as the nations within allows the chapter to focus on the dynamics and postcolonial logic of Indigenizing citizenship by way of Indigenous citizenship models. Particular attention is directed at the Nisga'a First Nations of British Columbia in demonstrating the viability of a postcolonial citizenship model based on the principle of Indigeneity-plus. Reference to Indigenous citizenship as a lens, a discursive framework, and a contested terrain of struggles and transformations allows this chapter to address the politics, processes, and conditions that include yet exclude the "citizens within" across the settler domains of Canada, United States, Australia, and New Zealand.

First Australians as Citizens-Minus

Australia's treatment of its First Inhabitants has shown overall if selective improvement (based on a Multicultural Policy Index, 2016). Nevertheless, the collective status of Indigenous Australians (namely, Aboriginal and Torres Strait Islanders) remains an uneven work in progress. Unlike Canada and New Zealand, there is no history of treaty making or a constitutional recognition of the First Australians. Such an omission ensures Indigenous Australians remain second class citizens in a systemic white society that denies their distinctiveness and heterogeneity, frames them as minorities with needs rather than peoples with rights, condemns them to patterns of assimilation or segregation, refuses to offer any meaningful self-determination pathways, and exposes them to bureaucratic control and surveillance (Briskman, 2014; Gerber, 2012; Webb, 2013; West-McGruer and Humpage, 2015). The impact of this institutionalized indifference and benign neglect in marginalizing their lives and life chances should not be underestimated. Like Indigenous peoples in Canada, the First Australians find themselves at the bottom of every socio-economic indicator while coping with assimilationist pressures that threaten their language, culture, and identity.

Promises of equal rights and full democratic citizenship for First Australians have proven a cruel hoax. They politely glossed over the lived-realities of an embedded inequality, a violent dispossesson, and ongoing marginalization, in the process reinforcing their collective status as citizens minus or citizens without rights (Chesterman and Galligan, 1997; Mercer, 2003; Peterson and Sanders, 1998; Tatz, 1999; Walter, 2014). What is particularly striking in reinforcing this citizen-minus status was the collusion of various Australian States in manipulating the law to deny citizenship rights, while curtailing the right of First Australians to work, move freely, receive an education or access to health care, marry, and consume alcohol. The Aboriginal and Torres Strait Islander Social Justice Commission, Mick Dodson, took white Australia to task when he described pre-1967 First Australians as citizens-minus (cited in Mercer, 2003: 431): "We were not free…to travel between imposed state borders or within states—no matter where the borders of our country lay—and we were not entitled to an Australian passport. We had to have permission to marry…".

Australian citizenship emerged as a legal category with passage of the Nationality and Citizenship Act in 1948. But while the First Australians were accorded formal citizenship rights under the Act, they were denied the substantive rights that render a citizenship meaningful rather than "hollow" in the words of John Chesterman and Brian Galligan (1997; also Peterson and Sanders, 1998). Not only were they excluded from Commonwealth citizenship entitlements due, in part, to a dearth of any constitutional or legislative recognition of their citizenship rights. They also were barred from State citizenship entitlements, including the right to vote in West Australia (granted in 1962) and Queensland (1965). Many were denied access to social security entitlements until 1959 (and not until 1966 for those deemed to be nomadic or primitive); others, in turn, were subject to intrusive levels of state surveillance to prevent waste, ensure conformity and discourage lawlessness (Chesterman and Galligan, 1997).

In short, formal citizenship rights were one thing, substantive citizenship outcomes were quite another. Conferral of formal citizenship removed many of the overt barriers to participation; nevertheless, blatantly discriminatory legislation remained in effect across the country. Despite government duplicity and mainstream indifference, the First Australians slowly moved toward a measure of substantive citizenship rights, albeit within the framework of anglo conformity and assimilationist ethos. In 1962, they received the right to vote at Commonwealth level although, unlike non-Aborigines, the First Australians were not required to register until 1983 (Mercer, 2003). The 1967 Citizenship Referendum endowed the Commonwealth (federal) government with the constitutional authority to make laws on behalf of the Indigenous Australians (until 1967, every state had the power to make laws exclusively for the First Australians [Brennan, 2011]). The referendum also voted to include First Australians in the national census; prior to that, the Commonwealth constitution had excluded them from the Australian population count. Nevertheless, birth registrations as a precondition for eventual voter registration remain an ongoing problem in outlying regions (also Chapman and Cannon, 2017 for Canada).

In hopes of expanding the substantive basis of citizenship for First Australians, the Whitlam government in 1972 introduced a policy of self-determination (Jupp, 2008). This initiative represented a major policy shift—at least in theory if not in practice. Promises of substantive change were offset by the imposition of a bureaucratic blanket with little in the way of community empowerment, institutional capacity-building, sustained funding, or power-sharing. It most certainly excluded any inclination toward a framework for advancing tribal models ofself-determining autonomy over land, identity, and political voice (Webb, 2013). Ironically, the principle of self-management as the capstone of government policy had a perverse effect. It reinforced the status of First Australians as a hapless population who must be prodded into more self-responsibility to overcome self-induced failures especially in those communities defined as crisis zones (Brigg and Curth-Bibb, 2017; MacDonald and Muldoon, 2006). Even Australia's belated recognition of native land title—including the Mabo decision in 1992 and the Wik decision in 1996—did not bolster their self-determining rights in any appreciable manner (Chesterman and Galligan, 1997; Webb, 2013). In other words, abolishing the doctrine of a terra nullius ("empty lands") that historically defined Australia-Indigenous people's relations did little to disrupt a corresponding psychological terra nullius (Behrendt, 2002). Such a debilitating mindset not only misrepresents Aborigine interests or ignores them (Hobbs, 2016; Wahlquist, 2016; Davidson, 2016). It also reinforces their status as citizen minus or citizens without rights of a constitutional nature (Webb, 2013).

The challenge is abundantly clear if Indigenous Australians are to contest a citizen-minus status. Their priority-plus status as First Australian with attendant powers and entitlements that flow from this recognition must be acknowledged and enforced (Peterson and Sanders, 1998). Such a commitments puts the onus on factoring Indigenous rights into a modern conception of Australian citizenship, not only to ensure formal recognition of their group-specific rights as the "first among equals" but also to secure their individual rights as Australian citizens (Dodson, 1993; Gunstone, 2016).

Citizen-Plus in Aotearoa New Zealand

The New Zealand state has long struggled to find a working balance between competing claims; on the one hand, the principle of Crown sovereignty; on the other hand, preexisting forms of Indigenous citizenship (Jones, 2016; Spoonley, 2016). Maori tribes who comprise the Indigenous peoples (*tangata whenua*) of New Zealand occupy a de facto dual (or differentiated) citizenship status as citizens-plus. This citizenship-plus status springs from the principle of *tino rangatiratanga* ("chiefly authority" or "self-determining autonomy") as stipulated by the Treaty of Waitangi/*Te Tiriti o Waitangi* which itself has acquired something of a constitutional status over the years (McMillan, 2004). Signed in 1840 but generally dismissed as constitutionally relevant until the mid-1970s, *Te Tiriti* continues to attract controversy, largely because the English and Maori versions convey diametrically opposed interpretations. Article 2 of the Treaty (Maori version) secured a guarantee of *tino rangatiratanga*, that is, continuation of Maori authority and control over land, dwelling places, *taonga* (ancestral treasures) in addition to protection of *tikanga* (customs, codes) under existing law and custom (Durie, 2006; Roughan, 2005; Salmond, 2012). By contrast, the English translation of Article 2 entitled Maori to full exclusive and undisturbed possession of land and resources until they saw fit to sell to the Crown. In Article 1 of the English version, Maori cede to Queen Victoria all rights and powers of sovereignty whereas Maori version relinquished only the *kawanatanga* (governorship) or right to appoint a governor (for example, the northern Ngapuhi tribes vehemently deny ceding sovereignty to the Crown). The third article in both Maori and English acknowledged the Queen's royal protection and conferral of rights and privileges of British subjects (Salmond, 2012; Stephens, 2016). These rights were once challenged on grounds that the communal nature of Maori land tenure disqualified them from enfranchisement, but subsequently restored and reaffirmed in the Native Rights Act,

1865. Nevertheless, full enjoyment by Maori of their citizenship rights was often compromised because of the gap between lofty political promises and the precariousness of Maori realities (Green, 2005; Thrupp, 2016).

A Maori reading of *Te Tiriti* points to the inescapability of a constitutionally defined dual Maori citizenship—both as British subjects/New Zealand citizens and as members of commununal organizations such as *iwi/hapu* (tribes/subtribes) with corresponding rights over land/resources/*taonga* (treasured things) (Pearson, 2010; Spoonley, 2007). Such a reading espouses Maori not as an ethnic minority with needs but as a peoples with rights including the right to ownership of pre-existing property, identity and culture, and de facto sovereignty (MacDonald and Muldoon, 2006). It also reinforces a territorialized sense of belonging and citizenship from which Maori as groups and individuals draw meaning, formulate identity, foster a sense of continuity, and construct their own cultural memories of space and time beyond the frames of official state narratives (Kidman, 2015). The citizenization of Maori under the Treaty yields two interpretations: Aotearoa New Zealand represents a binational state of differentiated citizenships where different political communities must negotiate their respective claims as nations in a spirit of wisdom and generosity rather than a competitive game of victors and vanquished (Fleras and Spoonley, 1999). Alternatively, it could be argued that Maori citizenship represents an "add on" ("citizens-plus") that is nested into a national citizenship rather than displacing it. This latter interpretation stakes out a middle ground between assimilation and parallelism in light of those policy and institutional arrangements that simultaneously acknowledge the citizen—plus status of Maori as the *tangata whenua o Aotearoa* yet reinforce a common citizenship that binds together all New Zealanders (also Cairns, 2001).

Indigenous Citizenship in the US: Native *and* American

Native Americans in the US possess an ambivalent relationship to the politics of citizenship (Lightfoot, 2013; Singer, 2013). Federal Indian Law was founded on the principle of Native American tribes as separate political entities (not simply minority communities or racial groups) within their territorial boundaries (Tsosie, 2016). Federally recognized Native Americans are thus not subject to constitutional restraints and largely exempt from state jurisdictional authority, thanks to their status as domestic dependent nations (semi-sovereign), with an attendant right to set their own citizenship criteria (Wilkins, 2014). But contradictions are rife. The federal government may have recognized tribal sovereignty as inherent, including the power to determine membership and citizenship, yet Congress continues to claim plenary (absolute) power over tribal nations. Moreover, the federal government has resorted to a series of interventions including trusteeship, assimilation, and termination to dispossess Native Americans of their land and resources (Lightfoot, 2013).

The relationship between Native Americans and federal government reflects an Indigeneity-minus model that reinforce the contentious politics of US citizenship and the demands of tribal self-determining autonomy (Tsosie, 2016). According to Rebecca Tsosie, four historical citizenship frames characterized—and continue to characterize—the status of Native Americans under federal Indian law: Native Americans as citizens of separate nations that constitute a third level of sovereignty alongside of the federal and state governments (Lightfoot, 2013; Tsosie, 2016); as wards of the federal government; as American citizens; and as a racialized minority groups. A fifth frame may be discerned that recognizes the right to self-determination which, paradoxically, marks a return to the first historical frame. It should be noted that all five frames may operate concurrently (Tsosie, 2016), in the process generating confusion and controversy because of overlapping and contested jurisdictional frames. Consider how Native Americans are treated as racial minorities for civil rights purposes, but as semi-sovereign members under federal Indian law with inherent rights to tribal authority. This commitment to a differentiated citizenship status tends to generate conflicts when courts must decide on whether to treat Native Americans as equal citizens for purposes of anti-discrimination law or as dual citizens of federally recognized tribal nations.

Prior to the Civil War, Native Americans found themselves in a jurisdictional limbo. They may have been subjects of the US, yet Native Americans were neither defined as citizens nor could they become naturalized as Americans since they were not foreigners (Ojibwa, 2010). The Fourteenth Amendment in 1868 seemingly conferred citizenship on Native Americans on grounds that "all persons born or naturalized in the United States, and subject to the jurisdiction of, are citizens of the United States and the state wherein they reside". But it become clear the Amendment was aimed at enfranchising now emancipated male black (former) slaves instead of Native Americans who were denied citizenship rights including the right to vote on grounds they did not fall under American jurisdiction. They were defined and dismissed, instead, as uncivilized members of foreign nations ("tribes") or as hapless wards of the state. It should be noted that some Native Americans did acquire citizenship by marrying out, while others eventually received citizenship through military service, payment of taxes, receipt of land allotments, or through special arrangements such as rejection of tribal life. For example, the Dawes Severalty Act of 1887 granted full citizenship to Native Americans who renounced both their tribal affiliations and claim to tribal lands (i.e. agreed to the division of tribal lands on a freehold basis). The 1890 Indian Territory Naturalization Act allowed any members of an Indian tribe in Indian Territory (now Oklahoma) to apply for citizenship through the federal courts without necessarily renouncing tribal membership—a nascent form of dual citizenship (Ojibwa, 2010). In 1919, Congress passed an act which conferred automatic citizenship to those Native Americans who served in the military during the First World War.

Passage of the 1924 Indian Citizenship Act consolidated the citizenization of all Native Americans, although it's estimated that about two thirds of all Native Americans had already acquired citizenship prior to this legislative change. The Act bestowed (or imposed) American citizenship on all Indians born in the US by automatically naturalizing all Native Americans who at that time were non citizens, while ensuring for all American-born Indians the same rights as natural-born citizens. As well, the provisions of the Act ensured that nothing would impair, supersede or remove Indigenous tribal rights, in effect establishing a framework for multilevel or dual citizenship status (Lightfoot, 2013). Accordingly, Native Americans did not have to apply for American citizenship nor did they have to relinquish their tribal affiliation. The Act ostensibly equipped Native Americans with the right to vote, obligation to do military service, and payment of taxes for off-reserve revenues. It also symbolized the political expression of America's assimilationist agenda by bringing Indigenous peoples into the fold through incorporation into civil and criminal law (Ojibwa, 2010).

Not all Native Americans concurred with this unilateral ("without their consent") conferral of a national citizenship (Lightfoot, 2013; Tsosie, 2016). The constituent tribes of the Iroquois Confederacy rejected the imposition of American sovereignty and citizenship preferring, instead, to assert their autonomous identity as preexisting sovereign nations on lands spanning the Canada and the US borders ("we didn't cross borders, borders crossed us"). They maintain that, by definition, treaties acknowledge and preserve their sovereignty as nations—a claim reinforced by a multi-country acceptance of Iroquois-issued passports as valid travel documents until 2001 (Lightfoot, 2013). Furthermore, the imposition of full citizenship rights on all Native Americans did not remove the stain of exclusionary practices. A number of the States took the position that the 1924 Act did not expressly grant state citizenship rights to Native Americans living on reservations (Tsosie, 2016). For example, seven states in 1938 refused to allow voting rights on grounds that Native Americans were exempted from paying real estate taxes, maintained tribal affiliations, and lived under federal guardianship. Neither Arizona nor New Mexico allowed Native Americans the right to vote in state elections despite their military duty during the Second World War. By 1948, however, all states with large Native American populations had extended voting and citizenship rights in compliance with federal court orders. Utah became the last state in 1957 to repeal the law against voting by allowing the Native American vote in the 1962 elections. And yet, citizenship disappointment outweigh citizenship promises. Although Native Americans possess a differentiated (tripartite) citizenship based on rights that derive from US citizenship, state citizenship and tribal nations citizenships (Wilkins, 2014), principles do not always match practices. Significant socio-economic gaps between Native Americans and non-Amerindians reinforce an Indigeneity-minus status, while providing a reminder of the distance to travel before an Indigeneity-plus status becomes a lived-reality.

Indigeneity-Plus Model in Canada

It is the right of the First Nations to determine their own citizenship and that no legislation of Canada can interfere with the right. Assembly of First Nations, September 1982, the House of Commons Subcommittee on Indian Women and the Indian Act

Canada's Indigenous people have long endured a frosty relationship to Canadian citizenship. To one side, a state-centric citizenship was understood as an institution of domination and exclusion that stratified members of society into a hierarchy of members and non-members. Indigenous peoples were marked for cultural (and possibly physical) extinction, often despised as little more than an unwelcome irritant (due to a lack of civilization, Christianity, and commerce) at odds with Canada's progress and prosperity. They were denied access to Canadian citizenship (including the right to federal vote until 1960) unless individuals voluntarily relinquished their Indian Act status and renounced their indigeneity, proved themselves sufficiently civilized by becoming self-sufficient farmers, and demonstrated a willingness to assimilate into mainstream Canada (Blackburn, 2009; Kornelsen, 2015; Thobani, 2007).

Contradictions prevailed, including an institutionalized gender bias. Indigenous women who married a Canadian male automatically became Canadian citizens, as did their children, but with an attendant loss of their Indian status and entitlements. In contrast, Indigenous males who married out did not lose their status. Conversely, female Canadian citizens who married status Indians lost their Canadian citizenship, likewise their children. In short, the Indian act encouraged enfranchisement and Canadian citizenship. Yet the price of admission was steep in accelerating the loss of Indigenous political status and corresponding entitlements. A rejection of Canadian citizenship on symbolic grounds reinforced an Indigenous apprehension that any commitment and participation could be interpreted as legitimizing an institution that historically excluded or oppressed (Green, 2016; Woons, 2014).

To the other side, the offer a national citizenship with its promise of inclusion, equality, and protection may have been tempting. But the benefits of formal entry in the Canadian political community proved illusory. From 1857 when Upper Canada passed an Act to Encourage the Gradual Civilization of the Indian Tribes to the 1969 White Paper, the objective of Canada's Indian policy rarely swayed from its central preoccupation: to extinguish Indigenous peoples distinctiveness through absorption into a common citizenship (Woons, 2014). But as far as Indigenous peoples were concerned, the universality of a national citizenship infringed on their unique identities, collective and inherent rights, constitutional and treaty rights, and rights to Indigenous models identity and belonging (Papillon, 2016; Scholtz, 2006). The bestowal of a national citizenship glossed over the injustices and oppressions of the colonial past and the chronic inequalities in a neocolonial present (Hebert and Wilkinson, 2002). It also compromised their collective rights to Indigenous models of self-determining autonomy over land, identity, and political voice (Lightfoot, 2013). In other words, to become a Canadian citizen ran the risk of forfeiting their recognition as the nations within, with a corresponding loss of constitutional priority and treaty rights (Fleras and Elliott, 1991; Henderson, 2002; MacDonald and Muldoon, 2006; Mhurchu, 2014).

Questions arise in debating Indigenous citizenship. How have colonial laws and policies including the 1876 Indian Act affected Indigenous notions of traditional citizenship? Are arrangements possible that entitle Indigenous peoples to reclaim self-autonomous communities as the primary locus of citizenship identity without repudiating the benefits of national citizenship? Alan Cairn's in his book Citizen-Plus (2001) has argued in defense of a framework that promotes Indigenous people's citizen-plus right to a citizenship that is both integrative and accommodative. Is there room for a distinctive Indigeneity oriented citizenship in a Canada that espouses a civic-based citizenship regime? (see Insight Post below) Despite incompatibilities, alternative citizenship models exist, based on the principle of Indigeneity-plus as basis for belonging, identity, and entitlements (Palmeter, 2017) and consistent with United Nations Declaration on the Rights of Indigenous Peoples in defending an Indigenous right to both autonomy and societal participation (Lightfoot, 2013).

Take for example, the case of the Nisga'a peoples who identify as Canadian through membership as Nisga'a First Nation citizens (Hanvelt and Papillon, 2005). The Nisga'a First Nation endorsed an Indigenous-plus citizenship model through a treaty settlement with the federal/BC provincial governments that come into effect in 2000 (Blackburn, 2009). The Nisga'a Citizenship Act secured Nisga'a control over membership criteria, with a corresponding right to call themselves "citizens of the Nisga'a nation" without revoking their status as citizens of Canada albeit through affiliation in the Nisga'a nation. Every Nisga'a participant who is a Canadian citizen or a permanent resident of Canada automatically becomes a Nisga'a citizen who must abide by the Oath of Nisga'a Citizenship "Will you be loyal to the Nisga'a Nation, uphold its values, protect and obey its constitution and fulfil your duties as a Nisga'a citizen?" The Nisga'a Citizenship Act defines who is a Nisga'a citizen (based on matrilineal ancestry), how a non-Nisga'a may acquire the right to vote and stand for office, who can own Nisga' a village entitlements, and who qualifies for benefits such as housing grants (McKay, 2011). Nisga'a citizens possess Indigeneity-plus rights such as self-government and land rights that elude other minorities in Canada, although the Nisga'a nation cannot claim exclusive jurisdiction or unrestrictive sovereignty (for example, it can't issue passports or control entry into Canada). Nevertheless, Nisga'a laws rather than provincial and federal laws exercise paramount authority over realms that impact Nisga'a lives and lived realties. Finally, the Nisga'a broke with Canadian convention by referring to themselves as citizens rather than as individual band members or as participants in land settlement agreements (Lightfoot, 2013).

The implications of this postcolonial turn acknowledges the duality of an Indigeneity-plus citizenship status. In moving from an Indian Act band to a self-determining autonomous nation, the Nisga'a nation has crafted a novel citizenship space in Canada whose jurisdictional authority is differently sourced from provincial and federal orders of government. The Royal Commission on Aboriginal Peoples (RCAP, 1996) also argued that Indigenous peoples are both Canadian citizens and citizens of their particular nation—a form of dual citizenship along the lines of the nations within (Fleras and Elliott, 1991; Maaka and Fleras, 2005). Admittedly, as Sheryl Lightfoot (2013) argues, Nisga'a citizenship is not strictly dual in the sense of formal citizenship in two separate sovereignties. More accurately, it represents a multilevel citizenship that aspires to a distinct form of self-determining political autonomy within the overarching territoriality of the Canadian state. At the core of this differentiated or dual citizenship is the right of Indigenous nations to define who belongs, how they belong, and what belonging entitles rather than relying on the Canadian state as the final arbiter of what constitutes membership, identity, and entitlements (also Dickson-Gilmore, 1999). A differentiated citizenship capitalizes on those collective and inherent rights that reflect the relationship of Indigenous peoples to ancestral land, their constitutionally and treaty based entitlements, and their identity as a preexisting political community (Blackburn, 2009; Henderson, 2002). The Indigeneity-plus logic behind Nisga'a citizenship also announces the possibility of a postcolonial citizenship as a discursive template for living together separately as power sharing partners (Fleras, 2017a). That, in turn, poses the question of Canada's forbearance in recognizing the concept of an ethnicity-based Indigenous citizenship model (jus sanguinis) at odds with Canada's civic-based national citizenship regime—as the next Insight Post demonstrates

Insight Post

The Politics of Blood Quantum and Kahnawa'ke Citizenship: Race or Survival?

"We are not Canadian citizens. We are North American Indians" Chief Clarence Simon, Kanesatake Mohawk (cited in Fleischmann and Styvendale 2011: xi)

This Insight Post examines the struggles over citizenship and membership in the Mohawk nation of Kahnawa'ke where issues of blood quantum, Indian status, and entitlement intersect and clash over the politics of belonging and entitlements (Dickson-Gilmore, 1999). The Post points out the challenges in reconciling competing models of citizenship—an ethnic model (blood and ethnicity) in defining First Nations identity (Napolean, 2001) vs a civic model that prevails in English speaking Canada based on individual choice, commitment to human rights, and rule of law. Do Indigenous models of citizenship have the right to define who belongs even if membership codes run afoul of national preferences or international human rights standards (Lightfoot, 2013)? The Post also demonstrates how the politics of citizenship in Canada are driven by debates over whose governance will prevail in defining who belongs, how they belong, and what belonging entitles (Curtis, 2015). In doing so, this case study grapples with the thorny issue of exercising and extending a sovereign state's powers without compromising the fair and just treatment of all its citizens (Singer, 2013)?

The Kahnawa'ke Mohawk on Montreal's South Shore are members of the 150,000 strong Iroquois (or Haudenosaunee) Confederacy, parts of which straddle the Canadian-American border in Ontario and Quebec. Like many other Iroquois peoples, including the community at Akwasasne/ St Regis which too is partitioned by an international border, the Kahnawa'ke First Nations engage in what Audra Simpson (2007, 2014) calls the "politics of refusal". They reject the legitimacy of Canadian law or Canada's sovereignty over them since the Mohawk nation neither relinquished its independence ("sovereignty") nor abdicated jurisdiction over territory or peoples. They also refuse to recognize or accept the validity of either Canadian or American citizenship, while insisting on their inherent rights to define who membership and entitlements. In that their status as sovereign both collective and inherent has never been usurped by treaty or declaration between Iroquois and Europeans, a distinctive relationship is proposed based on the Two Row Wampum Treaty with the Dutch in 1613 which affirmed the partnership of two distinct peoples coexisting separately on shared land.

Ottawa may claim that it alone has final say over who is a member of the Kahnawa'ke Mohawk. Nevertheless, the federal government seems unwilling to force the issue by compelling the Kahnawa'ke Mohawk to stand down. Several consequences follow from this political expediency. First, Mohawk prefer to travel on a Haudenosaunee passport issued by their confederacy as a symbol of their identity and citizenship as a sovereign peoples, although these passports are now rejected by the UK, USA, and Canada because they no longer meet post 9/11 security requirements). Second, Canadian authorities rarely interfere in businesses considered illegal by the Canadian state (from online gaming operations to cigarette smuggling) if practiced on Mohawk land as an extension of their territorial sovereignty (Horn-Miller and Horn-Miller 2014). Third, a band council decision to evict non Mohawk married to Mohawk was deemed regrettable by the federal government, but legal (or at least understandable), because of a Mohawk constitutional right to define membership codes and secure their cultural integrity.

In 1981, the Kahnawa'ke council imposed a moratorium on band member intermarriage to non-Indians or the adoption of non-Indians. According to the ban, any Kahnawa'ke Mohawk who married, cohabited or lived in common law with a non-Indian would lose membership benefits and privileges such as access to land allotment or voting rights. Three years later, in anticipation of impending changes to the Indian Act provisions regarding Indian status and band memberhip, the Mohawk council unilaterally declared full power and control over Kahnawa'ke membership and citizenship, including the rights of residence on band land, right to vote in Council elections, access to a burial plot in Kahnawa'ke territory, and some services administered by the council (Dickson-Gilmore, 1999). The loss of franchise—perhaps the most fundamental of citizenship rights—was appealed by affected members, but to little avail as the then Department of Indian Affairs and Northern Development recoiled from any involvement, dismissing the controversy as a local matter (Dickson-Gilmore, 1999). The subsequent removal of unattached "non-Indians" from the reserves proved relatively straightforward; more perplexing was the problem of what to do with "non-Indians" whose presence on reserve territory was acquired through mixed race marriage or adoption into the community.

To address this challenge, the council ruled on mixed race marriages as illegal ("marry out, get out"). This ruling was followed by a moratorium on such marriages. The 1984 the Mohawk Citizenship Law demanded a 50 percent blood quantum as grounds for incorporation into the Mohawk registry, although exceptions for non-Indians were possible if resolved through community deliberations (Social Development Unit, 2007). The 2003 Kahnawa'ke Membership Law replaced the 1984 Mohawk Law. It focused less on blood quantum but more on addressing the eligibility of those who could become members or reside in the community (for example reinstatement of membership if a Mohawk divorces a non-Indigenous partner) through assistance in rebuilding their ancestry and family ties (Social Development Unit, 2007). Both the moratorium and the citizenship law that limits the rights of non-Indian residents continue to generate controversy (Curtis, 2015; Deer, 2016; Horn-Miller and Horn-Miller, 2014; also ICMN Staff, 2003).

To be sure, the Mohawk council's requirement that a resident person possess 50 percent Indigenous ancestry is not without precedent. Canada itself through the 1876 Indian Act had imposed (and continues to apply) a similar formula to determine who is a status Indian (Curtis, 2015). The US during the late 19th century also employed one-half Indian blood quantum criteria to restrict the redistribution of land to Native Americans (ICMN Staff, 2003). Nevertheless, reaction to the "marry out, get out" ruling has proven fierce and contested. On one side is the exclusive membership perspective that views lineage (descent or blood) as the crucial indicator of belonging (King and Deer, 2015). Restrictions over membership and belonging are animated by a fear of losing what little is left of Mohawk indigeneity in a Canada that remains hostile to Indigenous sovereignty claims (Simpson, 2014). Additional concerns include worries that too much intermarriage will create a community so ethno-racially diluted that its distinctiveness as a culture, language and identity would be imperilled (Kahanwa'ke Mohawk Chief Michael Delisle, cited in Kay, 2015).

On the other side is an inclusive perspective among those Indigenous folk who disagree with the idea of blood quantum as a measure of Indigenous identity (Horn-Miller and Horn-Miller, 2014). According to the critics, the Kahnawa'ke "marry out, get out" ruling is a racist violation of human rights that cowers behind the smokescreen of cultural survival and community preservation to justify its bias toward racial purity. What's proposed instead is a right to an identity and belonging based on a more open community concept, not circumscribed by strict ancestral connection, but animated by principle of justice and human rights (King and Deer, 2015; Palmeter, 2017). This position is consistent with the conclusion of RCAP Report (1996) including the right of Indigenous nations to determine their own citizenship model as an existing Aboriginal and treaty right as set out in section 35(1) of the Constitution Act, 1982. But in determining the membership of who belongs RCAP proposes Indigenous nations develop a complex of criteria that reflect their status and existence as inclusive political and cultural entities. To do otherwise by relying on blood quantum as a general precondition is criticized as unconstitutional, wrong in principle, inconsistent with many Indigenous traditions, and an impediment to their development and status as autonomous political communities.

References

Alfred, Taiaiake. "First Nations Perspective on Political Identity." *First Nations Citizenship Research and Policy Series*. June 2009.

Barreto, A.A. and K. Lozano. "Hierarchies of Belonging: Intersecting Race, Ethnicity, and Territoriality in the Construction of US Citizenship." *Citizenship Studies* Published online, 3 August (2017):1–16.

Behrendt, Larissa. "Mabo Ten Years On: A Psychological Terra Nullius Remains." *Impact* July 2002: 1, 8–9.

Blackburn, Carole. "Differentiating Indigenous Citizenship: Seeking Multiplicity in Rights, Identity and Sovereignty in Canada." *American Ethnologist* 36, no. 1 (2009): 66–78.

Brennan, Elliot. "On this Day, Indigenous People Get Citizenship." *Australian Geographic* May 27, 2011.

Brigg, Morgan and Jodie Curth-Bibb. "Recalibrating Intercultural Governance in Australian Indigenous Organisations: The Case of Aboriginal Community Controlled Health." *Australian Journal of Political Science*. Published online January 31, 2017: 1–19.

Briskman, Linda. "Citizens or Denizens: The Stolen Generations in Australia." In *Reconfiguring Citizenship: Social Exclusion and Diversity within Inclusive Citizenship Practices*, edited by L. Dominelli and M. Moosa-Mitha, 105–116. Burlington, VT: Ashgate, 2014.

Cairns, Alan. *Citizen-Plus: Aboriginal Peoples and the Canadian State*. Vancouver: UBC Press, 2001.

Cattelino, Jessica R. "Thoughts on the U.S as a Settler Society." *Plenary Remarks*, *Society for the Anthropology of North America* 14, no. 1 (April 2010):1–6.

Chabot, Lynn. "The Concept of Citizenship in Western Liberal Democracies and in First Nations: A Research Paper." Prepared for the Governance Policy Directorate, Lands and Trusts Services. INAC, March 2007.

Chapman, Don and Chris Cannon. "Canadian Citizenship Must Be a Constitutional Right." *Globe and Mail* February 25, 2017.

Chesterman John and Brian Galligan. *Citizens without Rights: Aborigines and Australian Citizenship*. Melbourne: Cambridge University Press, 1997.

Curtis, Christopher. "Kahnawake Evictions: Mohawks, Feds on Collision Course." *Montreal Gazette* December 11, 2015.

Davidson, Helen. "Indigenous Affairs: Kenbi Land Claim Settled after 37 Year Battle." *The Guardian* April 6, 2016.

Deer, Jessica. "Membership Scraps Blood Quantum, But Not Really.". *The Eastern Door*, June 10, 2016.

Dickson-Gilmore E. J. "Iati-Onkwehonwe: Blood Quantum, Membership, and the Politics of Exclusion in Kahnawake." *Citizenship Studies* 3, no. 1 (1999): 27–43.

Dodson, Mick. "Aboriginal and Torres Strait Islander People and Citizenship." Speech at the Complex Notions of Civic Identity Conference, University of New South Wales, August 20, 1993.

Durie, Mason. "Measuring Maori Well-Being." New Zealand Treasury Guest Lecture Series. August 1, 2006.

Fleischmann, Aloys N. M. and Nancy van Styvendale. "Introduction." In *Narratives of Citizenship: Indigenous and Diasporic Peoples Unsettle the Nation State*, edited by Aloys Fleischmann, Nancy van Styvendale, and Cody McCarroll. 1–15, Edmonton: University of Alberta, 2011.

Fleras, Augie. *Unequal Relations*. 8th edition. Toronto: Pearson, 2016.

Fleras, Augie. *Inequality Matters*. Toronto: Oxford University Press, 2017a.

Fleras, Augie. "Rethinking Citizenship Through Transnational Lenses." In *Citizenship in a Transnational Perspective*, edited by J. Mann, 15–48. New York: Palgrave Macmillan, 2017b.

Fleras, Augie and Jean Leonard Elliott. *The Nations Within*. Toronto: Oxford University Press, 1991.

Fleras, Augie and Paul Spoonley. Recalling Aotearoa. Melbourne: Oxford University Press, 1999

Forte, M. *Indigenous Cosmopolitans*. New York: Peter Lang, 2010.

Gerber, Paula. "Aboriginal People are Still Denied Full Citizenship." *The Drum* (Australian Broadcasting Corporation), October 31, 2012.

Green, David. "Te Ara—The Encyclopedia of New Zealand." *Citizenship—1840–1948: British Subjects*. February 8, 2005.

Green, Joyce. "Introduction: Honoured in their Absence: Indigenous Human Rights." In *Indivisible: Indigenous Human Rights*, edited by J. Green, 1–16. Halifax: Fernwood, 2014.

Green, Joyce. "The Impossibility of Citizenship Liberation for Indigenous Peoples." Paper presented to the Citizenship in Transnational Perspective Conference, Edmonton, University of Alberta, Edmonton, July 6–7, 2016.

Gunstone, Andrew. "The Australian Reconciliation Process: A Case Study of Community Education." In *The Palgrave International Handbook of Education for Citizenship and Social Justice*, edited by A. Peterson, R. Hattam, M. Zembylas, and J. Arthur, 187–204. New York: Palgrave Macmillan, 2016.

Hanvelt, Marc and Martin Papillon. "Parallel or Embedded? Aboriginal Self-Government and the Changing Nature of Canadian Citizenship. *In Insiders and Outsiders:Alan Cairns and the Reshaping of Canadian Citizenship*. edited by G. Kernerman and P. Resnick. Pp. 242–257. Vancouver: UBC Press

Hebert, Yvonne M. and Lori Wilkinson. "The Citizenship Debates: Conceptual, Policy, Experiential, and Educational Issues." In *Citizenship in Transformation in Canada*, edited by Y. M. Hebert, 3–36. Toronto: University of Toronto Press, 2002.

Henderson, Sakej Youngblood. "Sui Generis and Treaty Citizenship". *Citizenship Studies* 6, no. 4 (2002): 415–440.

Hobbs, Harry. "The Uluru Decision Highlights What's So Wrong with Indigenous Policy." *The Guardian*, April 21, 2016.

Horn-Miller, W. and K. Horn-Miller. "Kahanwake First Nation Attacking the Human Rights of its Citizens." *CBC News*, November 3, 2014.

Humpage, Louise. "Revision Required: Reconciling New Zealand Citizenship with Maori Nationalisms." *National Identities* 10, 3. (2008): 247–261.

Humpage, Louise. *Policy Change, Public Attitudes and Social Citizenship*. Boston: Polity Press, 2015.

ICMN Staff. "Blood Quantum Wins at Flathead, Membership Decline Predicted." *Indian Country Today*, January 24, 2003.

Isin, Engin F. and Peter Nyers. "Introduction: Globalizing Citizenship Studies." In *Routledge Handbook of Global Citizenship Studies*, edited by E. Isin and P. Nyers. New York: Routledge, 2014.

Jones, Carwyn. "'All the Rights and Privileges of British Subjects': Maori and Citizenship in Aotearoa New Zealand." Paper presented to the Citizenship in Transnational Perspective Conference, University of Alberta, Edmonton, July 6–7, 2016.

Jupp, James. "Citizenship in Australia." *Canadian Diversity* 6, no. 4 (2008): 21–26.

Kay, Barbara. "Kahnawake's 'Marry out, stay out' Policy is About Survival, Not Race." *National Post*, May 27, 2015.

Kidman, Joanna. "Maori Young People, Nationhood and Land." *Geographies of Children and Young People* 3 (2005):1–19

King, Hayden and Jessica Deer. "Who Belongs on a Reserve: First Nations Will Decide." *Globe and Mail*, May 21, 2015.

Kornelsen, Derek Wayne. "Postcolonial Citizenship: Reconceiving Authority and Belonging in Settler Societies." PhD Thesis, Vancouver, UBC, 2015.

Kymlicka, Will and Wayne Norman (ed.). *Citizenship in Diverse Societies*. New York: Oxford University Press, 2000.

Levi, J. M. and E. Durham. "Indigeneity and Global Citizenship." In *Indigenous Education*, edited by W. J. Jacob et al. 395–437. Dordrecht: Springer Science + Business Media, 2015.

Lightfoot, Sheryl. "The International Indigenous Rights Discourse and its Demand for Multilevel Citizenship." In *Multilevel Citizenship*, edited by Willem Maas, 127–146. Philadelphia: University of Pennsylvania Press, 2013.

Maaka, Roger, and Augie Fleras. The Politics of Indigeneity: Challenging the State in Canada and Aotearoa New Zealand. Dunedin, NZ: University of Otago Press, 2005.

Maas, Willem. *Multilevel Citizenship*. Philadelphia: University of Pennsylvania Press, 2013.

MacDonald, Fiona and Ben Wood. "Potential Through Paradox: Indigenous Rights as Human Rights." *Citizenship Studies*. Published online, February 9, 2016.

MacDonald, Lindsay, Te Ata O Tu and Paul Muldoon. "Globalisation, Neo Liberalism, and the Struggle for Indigenous Citizenship." *Australian Journal of Political Science*. Published online, August 15, 2006.

Mann, Jatinder. "Introduction." In *Citizenship in a Transnational Perspective*, edited by J. Mann, 1–14. New York: Palgrave Macmillan, 2017.

McKay, Kevin. "Nisga'a Citizenship—Negotiation, Implementation and Administration." Presented by the Chair of the Nisga'a Lisims Parliament for AFN National Forum on First Nations Citizenship. November 2011.

McMillan, Kate. "Developing Citizens. Subjects, Aliens, and Citizens in New Zealand since 1840." In *Tangata, Tangata: the Changing Ethnic Contours of New Zealand*, edited by P. Spoonley and C. Macpherson, 267–290. Auckland: Thomson, 2004.

Menon, Nivedita. "Thinking Through the Postnation." *Economic and Political Weekly* 44, no. 10 (2009): 70–77.

Mercer, David. "Citizen Minus? Indigenous Australians and the Citizenship Question." *Citizenship Studies* 7, no. 4 (2003): 421–425.

Merry, Michael S. *Equality, Citizenship, and Segregation. A Defense of Separation*. New York: Palgrave Macmillan, 2013.

Mhurchu, Aoileann Ni. "Citizenship Beyond State Sovereignty." In Routledge Handbook of Global Citizenship Studies. edited by E Isin and P Nyers (eds.). 275–284. New York: Routledge.

Multiculturalism Policy Index. "Multiculturalism Policies in Democratic Countries." Retrieved from http://www.queensu.ca/mcp. June 18, 2016.

Napolean, Val. "Extinction by Number: Colonialism Made Easy." *Canadian Journal of Law and Society* 16, no. 1 (2001): 113–145.

Ojibwa. "Native American Netroots." *American Indian Citizenship*. Posted February 28, 2010.

Palmeter, Pam. "Indigenous Identity and Citizenship." *Summary of Research Project Funded by SSHRC, Canada*. Toronto: Ryerson University, 2017.

Papillon, Martin. "Abstract: From Second-Class to Multilevel Citizenship: Indigenous Peoples and Canada's Neocolonial Citizenship Regime." Paper presented to the CPSA 2016 Annual Conference Programme. June 2016. University of Calgary.

Pearson, David. "Citizenship, 'Culturalisms" and Civic Pluralism: Comparing New Zealand and Australia." In *Cultural Citizenship and the Challenges of Globalization*, edited by W. Ommundsen, M. Leach, and A Vandenberg, 147–164. Cresskill, NJ: Hampton Press, 2010.

Peterson, Nicolas and Will Sanders (eds.). *Citizenship and Indigenous Australians: Changing Conceptions and Possibilities*. Cambridge: Cambridge University Press, 1998.

Richardson, Diane. "Rethinking Sexual Citizenship." *Sociology*. Published online before print, November 11, 2015.

Roughan, Nicole. "Te Tiriti and the Constitution: Rethinking Citizenship, Justice, Equality, and Democracy." *New Zealand Journal of Public and International Law* 3 (2005): 285–303.

Royal Commission on Aboriginal Peoples. "Report: Restructuring the Relationship." 2, Part 1. Ottawa, 1996.

Salmond, Anne. "Ontological Quarrels: Indigeneity, Exclusion, and Citizenship in a Relational World." *Anthropological Theory* 12, no. 2 (2012): 115–141.

Scholtz, Christa. *Negotiating Claims*. New York: Taylor and Francis, 2006.

Simpson, Audra. "On Ethnographic Refusal: Indigeneity, 'Voice', and Colonial Citizenship." *Junctures* 9 (2007): 67–76.

Simpson, Audra. *Mohawk Interruptus: Political Life Across the Borders of Settler States*. Durham, NC: Duke University Press, 2014.

Singer, Joseph William. "Tribal Sovereignty and Human Rights." *Michigan State Law Review*. (2013): 307–334.

Social Development Unit. "Membership. Mohawk Council of Kahnawa'ke." October 2007.

Spoonley, Paul. "UNESCO." *Migration and the Reconstruction of Citizenship in Late Twentieth Century Aotearoa. Migration and Citizenship—Aotearoa—APMRN*, 2007. Retrieved from http://www.unesco.org.

Spoonley, Paul. "New Diversity, Old Anxieties in New Zealand: the Complex Identity Politics and Engagement of a Settler Society." *Ethnic and Racial Studies* 38, no. 4 (2015): 650–661. Originally published online, November 19, 2014.

Spoonley, Paul. "Renegotiating Citizenship: Twenty-First Century Citizenship and Indigeneity in Aotearoa New Zealand." Paper presented to the Citizenship in Transnational Perspective Conference, University of Alberta, Edmonton, July 6–7, 2016.

Stephens, Mamari. "'To Work Out Their Own Salvation.' Maori Citizenship and the Quest for Welfare in the Modern New Zealand State." Paper presented to the Citizenship in Transnational Perspective Conference, University of Alberta, Edmonton, July 6–7, 2016.

Tatz, Colin. Genocide in Australia. Research Paper No 8. Published by AIATSIS, Canberra, 1999.

Tawhai, Veronica M. H. "Indigenous Peoples and Indigeneity." In *The Palgrave International Handbook of Education for Citizenship and Social Justice*, edited by A. Peterson, R. Hattam, M. Zembylas, and J. Arthur, 97–119. New York: Palgrave Macmillan, 2016.

Thobani, Sunera. *Exalted Subjects*. Vancouver: UBC Press, 2007.

Thrupp, Martin. "The Political Rhetoric and Everyday Realities of Citizenship in New Zealand Society and Education." In *The Palgrave International Handbook of Education for Citizenship and Social Justice*, edited by A. Peterson, R. Hattam, M. Zembylas, and J. Arthur, 509–521. New York: Palgrave Macmillan, 2016.

Tsosie, Rebecca. "The Politics of Inclusion: Indigenous Peoples and U.S. Citizenship." *UCLA Law Review* 63 (2016): 1692–1755.

Wahlquist, Calla. "Indigenous Owners Outraged at Site Earmarked for Australia's First Nuclear Waste Dump." *The Guardian*, April 29, 2016.

Walter, Maggie. "The Race Bind: Denying Australian Indigenous Rights." In *Indivisible: Indigenous Human Rights*, edited by J. Green, 43–64. Halifax: Fernwood, 2014.

Webb, Jill. "Indigenous Peoples and the Right to Self Determination." *Journal of Indigenous Policy* no. 13 (2013): 75–91.

West-McGruer, Kiri and Louise Humpage. "Indigenous Stakeholders? Theorizing External Citizenship for Maori in Australia." *MAI Journal* 4, no. 2 (2015): 104–118.

Wilkins, David E. "Dismembering Natives: The Violence Done by Citizenship Rights." *Indian Country*. Posted May 16, 2014.

Wood, Patricia K. "Aboriginal/Indigenous Citizenship: An Introduction." *Citizenship Studies* 7, no. 4 (2003): 371–378.

Woons, Marc. "Decolonizing Canadian Citizenship: Shared Belonging, Not Shared Identity." *Settler Colonial Studies* 4, no. 2 (2014): 192–208.

Yashar Deborah J. "Citizen Regimes and Indigenous Politics in Latin America." Proto-Paper prepared for "Claiming Citizenship in America." A Conference Organized by the Canadian Research Chair in Governance and Citizenship. May 27, 2005.

· 8 ·

RETHINKING CITIZENSHIP IN A POSTCITIZENSHIP AGE

Introduction: The Postcitizenship Politics of Citizenship

To say we live in provocative and perplexing times is (to borrow a phrase) a cliché of understated proportions. The movement of people and diversification of mobility on an unprecedented scale elevates the politics of citizenship into one of the more perplexing and provocative challenges of the 21st century (Fleras, 2017b; Mann, 2017). The border-busting dynamics of transmigration and transnationalism are unsettling conventional citizenship models as sources of social control, national identity, and societal unity. Orthodox patterns of belongings and identities are increasingly contested in a diasporic and hyperdiverse world of contradictions and confusions as both crossings and connections encounter stricter citizenship protocols and ramped-up border surveillance. Irregular migrants (from asylum seekers to undocumented workers to stateless persons) are blurring the boundaries of citizenship by stretching the parameters of who belongs and how. Claims-making activities and identity politics create unique sovereign spaces and sites of resistance that generate new subjectivities of identity and belonging. No less disruptive to the society-building project is the growing popularity of the cosmopolitan principle in forging new patterns of membership and entitlements (Kymlicka and Walker, 2012). This humanistic commitment to universal personhood and a global citizenship without borders adds yet another layer of complexity to an already complicated world (Fleras, 2014).

That the domain of citizenship represents a site of contestation, change, and contradiction is hardly surprising (Isin and Nyers, 2014). The citizenship field is littered with paradoxes and perplexities that render it difficult to arrive at any sweeping generalizations. This assessment exposes how the politics of citizenship in defining who belongs, how they belong, and what belonging entitles are politicizing citizenship in ways unimaginable just a few years ago. The politics of how we think, talk, and do citizenship remain as contested as ever because of unresolved tensions that politely paper over inconvenient truths. The following disjunctures are particularly noteworthy: (a) citizenship remains territorially bounded despite the realities of an increasingly unbounded world (b) legal citizenship rights neither lead to substantive equality nor reflect group aspirations (c) an abstract or formal citizenship does not always connect with people's lived-realities (d) a static and singular citizenship may not prove a good fit with a "multiversal" world of hyper-diversities (e) a one-size-fits-all citizenship compromises the prospect of a differentiated citizenship (f) the promise of a cosmopolitan ("global") citizenship clashes with the realities of state-centric citizenship regimes and (g) a commitment to universalism masks a systemic bias, while subjecting it to criticism as assimilationist, marginalizing and controlling. No less contested are competing conflicts of interest. Those Indigenous, racialized, ethnic, sexual, dis/ableist, and gender identities at the margins of society demand recognition and accommodation through counterclaims that expose the Eurocentricity of a national citizenship model (Fleischmann et al., 2011; Isin, 2015). Of particular note in unsettling settler citizenship regimes are Indigenous peoples' insistence on regime-changes that prioritize their group-differentiated rights as the nations within without forfeiting their individual citizen rights (Maaka and Fleras, 2005).

Clearly, then, the concept of citizenship is both political and increasingly politicized. Conceptualizing citizenship as politics provides a useful interpretive lens for exposing power and unequal relations, assessing the dynamics and structures of oppression, and developing claims-making strategies that resist, disrupt, and transform (Field, 2007; Hines, 2009; Peled, 2007; Wood, 2003). Issues of equality and inclusiveness among racialized minorities, immigrants and refugees, and Indigenous peoples are now constructed and framed as a right of citizenship (Ang, 2009). The politics of citizenship also acknowledge that how we frame and explain citizenship no longer coincides with the priorities and legalities of national citizenship but reflect assumptions that go beyond a universalistic citizenship to embrace a particularistic, contingent, and culturally constructed version (Ivic, 2016).

Contemporary debates about identity and belonging as well as entitlements and social justice increasingly revolve around citizenship politics. Hardly surprising; after all, if membership in a political community constitutes the primary social good from which all other goods flow ("the right to *claim* rights" as insightfully rephrased by Isin and Nyers (2014), the politics of citizenship play a pivotal role in redefining who gets what and why. Assumed initially as a mark of membership and corresponding rights within a bounded political community, the politicization of citizenship as discourse (narrative) and doing (performance) subjects it to multiple meanings over time and across space, in response to internal pressures (Simmons, 2010) and in reaction to external dynamics (Jackson, 2015). Normative citizenship frameworks grounded in the primacy of the territorially bounded nation-state no longer speak with authority to the multiplicities of belonging and modalities of identity in a transnational world of flux and fluidity. Singular and static versions of citizenship have come under scrutiny as outdated and counterproductive in a changing and hyperdiverse world, in effect shifting the discursive frame of reference from legal definitions and formal attributes to contested narratives that unsettle and resist dominant imaginaries of belonging and identity (Cho, 2007; Delanty, 2007a,b; Edmundson et al., 2009; Tan, 2015; Theophanous, 1994).

Challenges to national citizenship models are putting pressure on deconstructing a settler-centric citizenship (Tonkiss and Bloom, 2015). The combination of international migration and the internationalization of human rights decentralizes the concept of membership and identity in a national group, although the state remains the most important location for legal citizenship (Tarozzi and Torres, 2016). Citizenships are increasingly viewed as coexisting in multiple forms and at multi-layered levels of political incorporation; intersecting with different axes of social division such as gender, race, and class; embodying both practice and performance as well as status and rights; and extending beyond the nation-state to incorporate the multi-national and the diasporic (Tonkiss and Bloom, 2015). The resultant identity crisis of confidence is hardly surprising. Most citizenship regimes were designed for a less complex, more immobile, and a diversity-aversive world that extolled the virtues of a national citizenship as the building blocks of society. Now, however, a commitment to the principle of universal human rights as the sine qua non of citizenship is challenging a belief in citizenship as a society building exercise. In attending to the crisis of a citizenship transitioning along postcitizenship lines, a key question captures the issue at hand. Are the CANZUS countries prepared to dislodge settler-centric citizenship models for more multicentric-inclusive citizenship models without impugning their status as immigration societies, a de facto commitment to multicultural principles, and claims to a postcolonial reality?

The transformations are palpable. Conventional models of citizenship are being contested in a rapidly changing and increasingly diverse world of posts, trans, and isms. We no longer live in Wesphalian citizenship world of a statist and homogenizing ("one-size-fits-all") logic, but increasingly in an emergent post-Westphalian (or postcitizenship) world organized around the primacy of globalization, the dilution of national identity and dispersal of authority in a transmigrant world of comings and goings, and the increased attention to a human rights agenda and the principle of universal personhood as basis for citizenship (Bloemraad, 2004). Nevertheless, citizenship as a legal status of formal rights (including the right to have rights or to claim rights) remains firmly under state control, thus confirming how the nation-state is not fading away but reinventing itself (Tarozzi and Torres, 2016). Scholars, too, are more receptive to the idea of a citizenship whose scope goes beyond the confines of a legal status. Citizenship is increasingly conceived as a performative practice embedded in everyday actions as people construct meaning, negotiate identity, and enact membership (Isin and Nyers, 2014; Stasiulis, 2017). For example, a duty based citizenship may have prevailed in the past when the good citizen acknowledged an obligation (such as voting), blind loyalty, and deference to authority. But the past few decades have heralded another set of citizenship norms—those of an engaged citizenship—with its focus on more direct approach to governance (activism), tolerance toward others, and concern for the well being of global others (Dalton, 2008). Young adults (millennials) are seemingly reluctant to adopt a citizenship mired in expectations of duty and obligation ("dutiful citizen model"). They prefer an actualizing citizenship model that favours a loosely network of community-based actions and activism (from anti-consumerism to community volunteering to transnational social movements) sustained through friends, peer relations, and social media ties (Bennett, 2007).

The paradoxes of citizenship are keenly experienced by those minorities at the margins. Citizenship as a key concept in debating social (in)justice looks very different to those on the outside looking in, compared to those securely inside and on the right side of the entitlement divide. For example, legally settled migrants enjoy a different citizenship reality than those undocumented or irregular who endure a punitive and restrictive set of exclusions (Urzi and Williams, 2016). Racialized immigrants and minorities perceive conventional citizenship models as systemically biased despite their claim to universality and inclusiveness. They may possess the same formal citizenship rights as all citizens; however, these rights must be exercised in a citizenship context neither designed to reflect their experiences or realities nor constructed to advance their interests or aspirations. Indigenous peoples, too, are chaffing against the Eurocentricity[1] implicit in a state-centric citizenship regimes preferring, instead, to endorse Indigenous-plus (or postcolonial) models of citizenship that acknowledge their inherent and collective rights as the nations within without foreclosing access to their constitutional citizenship rights. In other words, just as there is considerable value in framing the politics of inequality through the prism of a postcitizenship lens, so too is it worthwhile to employ a postcitizenship lens to reframe the inequities of racialization, immigrant status, and Indigeneity.

The accelerated realities of a postcitizenship world are dislodging those citizenship frames that no longer apply, although new citizenship models are not yet ready to dominate (also Isin and Nyers, 2014). At the crux of this pending erasure is the discursive demise of static, singular, and state-centric notions of citizenship that historically informed national models, yet can no longer abide by the realities and demands of a rapidly changing and increasingly hyperdiverse world. Another conundrum in the making reflects the push of transnationalism, a proliferation of diasporic linkages, and the ideals of universal personhood in globalizing the citizenship concept, in contrast to the particularist pull of ethnonationalism, the politics of Indigeneity, and the intensification of a multiversal world of diverse-diversities. The cumulative impact of a world of mobility, cosmopolitanism, and multicentricity unsettles the relevance of a territorially-bounded citizenship model, especially when peoples' notions of belonging and identity are gradually uncoupled and despatialized by transnational dynamics and postnational discourses. Debates and discourse about citizenship increasingly revolve around a post-structuralist understanding of individuals as a complex intersection of multiple, situated, and shifting subject positions; an anti-essentialist focus on identity as a social construct; a postcolonial emphasis on hybridity and third space; Foucauldian references to power as dispersed and capillary; and the Derridean idea of meaning as shaped by shifting contexts (Ang, 2011). Equally disruptive to the national citizenship project is a growing awareness that we longer occupy homogeneous, bounded, and stable "thick" communities, but rather coexist in "light" communities of individuals who construct and engage, yet share little beyond these situated experiences (Perez-Milans and Soto, 2017). These social and ideological transformations put the onus on rethinking (a) the meaning of citizenship in light of identities and belongings that are transitioning along transnational lines; (b) the evolving and contested relationship between citizens and the state in the 21st century world of posts, trans, and isms, and (c) the possibility of an inclusive postcitizenship as a discursive framework for differently accommodating a diversity of belongings.

The theme of no longer but not yet is inescapable. Ours may be a postcitizenship era in terms of how we think, talk, and do citizenship; nevertheless, the paramountcy of a national citizenship persists. The assumptions, logic, and characteristics of national citizenship are increasingly out of touch with the emergent realities, discourses and practices of a postcitizenship (or a postWestphalian) world. The centuries-long covenant (or social contract) between citizen and state in circumscribing the parameters of membership, commitments, and entitlements is now unravelling and contested (Stoker, 2011). Not surprisingly, a national citizenship no longer commands the clout it once did in framing references to access, membership, and entitlements; in defining patterns of becoming, being, and doing citizenship; and in specifying the parameters of a meaningful citizenship in a world whose conceptual moorings are increasingly adrift. Consider the politics at play because of the social, economic, and spatial transformations associated with globalization and the incorporation of new forms of mobility, transnationality and the connectivity of universal personhood (Clark and Savage, 2016; Gans, 2005). To one side of the political divide is the persistence of a national world of borders, the homogenizing logic of nation-state, and commitment to the principles of a spatialized national citizenship. To the other side of the divide is an emergent postcitizenship citizenship defined as dynamic and despatialized, textured and hybridic, multiversal and multicentric, and rooted in people's lived-experiences consistent with diversifying and changing world. Rather than being displaced or discredited, however, conventional notions of citizenship are being challenged and stretched in new and more inclusive way, in part by drawing attention to the need for a new vocabulary with which to build upon the positives of a national citizenship yet move positively forward (Levy and Massalha, 2012).

This chapter is themed accordingly: The emergence of a postcitizenship world suggests we can no longer assume easy answers to the question of 'what is citizenship for', but must disclose tacit assumptions and deconstruct hidden agendas. The chapter proposes that understanding a postcitizenship world requires the onset of a discursive citizenship frame consistent with the realities of postnationalism and transnationalism as well as postcolonialism and postmulticulturalism. In acknowledging a discursive shift in talking, thinking, and doing citizenship (McBean, 2013), this chapter emphasizes the utility of a postcitizenship *lens* for reframing the issues of identity, belonging, and entitlements in a 21st century world of posts, trans, and isms. The chapter also addresses the benefits and insights of reframing citizenship along postcitizenship lines: first, to demonstrate how the paradoxes and possibilities of inclusive citizenship models capitalize on the strengths of national citizenship ("fit into"); second, to move positively beyond Euro/state-centric regimes by advancing a postcitizenship narrative of inclusivity that refits the rules of an identity/belonging/entitlements nexus. In terms of content, the chapter explores the concept of postcitizenship in a postWestphalian world; explains why we no longer occupy a national citizenship world but live in a postcitizenship citizenship era; discusses the nature and characteristics of a postcitizenship lens as a discursive shift; and problematizes the concept of inclusiveness to yield new insights into belonging together with/in/through our differences.

A Postcitizenship Citizenship: Building on, Moving Beyond

We are less interested in throwing everything out than in seeing everything anew
(Shohat and Stam, 1994)

There is a certain futility in trying to understand new and evolving ideas, discourses, and practices by relying on antiquated models and dated concepts. A national citizenship model reflects a geopolitical logic that partitions the world into sovereign and distinctive states separated by inviolate boundaries so that, ideally, a state/nation/borders nexus prevails. Citizenship is framed as a state-centric entity, associated with a singular membership, exclusive loyalty, and legal status in territorially bounded political community with an already settled identity that privileges insiders by excluding outsiders (Atac, Rygiel, Stierl, 2016). But we no longer relate to a citizenship world if this means every citizen possesses the same rights and entitlements ("universal") since everybody is thought to occupy a similar relationship to the nation-state ("unitary") (Ivic, 2016). The homogenizing logic behind traditional citizenship models is now being challenged from above by the forces of transmigration and transnationalism, cosmopolitan ideologies and the principle of universal personhood, and the dynamics of globalization. Challenges from below are no less evident in disrupting the notion of coherent political community, including the politics of Indigeneity, the multiversality at the heart of a post-multiculturalism, and growing appeal of denizenship (conferral of rights to permanent residents similar to that of citizens [Soysal, 1994]).

The concept of citizenship is now experiencing an identity crisis and a crisis of confidence in terms of what it is and what it should be doing. The citizenship domain confronts a host of unruly tensions as it hovers in the liminal space ("no longer, not yet") between the plural and the singular, the universal and the multiversal, the local and the global, the national and the cosmopolitan (Camilleri, 2015). Yet moves toward resolving the conflict and constructing an inclusive postcitizenship beyond the confines of the nation-state will be prove a daunting endeavor. The tenacity of Westphalian citizenship regimes and the language of nation-states continue to dominate the discursive domain. Even the word "citizen" is deeply Eurocentric. It evokes a particular legacy associated with European history and scholarship, Enlightenment values of reason, science, and progress, and liberal notions of rights and democracy (Isin, 2015). Moreover, as long as the nation-state claims exclusive authority over a bounded polity and the narratives of right and membership, a state-centric citizenship model will remain open to criticism as controlling, selectively exclusionary, and systemically biasing (Gaucher 2016; Hoffman, 2004). But a rethinking of citizenship along postcitizenship lines promises to broach the stale polarity between the old and the new, theory and practice, inclusive and exclusive (Soysal, 2004). Creating new spaces for claims making and active mobilization offers a more inclusive postcitizenship space that bolsters the rights and realities of Indigenous peoples, transmigrants, and racialized minorities in reclaiming citizenship rights within contexts of overlapping jurisdictions, differential accommodations, and multilayered governances. (Maas, 2013; Anderson, 2000).

Reference to postcitizenship as reality, discourse and practice provides an entry point for deconstructing the citizenship concept while advancing its emancipatory potential (Kornelsen, 2015). A postcitizenship prism imparts a new perspective on patterns of belonging, identity, and entitlements that transcend national models. It proposes an explanatory lens for rethinking citizenship by way of playful inversions in hopes of uncovering fresh perspectives.

For example, while citizenship is normally framed as a thing or noun, it may be more insightful to reframe the citizenship in a postcitizenship discourse as an activity or *verb*, if only to capture its constructed, contested, and dynamic properties. Admittedly the "post" in postcitizenship is not what it seems to be. This book employs the term "post-" in a manner contrary to its popular use as "after" (a clean break with the past) or "rejection" (a repudiation of a preceding episode). Rather, "post" is employed in the sense of critically and constructively engaging with the past by moving positively beyond it, albeit with little assurance of what might lie in store. A synthesis (hybrid) is proposed that speaks to the possibilities of a liminal space between the older settled domain ("no longer") and new unexplored territory ("not yet") but waiting to be finalized (Isin and Nyers, 2014; Pinder, 2010). This Insight Post delves more deeply into the discursive frame known as postcitizenship.

Insight Post

Postcitizenship as a Discursive Frame:
A Discourse Whose Time Has Come

The term, postcitizenship, may strike the reader as odd, confusing, or even oxymoronic. But an online search reveals several references to post-citizenship in the literature. They include (Peled, 2007) and Stevenson (2015) who use the term to criticize the hollowing out of citizenship rights owing to the toxicity of neoliberalism and the erosion of social, political, and civil rights. Yoav Peled (2007) laments the rise of a post-citizenship society based on the toxic combination of neoliberal agendas, a global "war on terror", extension of citizenship rights to non citizens (Kivisto, 2015; Spiro, 2008), splintered identities because of globalization and universal personhood, and the emergence of sub-state or supra-national collectivities as competing frames of reference. Stevenson (2015) also employs post-citizenship in advancing the idea of more participatory forms of citizenship within the context of a radicalized democratic regime. Another reference to postcitizenship is somewhat unorthodox. In their article on animal rights as a postcitizenship protest, Lowe and Ginsberg (2002) capitalize on the work of Jasper (1997) to define postcitizenship as a specific type of social movement. Reference to postcitizenship encompasses those relatively affluent and altruistically inclined citizens who advocate goals

> of little direct benefit to themselves, while pursuing cultural changes by engaging in the thrill of protest to achieve a moral vision.
>
> The concept of postcitizenship is differently employed in this book. Postcitizenship at one level represents an umbrella term that collapses into a single word those much analyzed ways of rethinking the meaning of citizenship, reframing what it means to be a citizen, and recasting what constitutes the parameters a meaningful 21st century citizenship. Or phrased somewhat differently, it encompasses the paradigmatic insights derived from the interplay of posts, trans, and isms in advancing a postcitizenship citizenship model beyond the pale of the conventional. Reference to postcitizenship as a reality, discourse, and practice also represents a shorthand that compresses into a single terms the interplay of postnationalism and transnationalism as well as postcolonialism and postmulticulturalism. The intersection of these dynamics give rise to a postcitizenship world that is rapidly changing, digitally networked, increasingly complex, and more diverse than ever. Lastly, reference to postcitizenship does not announce a new political reality or a new legal citizenship status. Rather it refers to a critical awareness that a conventional citizenship world has conceded ground to world reorganized around new and emergent realities, contested discourses and evolving practices.

Reference to a postcitizenship citizenship does not imply the end of citizenship. To the contrary, it refers to the end of citizenship as we know it, namely, as an instrument of control and standardization aligned with the governance logic of "seeing like the state" (Fozdar, 2013; Joppke, 2008; Kivisto, 2015; Scott, 1999). With postcitizenship, we are reminded that the national, colonial and multicultural world that once informed citizenship models is now sharply contested, although it remains in effect at the present, albeit in altered forms (Tarozzi and Torres, 2016). Our diversely complex world is increasingly informed by new ways of reconceptualizing citizenship commensurate with the realities and challenges of a complexly diverse world of posts, trans, and isms. Once viewed a life-long and insoluable allegiance, citizenship is now perceived as a modifiable trait in response to situational circumstances, shifting national agendas, and evolving international laws, including a discursive shift from absolute state sovereignty as the primary citizenship source to the centrality of individual rights relative to state interests (Macklin and Crepeau, 2010). Alternative ways of framing citizenship along postcitizenship lines and lenses acknowledge the global connectedness and transcendent identities of transmigrant link-ages within transnational spaces/contexts, yet do so without minimizing the importance and utility of conventional (national) models. A postcitizenship citizenship capitalizes on the principles of universal personhood and the inter-nationalization of human rights in extending citizenship narratives beyond the boundaries of the nation-state and national citizenship. In short, in acknowl-edging that the potential of a truly inclusive citizenship must be disassociated from the controlling logic of the nation-state (Faulks, 2000; Hoffman, 2004), a postcitizenship model capitalizes on the strengths of national citizenship yet moves positively beyond them by advocating new patterns of entitlement, the legitimacy of new identities, and new possibilities for belonging.

Postcitizenship as a reality, discourse, and practice offers a new discursive framework for thinking, talking, and doing citizenship. Just as a transnational perspective provides insights that enrich our understanding of citizenship on a global stage, so too does reference to a postcitizenship secure a lens that fur-ther expands the meaning of citizenship within existing citizenship regimes and evolving global realities. Let's begin with the obvious. The exclusive importance of a sovereign nation state as the final authority is being gradu-ally whittled away by postnational possibilities and transnational dynamics in addition to postcolonial politics and postmulticultural realities (Banerjee, 2014). State-centric citizenship models and Eurocentric citizenship regimes cannot possibly cope with the complex, diverse, and changing world of multiple and intersecting universes, shifting and deterritorialized loyalties, hybridic identities and identity politics, the politics of indigeneity and sub-state national politics, and multiple and overlapping belongings and identities (Camilleri, 2015). The complex ways in which globalization is reconfiguring citizenship exposes yet another paradox: To one side, governments can no longer guarantee the security or prosperity of citizens in the new global order, despite monopolizing a legal citizenship status. To the other side, citizens' identity and belonging are no longer fixated on the loyalty to the nation-state, especially when social, political, and economic activities are stretched across national borders and beyond a territorial logic (Stoker, 2011). The unprec-edented movement of diverse groups within and across nation states has yielded a matrix of multilayered links and politicized claims that unsetttle the meaning of a meaningful citizenship in a postcitizenship world (Ng-A-Fook et al., 2013). Ien Ang (2009: 2) confirms how Australians no longer reside in a world of pluralism but rather in a network of multiversal complexities that are proving difficult to define, control, and citizenize:

> Today, however, Australia as a nation is vastly more de facto multicultural than 15 years ago, but at the same time diversity is also more multi-layered, more internally contradictory, more brittle and dynamic, more entangled within webs of transnational links and tensions. Migrants today come from a vastly greater range of countries and they come for many different purposes. Many of them do not settle permanently but come and go as they pursue opportunities elsewhere or as their visas expire. Ethnicity, which was supposed to signify the collective difference of immigrants in the era of high multiculturalism is no longer what it used to be; migrant identities are now much more mutable, differentiated, and individualized. This dynamic, hyper-diverse reality can no longer be captured by the singular term multiculturalism with its rather state connotation of coexisting but mutually exclusive cultural communities. *What can replace it?* (Emphasis, mine)

In short, the interplay and impact of globalization and the internationalization of human rights, together with the politicization of substate nations, the politics of Indigeneity, and realities of transnationalism, have blurred the conventional distinction between national and global, citizen and non-citizen, and inclusion and exclusion. Their combined effect are spurring demand for rethinking the meaning of citizenship along postcitizenship lines and through postcitizenship lenses (Krisch, 2012).

Postcitizenship Inclusiveness: Inclusivity and Inclusion

At the heart of a postcitizenship model of citizenship is a commitment to the principle of inclusiveness. Inclusiveness as diversity governance yields two analytically distinct yet mutually related approaches to accommodating diversity: inclusion and inclusivity (Fleras, 2017a). *Inclusion* as inclusiveness is about fitting into. It's predicated on the principle of removing discriminatory barriers to ensure a uniform (one-size-fits-all) integration into the existing system. Such a commitment reflects a belief that, to achieve individual fairness and maintain national unity, citizenship regimes must be difference-blind to the particularities of race, ethnicity or nationality. According to the principle of inclusion, no one should be excluded because of their differences since everyone deserves similar treatment and protections regardless of background (Bloemraad, 2015). By the same token, no one should be included or accorded special treatment for reasons of race or ethnicity. A commitment to inclusion also acknowledges that everyone is equal before the law; therefore, true equality arises from applying the law equally and without favour, although exemptions may be allowed in extenuating circumstances.

The principle of *inclusivity* differs: A commitment to inclusivity insists that everyone should be differently treated and included precisely because of their differences-based needs and rights. In necessitating interventions that take differences into account when necessary, reference to inclusivity as inclusiveness focuses on refitting the citizenship system by redesigning patterns of belonging, identity, and entitlement along more accommodative lines. Institutional design, organization, assumptions, operations, outputs, opportunity and reward structures are modified to reasonably accommodate ("within limits and without undue hardship") those formerly excluded through no fault of their own. With inclusivity, an inclusive citizenship is proposed that is *reflective of, respectful of and responsive to* a diversity of diversities through the provision of entitlements that are *available, accessible, accountable, and appropriate* (Fleras, 2017a).

The concepts of inclusivity and inclusion as ideal-typical constructs embody competing models of inclusiveness. Inclusion models of inclusiveness begin with the assumption that the existing system is essentially sound and fundamentally equitable, despite the necessity of a few tweaks to level the playing field. Any inequalities or exclusions are largely the fault of individuals who must be "fixed" for fitting them into the status quo (Harmon, n.d.). To the extent differences are recognized, they tend to be dismissed as largely superficial and irrelevant since our commonalities as individuals under a liberal universalism framework outweigh our group differences—at least for purposes of recognition, relationships, and reward. By contrast, inclusivity-based citizenship models entail a fundamentally different logic. Citizenship as principle and as regime must be re-imagined and restructured to differently accommodate the needs of an extremely diverse demographic by ensuring a better fit between ideals and reality, principles and practise. Cosmetic changes to citizenship conventions such as dual citizenships are a good start, according to inclusivity principles, but they are unlikely to dislodge those foundational rules that reinforce power relations and institutional culture. Finally, an inclusivity principle commits to the principles of deep diversity (that is, differences that stand in a fundamentally different relationship to the state) and that of ethnic particularism (group based differences complement the value of individualism as basis of entitlement and identity) as a basis for differently living together. In short, the principle of inclusion and inclusivity articulate fundamentally different patterns of inclusiveness when applied to citizenship including:

- Inclusion is associated with principle of equal treatment: that is, true equality arises from treating everyone the same (*"equally"*) because everyone is equal before the law, regardless of their differences. To the extent accommodations are made, a one-size-fits-all-format prevails, although exceptions and exemptions are possible provided they are temporary, needs-based, and focused on the individual rather than on specific groups. For inclusivity, however, the principle of treatment *as equals* acknowledges that, at times, peoples' difference-based disadvantages must be accommodated to ensure genuine equality. A commitment to inclusivity/ equity (as equals) invariably draws attention to the principle of differential accommodation, namely, accommodating different ways of accommodating a diversity of differences (also Blommaert, 2015).

- Inclusion tends to frame diversity as a problem to solve or an obstacle to surmount. Or put more candidly, how to neutralize differences so they no longer pose a problem. A commitment to inclusivity goes beyond simple recognition of diversities or their treatment as abstractions with no history or context. Inclusivity as principle endorses the value of diversity, neither as a problem to solve nor a challenge to surmount, but as an asset to nurture for improving citizenship outcomes (Fleras and Spoonley, 1999). This commitment creates a citizenship climate that recognizes, respects, and values a diversity-of-diversities by modifying institutions accordingly.

- A commitment to inclusivity as citizenship governance is about changing the rules that inform the conventions; by contrast, inclusion as principle is focused on tweaking the conventions that refer to the rules. Inclusivity is transformative in bringing about major change, whereas inclusion is more reform oriented in modifying the existing status quo. Instead of simply adding to something that already exists, inclusivity promotes the prospect of breaking with the past by changing patterns of culture, structure, environment, and social-organizational life. Or to phrase it a bit differently: inclusion is about fitting individuals into the existing system; inclusivity is about re-fitting the citizenship regime to accommodate diverse patterns of belonging and identity. Reference to inclusivity proposes a difference model that questions existing arrangements, posits a multiversal view of diversity, acknowledges the demands of an internally diverse and fractious demographic, and frames diversities within contexts of power and inequality (Berns-McGown, 2007–2008), Access and membership are rooted in the principle of rights and relations rather than those of obligations, needs or cultural differences.

Towards a Postcitizenship Citizenship Regime

We are living in a contested and evolving citizenship world that might be described as postcitizenship in reality, discourse and practice. Existing ideas of citizenship are experiencing an identity crisis of confidence in addressing 21st century challenges related to the war on terror, ecological crisis, neoliberalism, identity politics, and globalization (Stevenson, 2015). A model embedded within the confines of western history, Westphalian nation-state building, and European theorizing (Hoffman, 2004; Isin and Nyers, 2014), the legitimacy of a national citizenship no longer resonates with authority in coping the principles of an inclusive citizenship, the realities of a transmigrant world of transnationalism, and the universality of a human rights discourse (Hettne, 2000). Dominant views of citizenship that prevailed in the past—based on blood, beliefs, and laws—are no longer sufficient in a world that frames citizenship as a recipe for political action, civic engagement, and duty to "fellow" citizens (Kingwell, 2001). A new vocabulary of citizenship is required that incorporates the effects of globalization in transforming how we think, talk, and do citizenship (Spiro, 2008; Tarozzi and Torres, 2016). In invoking notions of contestation and redefinition across multiple domains and different time frames, the status of citizenship is discursively reframed from a thing (noun) to that of a verb (process or activity)—from being to becoming (and vice versa), from done to doing, from passive to active. Reference to postcitizenship calls into question the tacit assumptions and traditional meanings once predicated on the principle of a static, singular and state-centric status of abstracted individuals in a nation state (Munday, 2009). It provides a reminder of the need for recasting citizenship as a performative practice by engaged citizens rather than a legal status bestowed by state (Isin, 2008), notwithstanding fears the social is being hollowed out by the rampant individualism of a neoliberalism ethic (also Brodie, 2002). Framing postcitizenship as a textured and ongoing process of becoming, being, and doing, as well as negotiating, participating, and claims-making also reinforces its dynamic dimension. Despite these discursive shifts, the attainment of an inclusivity-based postcitizenship regime may prove too elusive a goal in the foreseeable future but, more realistically, reflect an aspirational ideal beyond our collective reach but still eminently worthwhile (Ramanathan, 2013).

Reference to postcitizenship as a lens or model as well as a principle and lived reality makes it abundantly clear. Citizenship as construct, discourse, and practices in a world of diverse complexities and complex diversities is sharply contested and deeply conflicted (Bloemraad, 2015; Cao, 2015). A discursive shift from a one-size-fits-all national citizenship to the emergence of postcitizenship principles and practice is profoundly transformative in the thinking, talking, and doing of citizenship. The onset of a postcitizenship discourse announces a new citizenship reality that no longer fits into conventional citizenship frameworks yet, paradoxically, remains fully conversant with it. Keep in mind the "post" in postcitizenship is not a rejection of national citizenship, which in any case is unlikely to disappear in the forseeable future. It refers instead to a constructive engagement between the past and the present as a pathway for the future of citizenship. In other words, a postcitizenship model that capitalizes on the strengths of a national citizenship model while jettisoning its weaknesses does not so much proclaim the end of citizenship, but rather the start of something new.

A find word: A postcitizenship perspective provides an interpretive lens for rethinking citizenship in a hyperdiversifying world of posts, trans, and isms. It speaks to the need of a citizenship cognizant of postcolonial Indigenous politics, postmulticultural commitments to differently accommodate a multiversality of diverse diversities, a postnational recognition that the nation-state no longer commands total control or exclusive loyalty, transmigrant linkages that foster transnational patterns of belonging, and a cosmopolitan world that espouses universal personhood. Such a perspective also points to a rethinking of citizenship discourses within the context of an imagined global community (Stromquist, 2009) whose borders do not exclude, whose identities are not mutually exclusive, where membership is multiple and layered, and where rights are portable across boundaries. A commitment to postcitizenship citizenship proclaims the inevitable: National citizenship models may have worked well in the past, but now are desperate for a reboot in a world that's increasingly complicated, connected and contested. It is in those postcitizenship space of across, beyond, and in between that the meaning of citizenship as identity and belonging will be defined, re-negotiated, and performed.

Of course, the prospect of conceptually overhauling the politically charged domain of national citizenship requires a dash of realism. The task of realigning national citizenship models along postcitizenship lines is dauntingly complex and not without pockets of fierce resistance among those who dislike transformational change or, conversely, who exhibit a passive resignation at the enormity of the challenge. Nevertheless, the postcitizenship ideal requires a leap of imagination neither constrained by the politics of the possible nor disheartened by calculations of what seems likely, but one energized by the prospect of what is just and fair, and a utopian confidence in the human capacity to exceed the realistic

(Cao, 2015: 61). But if we define ourselves as active and progressive agents of change whose reach should exceed our grasp, it's time to take action. Time will tell if the citizens of the CANZUS countries possess the courage of conviction to contest the rules that define citizenship conventions rather than simply fine-tuning the conventions that inform the rules of membership and entitlements. Our future as citizens of an expanding yet simultaneously shrinking world depends on striding boldly into this journey of unknown yet promising possibilities.

Note

1. Eurocentrism is defined by Shohat and Stam (1994) as that interlocked constellation of buried premises, entrenched interests, embedded narratives, and submerged tropes that constitute a broadly shared epistemology of ideas and ideals about what is normal, desirable, and acceptable.

References

Anderson, Kay. "Thinking "Postnationally:" Dialogue Across Multicultural, Indigenous, and Settler Spaces." *Annals of the Association of American Geographers* 90, no. 2 (2000): 381–391.

Ang, Ien. "Provocation: Beyond Multiculturalism: A Journey to Nowhere." *Humanities Research* 15, 2 (2009): 17–21.

Ang, Ien. "Navigating Complexity: From Cultural Critique to Cultural Intelligence." *Continuum: Journal of Media & Cultural Studies* 25, no. 6 (2011): 779–794.

Atac, Ilker, Kim Rygiel, and Maurice Stierl. "Introduction: The Contentious Politics of Refugee and Migrant Protest and Solidarity Movements: Remaking Citizenship From the Margins." *Citizenship Studies* 20, no. 5 (2016): 527–544.

Banerjee, Kiran. "Toward Post-National Membership? Tensions and Transformations in German and EU Citizenship." *Journal of International Law and International Relations* 10 (2014): 4–30.

Bennett, W. Lance. "Changing Citizenship in the Digital Age." Prepared for OECD/INDIRE Conference at Millenial Learners, Florence, March 5–6, 2007.

Berns-McGown, Rima. "Redefining 'Diaspora': The Challenge of Connection and Inclusion." *International Journal* 63, no. 1 (2007–2008): 3–21.

Bloemraad, Irene. "Who Claims Dual Citizenship? The Limits of Postnationalism, The Possibilities of Transnationalism, and the Persistence of Traditional Citizenship." *IMR* 38, no. 2 (2004): 389–426.

Bloemraad, Irene. "Theorizing and Analyzing Citizenship in Multicultural Societies." *The Sociological Quarterly* 56, no. 4 (2015): 591–606.

Blommaert, Jan. "Commentary Article: Culture and Superdiversity." *Journal of Multicultural Discourse* 10, no. 1 (2015): 22–24.

Brodie, Janine. "Citizenship and Solidarity: Reflections on the Canadian Way." *Citizenship Studies* 6, no. 4 (2002): 377–394.

Camilleri, Joseph. "Dialogical Citizenship: Dancing Toward Solidarity." A Great Transition Initiative Essay, 2015. Retrieved from http://www.greattransition.org

Cao, Benito. *Environment and Citizenship*. New York: Routledge, 2015.

Cho, Lily. "Diasporic Citizenship. Inhabiting Contradictions and Challenging Exclusions." *American Quarterly* 59, no. 2 (2007): 467–478.

Clark, Emily B. and Glenn C. Savage. "Problematizing 'Global Citizenship' in an International School." In *Educating for the 21st Century*, edited by S. Choo, D. Sawch, A. Villanueva, R. Vinz, 405–424. New York: Springer Link, 2016.

Dalton, Russell J. *The Good Citizen: How a Younger Generation is Reshaping American Politics*. Washington DC: CQ Press, 2008.

Delanty, Gerard. "European Citizenship: A Critical Assessment." *Citizenship Studies* 11, no. 1 (2007a): 63–72.

Delanty, Gerard. "Theorising Citizenship in a Global Age." In *Globalisation and Citizenship: The Transnational Challenge*, edited by W. Hudson and S. Slaughter, 15–29. New York: Routledge, 2007b.

Edmundson, Anna, Kylie Message, and Ursula Frederick. "Introduction. Compelling Cultures: Representing Cultural Diversity and Cohesion in Multicultural Australia." *Humanities Research* XV, no. 1 (2009): 1–6.

Faulks, Keith. *Citizenship*. London: Routledge, 2000.

Field, Ann-Marie. "Counter-Hegemonic Citizenship: LGBT Communities and the Politics of Hate Crimes in Canada." *Citizenship Studies* 11, no. 3 (2007): 247–262.

Fleischmann Aloys NM, Nancy van Styvendale, and Cody McCarroll (eds.). *Narratives of Citizenship: Indigenous and Diasporic Peoples Unsettle the Nation State*. Edmonton: University of Alberta, 2011.

Fleras, Augie. *Immigration Canada*. Vancouver: UBC Press, 2014.

Fleras, Augie. *Inequality Matters*. Toronto: Oxford University Press, 2017a.

Fleras, Augie. "Rethinking Citizenship Through Transnational Lenses." In *Citizenship in a Transnational Perspective*, edited by J. Mann, 15–48. New York: Palgrave Macmillan, 2017b.

Fleras, Augie and Paul Spoonley. *Recalling Aotearoa*. Auckland: Oxford University Press, 1999.

Fozdar, Farida. "Constructing Australian Citizenship as Christian: Or How to Exclude Muslims from the National Imagining." In *Migration, Citizenship, and Intercultural Relations: Looking Through the Lens of Social Citizenship*, edited by F. Mansouri and M. Lobo, 33–49. Burlington, VT: Ashgate Publishing, 2013.

Gans, Judith. "Citizenship in the Context of Globalization." Immigration Policy Working Papers, June. University of Arizona, 2005.

Gaucher, Megan. "Monogamous Canadian Citizenship, Constructing Foreigness, and the Limits of Harm Discourse." *Canadian Journal of Political Science* 49, 3 (2016): 519–538.

Hettne, Bjorn. "The Fate of Citizenship in Post-Westphalia." *Citizenship Studies* 4, no. 1 (2000): 35–46.

Hines, Sally. "A Pathway to Diversity?: Human Rights, Citizenship, and the Politics of Transgender." *Contemporary Politics* 15, no. 1 (2009): 87–102.

Hoffman, John. *Citizenship Beyond the State*. Thousand Oaks CA: Sage, 2004.

Isin, Engin F., Janine Brodie, Danielle Juteau, and Daiva Stasiulis. "Recasting the Social in Citizenship." In *Recasting the Social in Citizenship*, edited by E. Isin, 3–19. Toronto: University of Toronto Press, 2008.

Isin, Engin F. *Citizenship After Orientalism: Transforming Political Theory*. London: Palgrave Macmillan, 2015.

Isin, Engin F. and Peter Nyers. "Introduction: Globalizing Citizenship Studies." In *Routledge Handbook of Global Citizenship Studies*, edited by E. Isin and P. Nyers. 1–11. New York: Routledge, 2014.

Ivic, Sanja. "Citizenship as Discursive Practice: The Postmodern Culture of Citizenship." *Journal of Philosophy, Culture, and Religion* 19 (2016):13–22.

Jackson, Lucy. "Intimate Citizenship? Rethinking the Politics and Experiences of Citizenship as Emotional in Wales and Singapore." *Gender, Place, & Culture* 23, no. 6 (2015): 817–833.

Jasper, James M. *The Art of Moral Protest*. Chicago: University of Chicago Press, 1997.

Joppke, Christian. "Dual Citizenship and Transnationalism in Europe." *Canadian Diversity* 6, no. 4 (2008): 17–20.

Kingwell, Mark. *The World We Want: Restoring Citizenship in a Fractured Age*. Blue Ridge Summit, PA: Rowman and Littlefield, 2001.

Kivisto, Peter. "The Puzzle of Incorporation and Solidarity." *Sociological Quarterly* 56, no. 4 (2015): 581–590.

Kornelsen, Derek Wayne. "Postcolonial Citizenship: Reconceiving Authority and Belonging in Settler Societies." PhD Thesis, Vancouver, UBC, 2015.

Krisch, Nico. *Beyond Constitutionalism: The Pluralist Structure of Postnational Law*. New York: Oxford University Press, 2012.

Kymlicka, Will and Kathryn Walker. "Rooted Cosmpolitanism: Canada and the World." In *Rooted Cosmpolitanism: Canada and the World*, edited by W. Kymlicka and K. Walker, 1–27. Vancouver: UBC Press, 2012.

Levy, Gal and Mohammad Massalha. "Within and Beyond Citizenship: Alternative Educational Initiatives in the Arab Society of Israel." *Citizenship Studies* 16, no. 7 (2012): 905–917.

Lowe, B. M. and C. F. Ginsberg. "Animal Rights as a Post-citizenship Movement." *Animals & Society* 10, no. 2 (2002): 203–215.

Maaka, Roger and Augie Fleras. *The Politics of Indigeneity*. Dunedin NZ: Otago University Press, 2005.

Maas, Willem. *Multilevel Citizenship*. Philadelphia: University of Pennsylvania Press, 2013.

Macklin, Audrey and Francois Crepeau. "Multiple Citizenship, Identity, and Entitlement in Canada." *IRPP*, June 22, 2010.

Mann, Jatinder. "Introduction." In *Citizenship in a Transnational Perspective*, edited by J. Mann, 1–14. New York: Palgrave Macmillan, 2017.

McBean, Sam. "Dragging Antigone: Feminist Revisions of Citizenship." In *Beyond Citizenship?: Feminism and the Transformation of Belonging*, edited by Sasha Roseneil, 21–38. Palgrave Macmillan, 2013.

Munday, Jennie. "Gendered Citizenship." *Sociology Compass* 3, no. 2 (2009): 249–266.

Ng-A-Fook, Nicholas, Linda Radford, and Tasha Ausman. "Living a Curriculum of Hyph-E-Nations: Diversity, Equality, and Social Media." *Multicultural Education Review* 4, no. 2 (2013): 91–128.

Peled, Yoav. "Towards a Post-Citizenship Society? A Report from the Front." *Citizenship Studies* 11, no. 1 (2007): 95–104.

Perez-Milans, M. and C. Soto. "Light Communities?: Implications for Research on Diversity & Activism.". *Urban Language and Literacies*. Working Paper No 224. Paper presented at the AILA World Congress of Applied Linguistics, July, 2017.

Pinder, Sherrow O. *The Politics of Race and Ethnicity in the United States*. New York: Palgrave Macmillan, 2010.

Ramanathan, Vaidehi. "Language Policies and (Dis)Citizenship: Who Belongs? Who is a Guest? Who is Deported?" *Journal of Language, Identity, and Education* 12 (2013): 162–166.

Scott, James. *Seeing Like the State*. New Haven CT: Yale University Press, 1999.

Shohat, Ella and Robert Stam. *Unthinking Eurocentrism*. New York: Routledge, 1994.

Simmons, Alan. *Immigration and Canada. Global and Transnational Perspectives*. Toronto: Canadian Scholars' Press, 2010.

Soysal, Yasemin Nuhoglu. *Limits of Citizenship: Migrants and Postnational Membership in Europe*. Chicago: University of Chicago Press, 1994.

Soysal, Yasemin Nuhoglu. "Postnational Citizenship: Reconfiguring the Familiar Terrain." In *The Blackwell Companion to Political Sociology*, edited by Kate Nash and Alan Scott. Oxford, UK: Blackwell, 2004.

Spiro, Peter J. *Beyond Citizenship. American Identity After Globalizations*. New York: Oxford University Press, 2008.

Stasiulis, Daiva. "Respatializing Social Citizenship and Security Among Dual Citizens in the Lebanese Diaspora." In *Citizenship in a Transnational Perspective: Canada, Australia, and New Zealand*, edited by J. Mann., 49–78. New York: Palgrave, 2017.

Stevenson, Nick. "Post-Citizenship, the New Left, and the Democratic Commons." Citizenship Studies, published online August 25, 2015.

Stoker, Gerry. *Prospects for Citizenship*. New York: Bloomsbury Academic, 2011.

Stromquist, Nelly P. "Theorizing Global Citizenship: Discourses, Challenges, and Implications for Education." *Inter-American Journal of Education for Democracy* 2, no. 1 (2009).

Tan, Kathy-Ann. *Reconfiguring Citizenship and National Identity in the North American Literary Imagination*. Detroit: Wayne State University Press, 2015.

Tarozzi, M. and C.A. Torres. *Global Citizenship Education and the Crisis of Multiculturalism. Comparative Perspectives*. New York: Bloomsbury Press, 2016.

Theophanous, Andrew C. *Understanding Social Justice: An Australian Perspective*. Carlton Victoria: Elikia Books, 1994.

Tonkiss, K. and T. Bloom. "Theorising Noncitizenship: Concepts, Debates, and Challenges." *Citizenship Studies* 19, no. 8 (2015): 837–852.

Urzi, Domenica and Colin Williams. "Beyond Post-national Citizenship: An Evaluation of the Experiences of Tunisian and Romanian Migrants Working in the Agricultural Sector of Sicily." *Citizenship Studies*, 136–150. Published online, November 10, 2016.

Wood, Patricia K. "Aboriginal/Indigenous Citizenship: An Introduction." *Citizenship Studies* 7, no. 4 (2003): 371–378.

INDEX